AMERICA ALONE

AMERICA ALONE

THE END OF THE WORLD AS WE KNOW IT

MARK STEYN

Since 1947
REGNERY
PUBLISHING, INC.
An Eagle Publishing Company • Washington, DC

Library of Congress Cataloging-in-Publication Data

Steyn, Mark.
  America alone : the end of the world as we know it / Mark Steyn.
    p. cm.
  Includes index.
  ISBN-13 978-0-89526-078-9
  ISBN-10 0-89526-078-6
  1. United States—Foreign relations—2001– 2. United States—Civilization—1970– 3. Europe—Civilization—1945– 4. World politics—1989– 5. Islam and politics. 6. Civilization, Western. 7. Twenty-first century—Forecasts. I. Title.
  E895.S84 2006
  303.48'273017670905—dc22

                                    2006024828

Published in the United States by
Regnery Publishing, Inc.
One Massachusetts Avenue, NW
Washington, DC 20001
www.regnery.com

Distributed to the trade by
National Book Network
Lanham, MD 20706
Manufactured in the United States of America

10 9 8 7

Books are available in quantity for promotional or premium use. Write to Director of Special Sales, Regnery Publishing, Inc., One Massachusetts Avenue NW, Washington, DC 20001, for information on discounts and terms or call (202) 216-0600.

FOR CECI, HECTOR AND RALPH

CONTENTS

"When people see a strong horse and a weak horse,
by nature they will like the strong horse."

OSAMA BIN LADEN

KANDAHAR, NOVEMBER 2001

"If we know anything, it is that weakness is provocative."

DONALD RUMSFELD

WASHINGTON, OCTOBER 1998

To Be or Not to Be

We know what we are, but know not what we may be.

WILLIAM SHAKESPEARE, *HAMLET* (1601)

Do you worry? You look like you do. Worrying is the way the responsible citizen of an advanced society demonstrates his virtue: he feels good about feeling bad.

But what to worry about? Iranian nukes? Nah, that's just some racket cooked up by the Christian fundamentalist Bush and his Zionist buddies to give Halliburton a pretext to take over the Persian carpet industry. Worrying about nukes is so eighties. "They make me want to throw up....They make me feel sick to my stomach," wrote the

British novelist Martin Amis, who couldn't stop thinking about them during the Thatcher Terror. In the introduction to a collection of short stories, he worried about the Big One and outlined his own plan for coping with a nuclear winter wonderland:

> Suppose I survive. Suppose my eyes aren't pouring down my face, suppose I am untouched by the hurricane of secondary missiles that all mortar, metal, and glass has abruptly become: suppose all this. I shall be obliged (and it's the last thing I feel like doing) to retrace that long mile home, through the firestorm, the remains of the thousand-miles-an-hour winds, the warped atoms, the groveling dead. Then—God willing, if I still have the strength, and, of course, if they are still alive—I must find my wife and children and I must kill them.

But the Big One never fell. And instead of killing his wife Martin Amis had to make do with divorcing her. Back then it was just crazies like Reagan and Thatcher who had nukes, so you can understand why everyone was terrified. But now Kim Jong-il and the ayatollahs have them, so we're all sophisticated and relaxed about it, like the French hearing that their president's acquired a couple more mistresses. Martin Amis hasn't thrown up a word about the subject in years. To the best of my knowledge, he has no plans to kill the present Mrs. Amis.

So what should we be cowering in terror over? How about—stop me if you've heard this one before—"climate change"? If you've seen Al Gore's acclaimed documentary *An Inconvenient Truth* you'll know that it begins with a searing, harrowing nightmare vision of the world to come:

> One day Chicken Little was walking in the woods when— KERPLUNK—an acorn fell on her head.
>
>   "Oh my goodness!" said Chicken Little. "The sky is falling! I must go and tell the king."

Whoops, my mistake. I must be mixing Al's movie up with a previous eco-doom blockbuster. They come rolling in like rising sea levels in the Maldives. You may have seen yet another example of the genre, the film *The Day After Tomorrow*, in which (warning: plot spoiler) a speech by Dick Cheney brings on the flash-freezing of the entire northern hemisphere. I'm not a climatologist so I'll take Dennis Quaid's word for it that that's scientifically possible. But the point is that from Chicken Little to Al Gore to Dennis Quaid, respected figures have been forecasting the end of the world pretty much since the beginning of the world. In Professor Little's day, the sky was falling. In Vice President Gore's time, it's the Earth that's falling apart. *Plus ça change* of direction, *plus c'est la même* prose. But, if you can't beat 'em, join 'em. So let me put it in a nutshell:

It's the end of the world!! Head for the hills!!!

No, wait. Don't head for the hills—they're full of Islamist terrorist camps. Let me put it in a slightly bigger nutshell: much of what we loosely call the Western world will not survive the twenty-first century, and much of it will effectively disappear within our lifetimes, including many if not most European countries. There'll probably still be a geographical area on the map marked as Italy or the Netherlands—*probably*—just as in Istanbul there's still a building known as Hagia Sophia, or St. Sophia's Cathedral. But it's not a cathedral; it's merely a designation for a piece of real estate. Likewise, Italy and the Netherlands will merely be designations for real estate.

That's just for starters. And, unlike the ecochondriacs' obsession with rising sea levels, this isn't something that might possibly conceivably hypothetically threaten the Maldive Islands circa the year 2500; the process is already well advanced as we speak. With respect to Francis Fukuyama, it's not the end of history; it's the end of the world as we know it. Whether we like what replaces it depends on whether America can summon the will to shape at least part of the emerging world. If not, then it's also the end of the American moment, and the dawn of the new Dark Ages (if darkness can dawn): a planet on which much of the map is re-primitivized.

Does that make me sound as nuts as Al Gore and the rest of the eco-doom set? It's true the end of the world's nighness isn't something you'd want to set your watch by. Consider some of Chicken Little's eminent successors in this field:

- In 1968, in his bestselling book *The Population Bomb*, distinguished scientist Paul Ehrlich declared: "In the 1970s the world will undergo famines—hundreds of millions of people are going to starve to death."

- In 1972, in their landmark study *The Limits to Growth*, the Club of Rome announced that the world would run out of gold by 1981, of mercury by 1985, tin by 1987, zinc by 1990, petroleum by 1992, and copper, lead, and gas by 1993.

- In 1976, Lowell Ponte published a huge bestseller called *The Cooling: Has the New Ice Age Already Begun? Can We Survive?*

- In 1977, Jimmy Carter, president of the United States (incredible as it may seem), confidently predicted that "we could use up all of the proven reserves of oil in the entire world by the end of the next decade."

None of these things occurred. Contrary to the doom-mongers' predictions, millions didn't starve and the oil and gas and gold didn't run out, and, though the NHL now has hockey franchises in Anaheim and Tampa Bay, ambitious kids are still unable to spend their winters knocking a puck around the frozen Everglades. But that doesn't mean nothing much went on during the last third of the twentieth century. Here's what *did* happen between 1970 and 2000: in that period, the developed world declined from just under 30 percent of the global population to just over 20 percent, and the Muslim nations increased from about 15 percent to 20 percent.

Is that fact less significant to the future of the world than the fate of some tree or the endangered sloth hanging from it? In 1970, very few non-Muslims outside the Indian subcontinent gave much thought to Islam. Even the Palestinian situation was seen within the framework of a more or less conventional ethnic nationalist problem. Yet today it's Islam a-go-go: almost every geopolitical crisis takes place on what Samuel Huntington, in *The Clash of Civilizations*, calls "the boundary looping across Eurasia and Africa that separates Muslims from non-Muslims." That looping boundary is never not in the news. One week, it's a bomb in Bali. The next, some beheadings in southern Thailand. Next, an insurrection in an obscure resource-rich Muslim republic in the Russian Federation. And then Madrid, and London, and suddenly that looping, loopy boundary has penetrated into the very heart of the West. In little more than a generation.

1970 doesn't seem that long ago. If you're in your fifties or sixties, as many of the chaps running the Western world today are wont to be, your pants are narrower than they were back then and your hair's less groovy, but the landscape of your life—the look of your house, the layout of your car, the shape of your kitchen appliances, the brand names of the stuff in the fridge—isn't significantly different. And yet that world is utterly altered. Just to recap those bald statistics: in 1970, the developed nations had twice as big a share of the global population as the Muslim world: 30 percent to 15 percent. By 2000, they were at parity: each had about 20 percent.

And by 2020?

September 11, 2001, was not "the day everything changed," but the day that revealed how much had already changed. On September 10, how many journalists had the Council on American-Islamic Relations or the Canadian Islamic Congress or the Muslim Council of Britain in their Rolodexes? If you'd said that whether something does or does not cause offense to Muslims would be the early twenty-first century's principal political dynamic in Denmark, Sweden, the Netherlands, Belgium, France, and the United Kingdom, most folks would have thought you were crazy. Yet on that Tuesday morning the top of the iceberg bobbed up and toppled the Twin Towers.

This book is about the seven-eighths below the surface—the larger forces at play in the developed world that have left Europe too enfeebled to resist its remorseless transformation into Eurabia and that call into question the future of much of the rest of the world, including the United States, Canada, and beyond. The key factors are:

1. Demographic decline
2. The unsustainability of the advanced Western social-democratic state
3. Civilizational exhaustion

Let's start with demography, because everything does.

●   ●   ●

PEOPLE POWER

If your school has two hundred guys and you're playing a school with two thousand pupils, it doesn't mean your baseball team is definitely going to lose, but it certainly gives the other fellows a big starting advantage. Likewise, if you want to launch a revolution, it's not very likely if you've only got seven revolutionaries. And they're all over eighty. But if you've got two million and seven revolutionaries and they're all under thirty, you're in business.

I wonder how many pontificators on the "Middle East peace process" ever run this number: the median age in the Gaza Strip is 15.8 years.

Once you know that, all the rest is details. If you were a "moderate Palestinian" leader, would you want to try to persuade a nation—or pseudo-nation—of unemployed poorly educated teenage boys raised in a UN-supervised European-funded death cult to see sense? Any analysis of the "Palestinian problem" that doesn't take into account the most important determinant on the ground is a waste of time.

Likewise, the salient feature of Europe, Canada, Japan, and Russia is that they're running out of babies. What's happening in the developed world is one of the fastest demographic evolutions in history. Most of us have seen a gazillion heartwarming ethnic comedies—*My Big Fat*

Greek Wedding and its ilk—in which some uptight WASPy type starts dating a gal from a vast, loving, fecund Mediterranean family, so abundantly endowed with sisters and cousins and uncles that you can barely get in the room. It is, in fact, the inversion of the truth. Greece has a fertility rate hovering just below 1.3 births per couple, which is what demographers call the point of "lowest-low" fertility from which no human society has ever recovered. And Greece's fertility is the healthiest in Mediterranean Europe: Italy has a fertility rate of 1.2, Spain, 1.1. Insofar as any citizens of the developed world have "big" families these days, it's the Anglo democracies: America's fertility rate is 2.1, New Zealand's a little below. Hollywood should be making *My Big Fat Uptight Protestant Wedding*, in which some sad Greek only child marries into a big heartwarming New Zealand family where the spouse actually has a sibling.

As I say, this isn't a projection—it's happening now. There's no need to extrapolate, and if you do it gets a little freaky, but, just for fun, here goes: by 2050, 60 percent of Italians will have no brothers, no sisters, no cousins, no aunts, no uncles. The big Italian family, with papa pouring the vino and mama spooning out the pasta down an endless table of grandparents and nieces and nephews, will be gone, no more, dead as the dinosaurs. As Noel Coward once remarked in another context, "Funiculi, funicula, funic yourself." By mid-century, Italians will have no choice in the matter.

Experts talk about root causes. But demography is the most basic root of all. Many of the developed world's citizens gave no conscious thought to Islam before September 11. Now we switch on the news every evening and, though there are many trouble spots around the world, as a general rule it's easy to make an educated guess at one of the participants: Muslims vs. Jews in "Palestine," Muslims vs. Hindus in Kashmir, Muslims vs. Christians in Africa, Muslims vs. Buddhists in Thailand, Muslims vs. Russians in the Caucasus, Muslims vs. backpacking tourists in Bali, Muslims vs. Danish cartoonists in Scandinavia. The environmentalists may claim to think globally but act locally, but these guys live it. They open up a new front somewhere on the planet with nary a thought.

Why? Because they've got the manpower. Because in the seventies and eighties, Muslims had children (those self-detonating Islamists in London and Gaza are a literal baby boom) while Westerners took all those silly doomsday tomes about "overpopulation" seriously. We still do. In 2005, Jared Diamond published a bestselling book called *Collapse: How Societies Choose to Fail or Succeed*. A timely subject, so I bought a copy. More fool me. It's all about Easter Island going belly up because they chopped down all their trees. That's why they're not in the G-7 or a permanent member of the UN Security Council. Same with the Greenlanders and the Mayans and Diamond's other curious choices of "societies." Indeed, as the author sees it, pretty much every society collapses because it chops down its trees.

Poor old Diamond can't see the forest because of his obsession with the trees. Russia's collapsing and it's nothing to do with deforestation. It's not the tree, it's the family tree. It's the babes in the wood. A people that won't multiply can't go forth or go anywhere. Those who do will shape the age we live in. Because, when history comes a-calling, it starts with the most basic question of all:

Knock-knock.

Who's there?

•   •   •

WELFARE AND WARFARE

Demographic decline and the unsustainability of the social-democratic state are closely related. In America, politicians upset about the federal deficit like to complain that we're piling up debts our children and grandchildren will have to pay off. But in Europe the unaffordable entitlements are in even worse shape: there are no kids or grandkids to stick it to.

In my town in New Hampshire, the population peaked in 1820 and then declined until 1940, when it started edging up again until it stands today almost at what it was two centuries ago. The opening up of the west killed Granite State sheep farming, and young people fanned out across the plains, or to the mill towns in southern New England. It's sad to see cellar holes and abandoned barns and meadows reclaimed by the forest. But it didn't kill my town because we had no extravagant social programs to which our old-timers had become partial. Similarly, in the post–Gold Rush Yukon, one minute the saloons are bustling and the garters of the hoochie-koochie dancers are stuffed with dollar bills; next they're all shuttered up and everyone's skedaddled out on the last south-bound dogsled. But the territory isn't stuck trying to figure who's going to pay for the hoochie-koochie gals' retirement complex. Unlike the emptying saloons of White Horse and Dawson City, demography is an existential crisis for the developed world, because the twentieth-century social-democratic state was built on a careless model that requires a constantly growing population to sustain it.

You might formulate it like this:

Age + Welfare = Disaster for you

Youth + Will = Disaster for whoever gets in your way

By "will," I mean the metaphorical spine of a culture. Africa, to take another example, also has plenty of young people, but it's riddled with AIDS and, for the most part, Africans don't think of themselves as Africans; as we saw in Rwanda, their primary identity is tribal, and most tribes have no global ambitions. Islam, however, has serious global ambitions, and it forms the primal, core identity of most of its adherents in the Middle East, South Asia, and elsewhere. Islam has youth and will, Europe has age and welfare.

We are witnessing the end of the late twentieth-century progressive welfare democracy. Its fiscal bankruptcy is merely a symptom of a more fundamental bankruptcy: its insufficiency as an animating principle for society. The children and grandchildren of those Fascists and Republicans who waged a bitter civil war for the future of Spain now shrug when a bunch of foreigners blow up their capital. Too sedated even to sue for terms, they capitulate instantly. Over on the other side of the equation, the modern multicultural state is too watery a concept to bind huge numbers of immigrants to the land of their nominal citizenship. So they look elsewhere and find the jihad. The Western Muslim's pan-Islamic identity is merely the first great cause in a world where globalized pathologies are taking the place of old-school nationalism.

For states in demographic decline with ever more lavish social programs, the question is a simple one: Can they get real? Can they grow up before they grow old? If not, then they'll end their days in societies dominated by people with a very different worldview.

●   ●   ●

FIGHTING VAINLY THE OLD ENNUI

Which brings us to the third factor—the enervated state of the Western world, the sense of civilizational ennui, of nations too mired in cultural relativism to understand what's at stake. As it happens, that third point is closely related to the first two. To Americans, it doesn't always seem obvious that there's any connection between the "war on terror" and the so-called "pocketbook issues" of domestic politics. But there is a correlation between the structural weaknesses of the social-democratic state and the rise of a globalized Islam. The state has gradually annexed all the responsibilities of adulthood—health care, child care, care of the elderly—to the point where it's effectively severed its citizens from humanity's primal instincts, not least the survival instinct. In the American context, the federal "deficit" isn't the problem; it's the government programs that cause the deficit. These programs would be wrong even if Bill Gates wrote a check to cover them each month. They corrode the citizen's sense of self-reliance to a potentially fatal degree. Big government is a national security threat: it increases your vulnerability to threats like Islamism, and makes it less likely you'll be able to summon the will to rebuff it. We should have learned that lesson on September 11, 2001, when big government flopped big-time and the only good news of the day came from the ad hoc citizen militia of Flight 93.

There were two forces at play in the late twentieth century: in the eastern bloc, the collapse of Communism; in the West, the collapse of confidence. One of the most obvious refutations of Francis Fukuyama's famous thesis *The End of History*—written at the victory of liberal pluralist democracy over Soviet Communism—is that the victors didn't see it as such. Americans—or at least non-Democrat-voting Americans—may talk about "winning" the Cold War but the French and the Belgians and the Germans and the Canadians don't. Very few British do. These are all formal NATO allies—they were, technically, on the winning side against a horrible tyranny few would wish to live under themselves. In Europe, there was an initial moment of euphoria: it was hard not to be moved by the crowds sweeping through the Berlin Wall, especially as so many of them were hot-looking Red babes eager to enjoy a Carlsberg or Stella Artois with even the nerdiest running dog of imperialism. But when the moment faded, *pace* Fukuyama, there was no sense on the Continent that our Big Idea had beaten their Big Idea. With the best will in the world, it's hard to credit the citizens of France or Italy as having made any serious contribution to the defeat of Communism. Au contraire, millions of them voted for it, year in, year out. And with the end of the Soviet existential threat, the enervation of the West only accelerated.

In Thomas P. M. Barnett's book *Blueprint for Action*, Robert D. Kaplan, a very shrewd observer of global affairs, is quoted referring to the lawless fringes of the map as "Indian territory." It's a droll joke but a misleading one. The difference between the old Indian territory and the new is this: no one had to worry about the Sioux riding down Fifth Avenue. Today, with a few hundred bucks on his ATM card, the fellow from the badlands can be in the heart of the metropolis within hours. Here's another difference: in the old days, the white man settled the Indian territory. Now the followers of the badland's radical imams settle the metropolis. And another difference: technology. In the old days, the Injuns had bows and arrows and the cavalry had rifles. In today's Indian territory, countries that can't feed their own people have nuclear weapons.

But beyond that, the very phrase "Indian territory" presumes that inevitably these badlands will be brought within the bounds of the ordered world. In fact, a lot of today's "Indian territory" was relatively ordered a generation or two back—West Africa, Pakistan, Bosnia. Though

Eastern Europe and Latin America and parts of Asia are freer now than they were in the seventies, other swathes of the map have spiraled backwards. Which is more likely? That the parts of the world under pressure will turn into post-Communist Poland or post-Communist Yugoslavia? In Europe, the demographic pressures favor the latter.

The enemies we face in the future will look a lot like al Qaeda: transnational, globalized, locally franchised, extensively outsourced—but tied together through a powerful identity that leaps frontiers and continents. They won't be nation states and they'll have no interest in becoming nation states, though they might use the husks thereof, as they did in Afghanistan and then Somalia. The jihad may be the first, but other transnational deformities will embrace similar techniques. September 10 institutions like the UN and the EU will be unlikely to provide effective responses.

I never thought I'd find myself in the Doom-Mongering section of the bookstore, and, to be fair to myself, there is one significant difference between what you're about to read and the frostbitten-population explosions-foraging for zinc scenarios above. I'll come to that difference in a moment, because it's critical to understanding the central equation in human development: the intersection of demography and will. Demography is mainly a matter of number-crunching, dry statistics. The second phenomenon—will—is a little less concrete, but just as important.

When Osama bin Laden made his observation about people being attracted to the strong horse rather than the weak horse, it was partly a perception issue. You can be, technically, the strong horse—plenty of tanks and bombs and nukes and whatnot—but, if you're seen as too feeble ever to deploy them, you'll be kitted out for the weak-horse suit. He wasn't thinking of Europe, whose reabsorption within the caliphate Islamists see as all but complete. Rather, he was considering the hyperpower. In late September 2001 Maulana Inyadullah was holed up in Peshawar awaiting the call to arms against the Great Satan and offered this pithy soundbite to David Blair of Britain's *Daily Telegraph*: "The Americans love Pepsi-Cola, we love death."

Compare Mr. Inyadullah with the acclaimed London novelist Margaret Drabble, also speaking in the *Daily Telegraph*, just after the Iraq war. She feels the same way, at least about carbonated beverages: "I detest Coca-

Cola, I detest burgers, I detest sentimental and violent Hollywood movies
that tell lies about history. I detest American imperialism, American infan-
tilism, and American triumphalism about victories it didn't even win."

Look at Ms. Drabble's list of grievances. If you lived in Poland in the
1930s, you weren't worried about the Soviets' taste in soft drinks or sentimental Third Reich movies. America is the most benign hegemon in history: it's the world's first non-imperial superpower and, at the dawn of
the American moment, it chose to set itself up as a kind of geopolitical
sugar daddy. By picking up the tab for Europe's defense, it hoped to prevent those countries lapsing into traditional power rivalries. Nice idea.
But it also absolved them of the traditional responsibilities of nation-
hood, turning the alliance into a dysfunctional sitcom family, with one
grown-up presiding over a brood of whiny teenagers—albeit (demographically) the world's wrinkliest teenagers. America's preference for
diluting its power within the UN and other organs of an embryo world
government has not won it friends. All dominant powers are hated—
Britain was, and Rome—but they're usually hated for the right reasons.
America is hated for every reason. The fanatical Muslims despise America because it's all lap-dancing and gay porn; the secular Europeans
despise America because it's all born-again Christians hung up on abortion; the anti-Semites despise America because it's controlled by Jews.
Too Jewish, too Christian, too godless, America is George Orwell's
Room 101: whatever your bugbear you will find it therein; whatever
you're against, America is the prime example of it.

That's one reason why its disparagers have embraced environmental-
ism. If Washington were a conventional great power, the intellectual class
would be arguing that the United States is a threat to France or India or
Gabon or some such. But because it's so obviously not that kind of power
the world has had to concoct a thesis that the hyperpower is a threat not
merely to this or that rinky-dink nation state but to the entire planet, if
not the entire galaxy. "We are," warns Al Gore portentously, "altering the
balance of energy between our planet and the rest of the universe."

Think globally, act lunarly. The "balance of energy" between Earth and
"the rest of the universe"? You wouldn't happen to have the statistical
evidence for that, would you? Universal "balance of energy" graphs for

1940 and 1873? Heigh-ho. America is a threat not because of conventional great-power designs, but because—even scarier—of its "consumption," its way of life. Those Drabble-detested Cokes and burgers are straining the Earth in ways that straightforward genocidal conquerors like Hitler and Stalin could only have dreamed of. The construct of this fantasy is very revealing about how unthreatening America is.

But others cast the hyperpower's geniality in a different light. Visitors to America often remark on that popular T-shirt slogan usually found below a bold Stars and Stripes: "These Colors Don't Run." To non-Americans, it can seem a trifle touchy. But for a quarter century the presumption of the country's enemies was that those colors did run—they ran from Vietnam, they ran from the downed choppers in the Iranian desert, they ran from Somalia. Even the successful campaigns—the inconclusively concluded 1991 Gulf War and the air-only 1999 Kosovo war—seemed manifestly designed to avoid putting those colors in the position of having to run. As Osama saw it, those colors ran from the African embassy bombings and the Khobar towers, just as Zarqawi figured those colors would run from the Sunni Triangle. Being seen not to run—or, if you prefer, being seen to show "resolve"—should be the indispensable objective of U.S. foreign policy. Were these colors to run from Iraq, it would be the end of the American era—for why would Russia, China, or even Belgium ever again take seriously a superpower that runs screaming for home at the first pinprick?

Don't take Osama's, or Saddam's, or Mullah Omar's, or the Chinese politburo's word for it. Consider those nations who (a) regard themselves as broadly well-disposed toward America and (b) share the view that Islamism represents a critical global security threat, yet (c) have concluded that the United States lacks the will to get the job done. You hear such worries routinely expressed by the political class in India, Singapore, and other emerging nations. The British historian Niall Ferguson talks about "the clay feet of the colossus." Admiral Yamamoto's "sleeping giant" has become harder to rouse—the La-Z-Boy recliner's a lot more comfortable and pampering than the old rocker on the porch. In Vietnam, it took 50,000 deaths to drive the giant away; maybe in the Middle East, it will only take 5,000. And maybe in the next war the giant will give up after 500, or 50, or not bother at all. Our enemies have made a bet—that the West in general and the United States in particular are soft and decadent and have no attention span. America has the advantage of the most powerful army on the face of the planet, but she doesn't have the stomach for war, so it's no advantage at all. After all, if you were a typical viewer of CNN International (which makes CNN's domestic service look like a 24/7 Michael Savage channel), what would have made the biggest impression on you since September 11? That America has the best, biggest, and most technologically advanced military on the planet? Or that the minute you send it anywhere hysterical congressmen are shrieking that we need an "exit strategy"? The corpulent snorer in the La-Z-Boy recliner may have a beautifully waxed Ferrari in the garage, but he hates having to take it out on the potholed roads. Still, it looks mighty nice parked in the driveway when he washes it.

●   ●   ●

ALTERNATIVE REALITIES

If Europe's dwindling manpower and will are a one-way ticket on the oblivion express, numbers plus will is the most potent combination of all: serious people power. What does it mean when the fastest-growing population on the planet is a group that, to put it at its mildest, has a somewhat fractious relationship with the characteristics of a free society?

Can the developed world get more Muslim in its demographic character without becoming more Muslim in its political character? And what consequences does that have for art and culture, science and medicine, innovation and energy...and basic liberties?

Perhaps the differences will be minimal. In France, the Catholic churches will become mosques; in England, the village pubs will cease serving alcohol; in the Netherlands, the gay nightclubs will close up shop and relocate to San Francisco. But otherwise life will go on much as before. The new Europeans will be observant Muslims instead of post-Christian secularists, but they will still be recognizably European. It will be like *Cats* after a cast change: same long-running show, new actors. Or maybe the all-black Broadway production of *Hello, Dolly!* is a better comparison: Pearl Bailey instead of Carol Channing, but the plot, the music, the sets are all the same. The animating principles of advanced societies are so strong that they will thrive, whoever's at the switch.

But what if it doesn't work out like that? In the 2005 rankings of Freedom House's survey of personal liberty and democracy around the world, five of the eight countries with the lowest "freedom" score were Muslim. Of the forty-six Muslim majority nations in the world, only three were free. Of the sixteen nations in which Muslims form between 20 and 50 percent of the population, only another three were ranked as free: Benin, Serbia and Montenegro, and Suriname. It will be interesting to follow France's fortunes as a fourth member of that group.

We can argue about what consequences these demographic trends will have, but to say blithely they have none is ridiculous. In his book *The Empty Cradle*, Philip Longman writes:

> So where will the children of the future come from? Increasingly they will come from people who are at odds with the modern world. Such a trend, if sustained, could drive human culture off its current market-driven, individualistic, modernist course, gradually creating an anti-market culture dominated by fundamentalism—a new Dark Ages.

Mr. Longman's point is well taken. The refined antennae of Western liberals mean that whenever one raises the question of whether there will be any Italians living in the geographical zone marked as Italy a generation or three hence, they cry, "Racism!" To agitate about what proportion of the population is "white" is grotesque and inappropriate. But it's not about race; it's about culture. If 100 percent of your population believes in liberal pluralist democracy, it doesn't matter whether 70 percent of them are "white" or only 5 percent are. But if one part of your population believes in liberal pluralist democracy and the other doesn't, then it becomes a matter of great importance whether the part that does is 90 percent of the population or only 60 percent, or 50, or 45 percent. Which is why that question lies at the heart of almost any big international news story of recent years—the French riots, the attacks on Danish embassies and consulates over the publication of cartoons of Mohammed, the murder of Dutch filmmaker Theo van Gogh, Turkey's membership in the European Union, Pakistani riots over *Newsweek*'s Koran-down-the-toilet story. Whenever I make that point, lefties always respond, "Oh, well, that's typical right-wing racism." In fact, it ought to be the Left's issue. I'm a "social conservative." When the mullahs take over, I'll grow my beard a little fuller, get a couple extra wives, and keep my head down. It's the feminists and gays who'll have a tougher time. If, say, three of the five judges on the Massachusetts Supreme Court are Muslim, what are the chances of them approving "gay marriage"? That's the scenario Europe's looking at a few years down the road.

The basic demography explains, for example, the critical difference between the "war on terror" for Americans and Europeans: in the U.S., the war is something to be fought in the treacherous sands of the Sunni Triangle and the caves of the Hindu Kush; you go to faraway places and kill foreigners. But in Europe it's a civil war. Neville Chamberlain dismissed Czechoslovakia as "a faraway country of which we know little." This time around, for much of Western Europe it turned out the faraway country of which they knew little was their own.

As for America, Shelby Steele sees the tentativeness of our performance in Iraq as a geopolitical version of "white guilt," a "secular penitence" for the sins of the past. Even while waging war, our culture has internalized the morbid syndromes of the age: who are we to liberate the Iraqis? We represent imperialism and all the other evils.

On that point, I wish we did represent imperialism, at least to this extent: there's a lot to be said for a great nation that understands its greatness is not an accident and that therefore it should spread the secrets of its success around; conversely, there's not much to be said for a great nation that chooses to hobble itself by pretending it's merely one vote among co-equals on international bodies manned by Cuba and Sudan—the transnational version of "affirmative action," to extend Shelby Steele's thought.

As clashes of civilizations go, this one's between two extremes: on the one hand, a world that has everything it needs to wage decisive war—wealth, armies, industry, technology; on the other, a world that has nothing but pure ideology and plenty of believers. Everything else it requires it can pick up at Radio Shack: cell phones and laptops, which, along with ATM cards and some dime-store box-cutters, were all it took to pull off September 11.

For this to be an existential struggle, as the Cold War was, the question is: are they a credible enemy to us?

For a projection of the likely outcome, the question is: are we a credible enemy to them?

You may recall a pertinent detail during the bogus controversy over the "torture" of prisoners at Guantánamo Bay: U.S. guards at Gitmo are under instructions to handle copies of the Koran only when wearing gloves. The reason for this is that the detainees regard infidels as "unclean." But it's one thing for the Islamists to think infidels are unclean, quite another for the infidels to agree with them—and, by doing so, to validate their bigotry. Far from being tortured, the prisoners are being handled literally with kid gloves (or simulated kid-effect gloves). The U.S. military hands each jihadist his complimentary copy of the Koran as delicately as white-gloved butlers bringing His Lordship the *Times* of London. It's not just unbecoming to buy in to Muslim psychoses; in the end, it's self-defeating. And our self-defeat is their surest shot at victory. Four years into the "war on terror," the Bush administration began promoting a new formulation: "the long war." Not a good sign. In a short war, put your money on tanks and bombs—our strengths. In a long war, the better bet is will and manpower—their strengths. Even a loser can win when he's up against a defeatist. A big chunk of Western Civilization, consciously or otherwise, has given the impression that it's dying to surrender to somebody, anybody. Reasonably enough, the jihadists figure: hey, why not us?

The longer the long war gets, the harder it will be, because it's a race against time, against lengthening demographic, economic, and geopolitical odds. By "demographic," I mean the Muslim world's high birth rate, which by mid-century will give tiny Yemen a higher population than vast empty Russia. By "economic," I mean the perfect storm the Europeans will face within this decade, because their lavish welfare states are unsustainable with their post-Christian birth rates. By "geopolitical," I mean that if you think the United Nations and other international organizations are antipathetic to America now, wait a few years and see what kind of support you get from a semi-Islamified Europe.

I said above that there is one difference between me and the other doom-mongers. For Al Gore and Paul Ehrlich and Co., whatever the problem, the solution is always the same. Whether it's global cooling, global warming, or overpopulation, we need bigger government, more regulation, higher taxes, and a massive transfer of power from the citizen to some unelected self-perpetuating crisis lobby. Not only does this not solve the problem, it is, in fact, a symptom of the real problem: the torpor of the West derives in part from the annexation by government of most of the core functions of adulthood. Even in America, too many Democrats take it as read that the natural destination of an advanced Western democracy is Scandinavia. If it is, we're all doomed. Every successful society is a balancing act between the private and the public, but in Europe and Canada the balance is way out of whack. When the foreign policy panjandrums talk about our enemies, they distinguish between "rogue states" like Iran and North Korea and "non-state actors" like al Qaeda and Hezbollah. But those distinctions apply on the home front too. Big governments are "rogue states," out of control and lacking the wit and agility to see off the threats to our freedom. Citizens willing to be "non-state actors" are just as important and, as we saw on Flight 93, a decisive part of our defense, nimbler and more efficient than the federal behemoth. The free world's citizenry could use more non-state actors.

So this is a doomsday book with a twist: an apocalyptic scenario that can best be avoided not by more government but by less—by government returning to the citizenry the primal responsibilities it's taken from them in the modern era.

The alternative is stark: Europe has all but succumbed to the dull opiate of multiculturalism. In its drowsy numbness, it stirs but has no idea what to do and so does nothing. One day, years from now, as archaeologists sift through the ruins of an ancient civilization for clues to its downfall, they'll marvel at how easy it all was. You don't need to fly jets into skyscrapers and kill thousands of people. As a matter of fact, that's a bad strategy, because even the wimpiest state will feel obliged to respond. But if you frame the issue in terms of multicultural "sensitivity," the wimp state will bend over backward to give you everything you want—including, eventually, the keys to those skyscrapers. Thus, during the Danish "cartoon jihad" of 2006, Jack Straw, then British foreign secretary, hailed the "sensitivity" of Fleet Street in not reprinting the offending representations of the Prophet.

No doubt he was similarly impressed by the "sensitivity" of Burger King, which withdrew ice cream cones from its British menus because Mr. Rashad Akhtar of High Wycombe complained that the creamy swirl shown on the lid looked like the word "Allah" in Arabic script. I don't know which sura in the Koran says, "Don't forget, folks, it's not just physical representations of God or the Prophet but also chocolate ice cream squiggly representations of the name," but ixnay on both just to be "sensitive."

And doubtless the British foreign secretary also appreciated the "sensitivity" of the owner of *France-Soir*, who fired his editor for republishing the Danish cartoons. And maybe he even admires the "sensitivity" of the increasing numbers of Dutch people who dislike the pervasive fear and tension in certain parts of the Netherlands and so have emigrated to Canada, Australia, and New Zealand.

One day the British foreign secretary will wake up and discover that, in practice, there's very little difference between living under Exquisitely Refined Multicultural Sensitivity and sharia. As a famously sensitive non-cartooning Dane once put it: "To be or not to be: that is the question."

And, in the end, the answer to that question is the only one that matters.

Part I

The Gelded Age

DEMOGRAPHY, DEMOCRACY, DESTINY

Chapter One

The Coming of Age

BIRTHS VS. DEARTHS

Civilizations die from suicide, not murder.

ARNOLD J. TOYNBEE, *A STUDY OF HISTORY* (1934–1961)

M y old—very old—friend George Abbott, the director of *On the Town*, *Damn Yankees*, and *Pal Joey*, died in 1995 at the age of 107 while working on a revival of *The Pajama Game*. A few years earlier, in his late nineties, he'd given up playing tennis because all his partners had died. That's the position America is facing in respect to its transnational social life: it'll be turning up to the G-8, NATO, and the EU-US summit only to find that all its partners have died.

The single most important fact about the early twenty-first century is the rapid aging of almost every developed nation other than the United States: Canada, Europe, and Japan are getting old fast, older than any functioning society has ever been and faster than any has ever aged. A society ages when its birth rate falls and it finds itself with fewer children and more grandparents. For a stable population—i.e., no growth, no decline, just a million folks in 1950, a million in 1980, a million in 2010—you need a total fertility rate of 2.1 live births per woman. That's what America has: 2.1, give or take. Canada has 1.48, an all-time low and a more revealing difference between the Great Satan and the Great White North than any of the stuff (socialized health care, fewer handguns, more UN peacekeepers, etc.) that Canucks usually brag about. Europe as a whole has 1.38; Japan, 1.32; Russia, 1.14. These countries— or, more precisely, these people—are going out of business.

There's nothing wrong with old folks: speaking for myself, if I'm at some soiree, I'd much rather Doris Day provided the evening's musical entertainment than the latest caterwauling gangsta rapper; I'd rather date Debbie Reynolds than Angelina Jolie. But even to put it in those terms is to become aware of how our assumptions about a society's health—about its innovative and creative energies—are based on its youthfulness. Picture the difference between a small northern mill town where the mill's closed down and the young people have moved away and a growing community in the Sun Belt. Which has the bigger range of stores and restaurants, more work opportunities, better school choice? Which problem would you rather have—managing growth or managing decline?

So what happens when the whole nation—and in Europe the entire continent—has a profile closer to the decrepit mill town than to the Sun Belt suburb?

And, if you're anti-capitalist, don't console yourself with the thought that you don't need all those businesses anyway. Big Government depends on bigger population: Americans have a relatively smallish government compared to Canada and Europe, but the U.S. Social Security system assumes a 30 percent population growth between now and 2075 or so and, even then, expects to be running a deficit after 2017. Now imagine you're Spain and you've got even bigger public pensions liabilities and a population that's going to be halving every thirty-five years. The progressive Left can be in favor of Big Government or population control but not both. That mutual incompatibility is about to plunge Europe into societal collapse. There is no precedent in human history for economic growth on declining human capital—and that's before anyone invented unsustainable welfare systems.

True, birth rates are falling all over the world, and it may be that eventually every couple on the planet decides to opt for the Western yuppie model of one designer baby at the age of thirty-nine. But demographics is a game of last man standing. The groups that succumb to demographic apathy last will have a huge advantage—and those societies with expensive social programs dependent on mass immigration will be in the worst predicament. It's no consolation for the European Union, with its deathbed birth statistics, if the Third World's demographics are also falling: they're your nursery, they're the babies you couldn't be bothered to have; if their fertility rate goes the same way yours has, that will be a problem for you long before it's a problem for them. Unless it corrects course within the next five to ten years, Europe by the end of this century will be a continent after the neutron bomb: the grand buildings will still be standing but the people who built them will be gone. By the next century, German will be spoken only at Hitler, Himmler, Goebbels and Goering's Monday night poker game in Hell. And long before the Maldive Islands are submerged by "rising sea levels" every Spaniard and Italian will be six feet under. But sure, go ahead and worry about "climate change."

More immediately, Europe will be semi-Islamic in its politico-cultural character within a generation.

In the fourteenth century, the Black Death wiped out a third of the Continent's population; in the twenty-first, a larger proportion will disappear—in effect, by choice. We are living through a rare moment: the self-extinction of the civilization which, for good or ill, shaped the age we live in. One can cite examples of remote backward tribes who expire upon contact with the modern world, but for the modern world

to expire in favor of the backward tribes is a turn of events future anthro-
pologists will ponder, as we do the fall of Rome.

●   ●   ●

THE MATH OF THE MAP

My interest in demography dates back to September 11, 2001, when a
demographic group I hadn't given much thought to managed to get my
attention. I don't mean the, ah, unfortunate business with the planes and
buildings and so forth, but the open cheering of the attacks by their co-
religionists in Montreal, Yorkshire, Copenhagen, and elsewhere. How
many of us knew there were quickly growing and culturally confident
Muslim populations in Scandinavia?

Demography doesn't explain everything, but it accounts for a good 90
percent—including the easy stuff, like why Jacques Chirac wasn't
amenable to Colin Powell's schmoozing on Iraq: if the population of your
cities was 30 percent Muslim, with spectacularly high youth unemployment rates and a bunch of other grievances, would you be so eager to send
your troops into an Arab country fighting alongside the Great Satan?
Stick a pin almost anywhere in the map, near or far: the "who" is the best
indicator of the what-where-when-why. Remember how it was when you
watched TV in the eighties? You'd be bombarded with commercials warning that the Yellow Peril was annexing America and pretty soon they'd be
speaking Japanese down at the shopping mall. It didn't happen and it's
never going to happen. In the nineties, I tended to accept the experts' line
that Japan's rising sun had gone into eclipse because its economy was riddled with protectionism, cronyism, and inefficient special-interest groups.
But so what? You could have said the same in the sixties and seventies,
when the joint was jumping. The only real structural difference between
Japan then and Japan now is that the Yellow Peril got a lot wrinklier.
What happened in the 1990s was what Yamada Masahiro of Tokyo's
Gakugei University calls the first "low birth-rate recession." It's not the
economy, stupid. It's the stupidity, economists—the stupidity of thinking

you can ignore demography. Japanese society aged, and aged societies, by their nature, are more cautious and less dynamic: old people weigh exposure to risk more than potential for gain.

Another example: will China be the hyperpower of the twenty-first century? Answer: no. Its population will get old before it's got rich.

Another: why did Bosnia collapse into the worst slaughter in Europe since World War Two? In the thirty years before the meltdown, Bosnian Serbs had declined from 43 percent to 31 percent of the population, while Bosnian Muslims had increased from 26 percent to 44 percent. In a democratic age, you can't buck demography—except through civil war. The Serbs figured that out—as other Continentals will in the years ahead: if you can't outbreed the enemy, cull 'em. The problem Europe faces is that Bosnia's demographic profile is now the model for the entire continent.

The literal facts of life are also what underpinned the so-called "cartoon jihad" of early 2006. It was a small portent of the future: the publication by one Danish newspaper of various cartoonists' mostly very mild representations of the Prophet Mohammed was the pretext for weeks of protests, lawsuits, death threats, rioting, torching, razing, and killing by disaffected Muslims from Calgary to Islamabad, London to Jakarta. On September 10, 2001, not many of us thought it would soon seem perfectly routine to hear news announcers read headlines like: "The Danish cartoon death toll is now up to nine."

No laughing matter, especially as that number multiplied into double and triple figures. But it's remarkable how quickly we've internalized the underlying demographic reality. Like all the mini-crises afflicting the Continent since September 11, its subtext derives from the belated realization among Europeans that they're elderly and fading and that their Muslim populations are young and surging, and in all these clashes the latter are putting down markers for the way things will be the day after tomorrow, like the new owners who have the kitchen remodeled before moving in. When it came to those cartoons, every Internet blogger was eager to take a stand on principle alongside plucky little Denmark. But there's only five million of them. Whereas there are twenty million Muslims in Europe—officially. That's the equivalent of the Danes plus the Irish plus the Belgians plus the Estonians. You do the math.

What's the Muslim population of Rotterdam? Forty percent. What's the most popular baby boy's name in Belgium? Mohammed. In Amsterdam? Mohammed. In Malmö, Sweden? Mohammed. By 2005, it was the fifth most popular baby boy's name in the United Kingdom. Yet most Europeans weren't even aware of the dominant demographic trend until September 11, and subsequent events in Madrid, Paris, and London.

Or to put it at its most basic: Why is the world we live in the way it is? Why is this book written in the language of a tiny island off the coast of northern Europe? Why is English the language of global business, of the Internet, of the paramount power of the age and of dozens of other countries from Belize to Botswana, Nigeria to Nauru? Why does Canada share its queen with Papua New Guinea? Why does a quarter of the world's population belong to the British Commonwealth and enjoy to one degree or another English Common Law and Westminster parliamentary traditions?

Because in the early nineteenth century the first nation to conquer infant mortality was England. Hitherto, the British Isles had been like the rest of the world: you had a big bunch of kids and a lot of them died before they could be of economic benefit to you or to society. But by 1820 medical progress and improvements in basic hygiene had so transformed British life that half the population was under the age of fifteen. In sheer numbers, the country was still a pipsqueak cluster of North Atlantic islands with 28 million people compared to China's 320 million. But it was the underlying demographic trend that proved decisive in the century ahead. Britain had the surplus manpower not just to settle Canada, Australia, and New Zealand, but also to provide the administrative and business class in the West Indies, Africa, India, and the Pacific. And, fortunately for the world, this demographic transformation occurred in a culture that even then had a long-established system of law, property rights, and personal freedom.

Imagine what the planet would look like if the first country to conquer infant mortality had been a country with a less sustained tradition of individual liberty—China, say, or Japan or Russia or Germany. The "what," "where," and "when" are important, but the "who" is critical. It's hard to have a big influence in the world when there's just a few of you and you're all getting on in years.

So who's in the situation of England at the beginning of the nineteenth century? What country today has half its population under the age of fifteen?

Spain and Germany have 14 percent, the United Kingdom 18 percent, the United States 21 percent—and Saudi Arabia has 39 percent, Pakistan 40 percent, and Yemen 47 percent. Little Yemen, like little Britain two hundred years ago, will send its surplus youth around the world—one way or another. Cultural relativists who sneer at the idea of English civilization should try to imagine what the world would be like if the U.S. Supreme Court and the Indian parliament and the Australian legal system, not to mention Harvard and Yale, Oxford and Cambridge, had been built on Yemeni values.

The state of our civilization manifests itself both in the non-problems that terrify us beyond all reason—rising sea levels—and in the real problems we pay no heed to. So David Remnick, editor of the famously fact-checked-to-death *New Yorker*, declares to the magazine's readers that the earth will "likely be an uninhabitable planet." In reality, much of the planet will be uninhabited long before it's uninhabitable. Yet environmentalists couldn't be less interested in the politics of people—people who need people. *Pace* Barbra Streisand, they're the unluckiest people in the world— as we're about to find out. When my second child was born, a neighbor said, "Well, you've got two. You can stop now." She was being enlightened and responsible. After all, for her entire adult life, the progressive-minded have worried about "overpopulation." And this view became so pervasive that, in an age of hysteria about "dwindling resources," it became entirely normal to look on our greatest resource—us—as a liability. So today we're the dwindling resource, not the oil. We're the endangered species, not the spotted owl. The "population explosion" is a prop of the Western progressive's bizarre death-cultism. We are so bad, so polluting, so exploitative, so violent, so destructive that we owe it to the world not to be born in the first place. As Dr. Sue Blackmore wrote (in Britain's *Guardian*) in an unintentional side-splitter of an enviro-doom column:

> In all probability billions of people are going to die in the next few decades. Our poor, abused planet cannot take much more....If we take the unselfish route and try to save everyone the outcome is likely to be horrific conflict in the fight over resources, and continuing devastation of the planet until most, or all, of humanity is dead.
>
> If we decide to put the planet first, then we ourselves are the pathogen. So we should let as many people die as possible, so that other species may live, and accept the destruction of civilization and of everything we have achieved.
>
> Finally, we might decide that civilization itself is worth preserving. In that case we have to work out what to save and which people would be needed in a drastically reduced population—weighing the value of scientists and musicians against that of politicians, for example.

Hmm. On the one hand, Dr. Sue Blackmore and the bloke from Coldplay. On the other, Dick Cheney. I think we can all agree which people would be "needed"—Al Gore, the board of the Sierra Club, perhaps Scarlett Johansson in a fur-trimmed bikini paddling a dugout canoe through a waterlogged Manhattan foraging for floating curly endives from once fashionable eateries.

Curiously, those environmentalists calling for a dramatically smaller population never seem to lead by example, and always manage to give the impression that no matter how small the ark is they're a shoo-in for a first-class stateroom. But, as it happens, Dr. Blackmore won't have to worry about whether to sacrifice Jacques Chirac and Vladimir Putin in order to save Sting and Bono. Given the plummeting birth rates in Europe, Russia, Japan, etc., a large chunk of the world has evidently decided to take pre-emptive action on climate change and opt for societal suicide. The crisis we face today is the precise opposite of "overpopulation": the developed world's population is shrinking faster than any human society not in the grip of war or disease has ever shrunk. Does the environmental movement sicken itself only over the black rhino and the green-cheeked parrot? Aren't people part of the environment? They certainly have environmental implications. For one thing, there'll be far fewer environmentalists around. By the end of this century, the demographically doomed Italians and Spaniards will be so few in number there won't be enough Continental environmentalists left to man the local Greenpeace office. The Belgian climate-change lobbyist will be on the endangered species list with the Himalayan snow leopard. And, from an American point of view, the blue-state ecochondriacs of Massachusetts and California will be finding the international sustainable-development conferences a lot lonelier.

As for the merits of scientists and artists over politicians, those parts of the world still breeding are notable for their antipathy to music, haven't done much in the way of science for over a millennium, and politics-wise incline mostly to dictators and mullahs, nuclear or otherwise. Scrap Scarlett Johansson's fur-trimmed bikini and stick her in a waterlogged burqa.

Most twenty-year projections (on economic growth, global warming, etc.) are laughably speculative, and thus most doomsday scenarios are too. The eco-doom-mongers get it wrong because they fail to take into account human inventiveness: *We can't feed the world!* they shriek. But we develop more efficient farming methods with nary a thought. *The oil will run out by the year 2000!* they warn. But we develop new extraction methods and find we've got enough oil for as long as we'll need it.

But human inventiveness depends on humans—and that's the one thing we really are running short of, at least in the self-flagellating developed world.

●　　●　　●

THE WEST RUNS OUT OF STOCK

Take an alphabetical list of nations of the world and start at the beginning:

1. Afghanistan. In 2005, the rate of births per 1,000 people in the country was 47.02.
2. Albania. In 2005, the rate of births per 1,000 people in the country was 15.08.

That means Albanians are breeding at a third of the rate of Afghans. As noted above, "replacement" fertility rate—i.e., the number you need for merely a stable population, not getting any bigger, not getting any smaller—is 2.1 babies per woman. Some countries are well above that: the global fertility leader, Niger, is 7.46; Mali, 7.42; Somalia, 6.76; Afghanistan, 6.69; Yemen, 6.58. Notice what those nations have in common? Starts with an *I*, ends with a *slam*. As in: slam dunk.

Go back to that Albanian fertility rate. It looks low compared to Afghanistan but it's the highest in Europe. And why would that be? Because it's Europe's only majority Muslim country. At the moment.

Scroll way down to the bottom of the Hot One Hundred top breeders and you'll eventually find the United States, hovering just at replacement rate with 2.11 births per woman. New Zealand's just below; Ireland's at 1.9; Australia, 1.7. But Canada's fertility rate is down to 1.5, well below replacement rate; Germany and Austria are at 1.3, the brink of the death spiral; Russia and Italy are at 1.2; Spain, 1.1—about half replacement rate. So Spain's population is halving with every generation. Two grown-ups have a total of one baby. So there are half as many children as parents. And a quarter as many grandchildren as grandparents. And an eighth as many great-grandchildren as great-grandparents. And after that there's no point extrapolating, because you're over the falls and it's too late to start paddling back. I received a flurry of letters from furious Spaniards when the government decided to replace the words "father" and "mother" on its birth certificates with the less orientationally offensive terms "Progenitor A" and "Progenitor B." This was part of the bureaucratic spring-cleaning of traditional language that always accompanies the arrival in law of "gay marriage." But with historically low numbers of progeny, the designations of the respective progenitors seem of marginal concern. No point renaming the teams if you no longer play the game. They might at least encourage young Spaniards to wander into the Barcelona singles bars and try out the line: "Do you want to come back to my pad and play Progenitor A and Progenitor B?" "Well, okay, but only if I can be Progenitor A..."

Just as revealing, in 2006 Spain's ruling Socialist Party introduced a bill in parliament legislating that apes be included in "the category of persons, and that they be given the moral and legal protection that currently are only enjoyed by human beings." The party's argument was that human Spaniards do, after all, share 98.4 percent of their genes with chimpanzees, 97.7 percent with gorillas, and 96.4 percent with orangutans. Unfortunately, the 2 percent Spaniards don't share apparently includes the urge to reproduce. For the new Europe, instead of Gibbon's *Decline and Fall*, maybe someone should write *Gibbons' Rise and Triumph*. But why stop there? Why not give sheep the right to an abortion? Or allow gerbils to contract gay marriage? With a cockatoo? Why does the king of Spain not simply declare that henceforth, by royal proclamation, pigs shall fly?

By 2050, Italy's population will have fallen by 22 percent, Bulgaria's by 36 percent, Estonia's by 52 percent—or more. Seventeen European nations are now at what demographers call "lowest-low" fertility: 1.3 births per woman. In theory, those countries will find their population halving every thirty-five years or so. In practice, it will be quicker than that, as the savvier youngsters figure there's no point sticking around a country that's turned into an undertaker's waiting room. Not every pimply burger flipper wants to support entire old folks' homes single-handed and, aside from the economic argument, there are cultural factors too: I love going into Viennese record stores where the main floor's full of waltzes and operetta, and the hip-hop section's one tiny bin down in the back of the basement. But if you're young and fancy a burg with more of a buzz on the cutting edge of the zeitgeist you're unlikely to find it in Western Europe circa 2020.

As for America, demographic trends suggest that the blue states ought to apply for honorary membership of the EU; in the 2004 election, the Bush-voting states had fertility rates 12 percent higher than Kerry-voting states. Barring a sudden change in electoral fortunes, Democrats are going to be even more depressed after the 2010 and 2020 reapportionments.

Those who pooh-pooh the United States' comparatively robust demographics say they reflect nothing more than the fecundity of Hispanic immigration—it's the legions of the undocumented who are filling the maternity wards. In fact, white women in America still breed at a greater rate—1.85 or so—than white women in Europe or Canada. And, from the Democrats' point of view, as they preside over dwindling school enrollments from San Francisco to rural Vermont, the reality is that red-state white Americans breed above replacement rate. In demographic terms, the salient feature of much of the "progressive agenda"—abortion, gay marriage, endlessly deferred adulthood—is that, whatever the charms of any individual item, cumulatively it's a literal dead end.

As fertility dries up, so do societies. Demography is the most obvious symptom of civilizational exhaustion, and the clearest indicator of where we're headed. These countries are fading to oblivion unless they can change their ways, or train those orangutan citizens to serve the food at the seniors' community center. The tax revenues that support the ever-growing numbers of the elderly and retired have to be paid by equally growing numbers of the young and working. The design flaw of the radically secularist Eutopia is that it depends on a religious-society birth rate.

So, if Europeans and Canadians can no longer be bothered to have children, where's that workforce going to come from?

Easy, say the complaceniks at Toronto's *Globe and Mail*. In 2004, reacting to the lowest Canadian fertility rate since records began and a 25.4 percent fall since 1992, the *Globe*'s editorialists wrote: "Luckily for our future economic and fiscal well-being, Canada is well-positioned to counter the declining population trend by continuing to encourage the immigration of talented people to this country from overcrowded parts of the world."

Phew! So there's nothing to worry about, eh? Thank goodness for that. Canadians can all go back to sleep while reading the "Celebrate Diversity" booklet from the Department of Multiculturalism.

But hang on a minute: "talented people" from "overcrowded parts of the world"? Okay, name some.

The "experts" of the Western world are slower to turn around than an ocean liner, and in Europe they were still yakking about the "population explosion" even as their 1970s schoolhouses, built in anticipation of traditional Catholic birth rates, were emptying through the nineties and oughts. In the ne plus ultra of doomsday tracts, *The Population Bomb* (1968), Paul Ehrlich begins with a blithely snobbish account of trying to reach his hotel in Delhi through the teeming hordes of humanity:

> People eating, people washing, people sleeping. People visiting, people arguing and screaming. People thrust their hands through the taxi window, begging. People defecating and urinating. People clinging to buses. People herding animals. People, people, people, people.

But in the twenty-first century, even Delhi's running out of people. Even Paul Ehrlich's hellhole of choice doesn't have a high enough birth rate to maintain its population in the long term. Yet the complaceniks cling to the long-held Euro-Canadian policy of using the Third World as a farm team and denuding developing societies of their best and brightest. In the 2004 election, John Kerry and John Edwards made a big hoo-ha about "outsourcing"—i.e., American companies setting up a customer call center in Ireland or India. Outrageous! Yet most of the West has outsourced its entire future to the Third World. Just as America relies on the Chinese to make cheap Elmos and Poohs, so Canada relies on them to make cheap human beings—the children that domestic manufacturers in Canada, Europe, and elsewhere have concluded are prohibitively expensive to produce at home. Personally, I've never seen what's so liberal and enlightened, rather than lazy and selfish, about fleecing the Third World of its doctors and engineers. But, even if you approve of it, it won't be an option much longer. The UN's most recent population report has revised the global fertility rate down from 2.1—i.e., replacement rate—to 1.85— i.e., eventual population decline. World population will peak in about 2050 (I'd hazard earlier) and then fall. For Europeans too self-absorbed or over-taxed to breed, the fallback position for their own barrenness—use the Third World as your nursery—is also dead.

Post-Christian hyper-rationalism turns out to be, in the objective sense, a lot less rational than Catholicism or Mormonism. Indeed, in its reliance on immigration to ensure its future, the European Union has adopted a twenty-first-century variation on the strategy of the Shakers, who were forbidden from reproducing and thus could increase their numbers only by conversion.

Birth rates in the so-called "overcrowded" parts of the world are already 2.9 and falling. India has a quickly growing middle class and declining fertility. In 2020 "talented people" will be much sought after by all countries within the developed-but-depopulating world: how sure can Canadians be that an educated Indian will prefer a high-tax, low-temperature jurisdiction to America or Australia? Or, come to that, to his own economically booming country, where the fruits of his labor won't be shoveled straight into paying the debts run up by the wheezing boomers. The Third Worlders being born now in all but the most psychotic jurisdictions will reach adulthood with a range of options. By 2015, a smart, energetic Chinaman or Brazilian will be able to write his own ticket anywhere he wants. How attractive will the prospect of moving to the European Union and supporting a population of geriatric ingrate Continentals be? If that ratio of workers to retirees keeps heading in the same direction, the EU will have the highest taxes not just in the Western world, but in most of the rest. A middle-class Indian or Singaporean or Chilean already has little incentive to come to the Continent. If the supposedly insane neocon plan to remake the Middle East comes off, even your wacky Arabs may stay home.

●   ●   ●

EAST MEETS WEST

There is no "population bomb." There never was. Even in 1968 Paul Ehrlich and his ilk should have understood that their so-called "population explosion" was really a massive population adjustment. The world's people are a lot more Islamic than they were back then and a lot less "Western." Islam is the fastest-growing religion in Europe and North America: in the United Kingdom, more Muslims than Christians attend religious services each week. Meanwhile, in areas of traditionally moderate Islam, from the Balkans to Indonesia, Muslims are becoming radicalized and fiercer in their faith.

If a society chooses to outsource its breeding, who your suppliers are is not unimportant. "I've heard those very silly remarks made about immigrants to this country since I was a child," said Lyn Allison of the Australian Democrats, after a political opponent, Danna Vale, warned that the country could be swamped by Muslims. "If it wasn't the Greeks, it was the Italians...or it was the Vietnamese." But those are races or nationalities. Islam is a religion, and an explicitly political one—unlike the birthplace of your grandfather, it's not something you leave behind in the old country. Indeed, for many of its adherents in the West, it becomes their principal expression—a pan-Islamic identity that transcends borders. "You can't find any equivalent in Italian or Greek or Lebanese or Chinese or Baltic immigration to Australia. There is no equivalent of raving on about jihad," said the Aussie prime minister, John Howard, stating the obvious in a way most political leaders can't quite bring themselves to do. "There is really not much point in pretending it doesn't exist."

Islam is now the principal supplier of new Europeans, and currently the second biggest supplier of new Canadians. So it's worth mulling over the question John Howard suggests: What proportion of Western Muslims is hot for jihad? Five percent? Ten, 12, 20 percent? The years roll by since September 11, and for the most part we're none the wiser. Nonetheless, except for the willfully blind, the distinctions between Ms. Allison's "Greeks and Italians and Vietnamese" and Muslim immigration are clear. Instead of a melting pot, there's conversion: a Scot can marry a Greek or a Botswanan, but when a Scot marries a Yemeni it's because the former has become a Muslim. In defiance of normal immigration patterns, the host country winds up assimilating with Islam: French municipal swimming baths introduce gender-segregated bathing sessions; Australian hospitals remove pork from the cafeteria menu.

It's fair to point out that in much of the West "Western Civilization" has been only recently acquired. Until the 1970s, southern Europe was mostly dictatorships—Portugal, Spain, Greece. A generation earlier, Italy was a gangster state and Germany a genocidal one. The Muslim critique of the West—that we're decadent vulgar narcissist fornicating sodomites—is not without more than a grain of truth. But when the fastest-breeding demographic group on the planet is also the one most resistant to the pieties of the social-democratic state, that presents a severe challenge, at least for the Left. In their bizarre prioritization of "a woman's right to choose," feminists have helped ensure that European women will end their days in a culture that doesn't accord women the right to choose anything. Non-Muslim females in heavily Muslim neighborhoods in France now wear headscarves while out on the streets. Yes, yes, I know Islam is very varied, and Riyadh has a vibrant gay scene, and the Khartoum Feminist Publishing Collective now has so many members they've rented lavish new offices above the clitorectomy clinic. I don't pretend to have all the answers, except when I'm being interviewed live on TV. But that's better than pretending that there aren't even any questions.

Forget the Jews and the gays and the women and reduce it to its most basic: in most Muslim jurisdictions, there is simply no culture of inquiry. No notion that challenging, questioning, testing the assumptions of that society has any value. This isn't a recent development. For Islam's first two or three centuries, scholars busied themselves figuring out what the divine revelations of the Koran actually meant for the daily routine of believers. But by the eleventh century all four schools of Islamic law had concluded they were pretty much on top of things and there was no need for any further interpretation or investigation. And from that point on Islam coasted, and then declined. The famous United Nations statistic from a 2002 report—more books are translated into Spanish in a single year than have been translated into Arabic in the last thousand—suggests at the very minimum an extraordinarily closed world. What books are among the few they do translate? *Mein Kampf* and *The Protocols of the Elders of Zion*, both of which are prominently displayed bestsellers in even moderate Muslim countries—and, indeed, even in the Muslim stores on Edgware Road in the heart of London. No Islamic nation could have flown to the moon or invented the Internet, simply because for a millennium the culture has suppressed the curiosity necessary for such a venture.

You don't have to subscribe to the view that every Muslim is a jihadist nutcake eager to hijack a 747 and head for the nearest tall building to acknowledge that at the very minimum these population trends put a large question mark over the future. Let me pluck two interesting numbers:

- In the fall of 2001, the *Ottawa Citizen* conducted a coast-to-coast survey of Canadian imams and found all but two insistent that there was no Muslim involvement in September 11. Oh, well. It was just a few weeks after the attacks; everyone was still in shock. Perfectly understandable in its way.
- Five years later, in the summer of 2006, a poll in the United Kingdom found that only 17 percent of British Muslims believed there was any Arab involvement in September 11.

Anyone who's traveled in the Middle East will recognize that moment—not with the wacky death-to-the-Great-Satan guys but with the hot-looking Westernized Bahraini lady doctor you're enjoying a little incendiary flirting with. And then—ten, twenty, forty-five minutes into the conversation—she says something nutty. Often what's nuttiest is that it's completely illogical: in the spring of 2002, I met many Arabs who believed simultaneously that (a) September 11 was pulled off by the Mossad and (b) it was a great victory for the Muslim people.

What that British poll suggests is that the same syndrome is very advanced among Western Muslims. You can be perfectly assimilated when it comes to clothes, sports, pop music, the state of the economy, the need for transport infrastructure spending, and a million other issues, but on one of the central questions facing the world today 83 percent of the fastest-growing demographic in the United Kingdom does not accept the same reality as their fellow British subjects. And competing versions of reality is never a good recipe for social stability. Western Muslims are playing their own 24/7 version of the children's game "Opposite Land."

So if a population "at odds with the modern world" (in Philip Longman's phrase) is the fastest-breeding group on the planet, how safe a bet is the survival of the "modern world"? The principal challenge to the United States in the years ahead is to avoid winding up the lonesomest gal in town. Given that most of its old allies—the ones John Kerry places so much stock in—are unlikely to conjure up the will to save themselves, it's important that new allies are found among the emerging nations. I'm a supporter of the Bush Doctrine, of bringing liberty to the Middle East. It's a long shot, but, whatever their problems, most Islamic countries have the advantage of beginning any evolution into free states from the starting point of relative societal cohesion. By contrast, European nations face the trickier task of trying to hold on to their freedom at a time of cultural disintegration. Many of them won't make it. Watching the scenes of the anti-Danish protests on TV, as angry implacable crowds marched through the streets denouncing freedom as "Western terrorism" and pledging that "the enemies of Islam" would "drown in their own blood," I thought back to those times I've been in the Arab world and rounded a corner and found something scary going on—excitable men prancing around the streets doing the old "Death to the Great Satan" dance. In the Middle East, you quickly learn the art of backing out of the room without catching the crazy guy's eye. The problem for Europe is that it's their room the crazy guys are now in.

●   ●   ●

THE SEVENTH AGE

A good way to look at what's happening is via Shakespeare's seven ages of man:

> All the world's a stage,
>
> And all the men and women merely players,
>
> They have their exits and entrances...

And right now some of us are a lot closer to the exits and some of us are still pouring through the entrances. Look at the Bard's various "ages":

> ...Then a soldier.
>
> Full of strange oaths, and bearded like a pard,
>
> Jealous in honour, sudden and quick in quarrel,
>
> Seeking the bubble reputation
>
> Even in the cannon's mouth.

They're the foot soldiers of the jihad, the excitable young men you see on the news jumping up and down in the streets of Gaza and Islamabad torching the Stars and Stripes—and also (and more important) the ones who take flight training so they can plough jets into skyscrapers, who take whitewater rafting breaks in Wales so they'll be at the peak of fitness when they self-detonate on the London Tube, the ones who define courage as the ability to look a seven-year-old Beslan schoolgirl in the eye and kill her: full of strange oaths, seeking the bubble reputation in the cannon's mouth, or even the canon's mouth—the incendiary imam urging them on to martyrdom. Over the next generation, that population of excitable young men will explode—demographically I mean, though very literally if the more severe mullahs have their way. By 2050, Muslim fertility rates will be in decline, as they already are in some of the more developed Islamic countries. But they'll be beginning their decline much later than Europe's, or Canada's, or Vermont's, and so they will have a huge demographic advantage. And given that that's the sole advantage they'll have—the Middle East's only other resource, oil, will be a fast-evaporating pool by mid-century—this is Islam's demographic moment and they have to make the most of it. If they're serious about the new caliphate and making the whole world part of the Dar al-Islam, they have to pull it off in the next quarter century.

What of America? The hyperpower, demographically, is in Shakespeare's middle age:

> In fair round belly with good capon lined...
> Full of wise saws and modern instances...

or, more accurately, divided between the two: blue-staters taking refuge in too many "modern instances," but with sufficient red-staters who still live by the "wise saws." The United States has demographic challenges of its own, but, even if one accepts the dubious proposition that its population's ability to maintain "replacement rate" fertility is largely dependent on Hispanic immigration, its native birth rate is still the highest in the developed world. So the United States's relatively healthy demographic profile is merely the latest example of American exceptionalism.

What of Europe?

> ...The sixth age shifts
> Into the lean and slippered pantaloon,
> With spectacles on nose and pouch on side,
> His youthful hose, well saved, a world too wide,
> For his shrunk shank; and his big manly voice,
> Turning again towards the childish treble, pipes
> And whistles in his sound...

That's the situation the Continent's in. In constructing the European Union, they've built a world too wide for their shrunk shank. Worse, it's constructed in a particular fashion: since 1945, the big manly voices of the perpetually warring Germans and French and Italians have been turned to socialized health care and welfare and paid vacations that enable modern European man to live his entire life in the childish treble. Unfortunately, such a society is hideously expensive to maintain, so

Europe's aging population requires ever more and ever younger immigrants to prop up the system.

How does Shakespeare conclude?

> ...Last scene of all,
> That ends this strange eventful history,
> Is second childishness and mere oblivion,
> Sans teeth, sans eyes, sans taste, sans everything.

That's Russia today: "the sick man of Europe," with falling life expectancy, riddled with HIV and tuberculosis and heart disease, its infrastructure crumbling, its borders unenforceable, and its wily kleptocracy draining its wealth Westward—a nation all but "sans everything."

How does Shakespeare begin?

> ...At first the infant,
> Mewling and puking in the nurse's arms...

Go to any children's store in Amsterdam or Marseilles or Vienna or Stockholm. Look at the women in headscarves or full abaya. That's the future.

Chapter Two

Going . . . Going . . . Gone

DEMOGRAPHY VS. DELUSION

Like a lecherous stud suddenly stricken with impotence, we are humiliated at the very heart of our faith in ourselves. For all our knowledge, our intelligence, our power, we can no longer do what the animals do without thought.

P. D. JAMES, *THE CHILDREN OF MEN* (1993)

The words are those of Theodore Faron, Fellow of Merton College, Oxford, in the first chapter of Baroness James's novel, set in 2021, when the human race is unable to breed. We seem to be approaching that situation a little ahead of schedule. The only difference between Lady James's dystopian fantasy and our current reality is that, in the fictional version, man is physically impotent.

In real life, we appear to be psychosomatically barren—at least in the non-red-state parts of the developed world. Almost every geopolitical challenge in the years ahead has its roots in demography, but not every demographic crisis will play out the same way. That's what makes doing anything about it even more problematic—different countries' reactions to their own particular domestic circumstances will impact in destabilizing ways on the international scene. In Japan, the demographic crisis exists virtually in laboratory conditions—no complicating factors; in Russia, it will be determined by the country's relationship with a cramped neighbor, China; and in Europe, the new owners are already in place—like a tenant with a right-to-buy agreement.

Let's start in the most geriatric jurisdiction on the planet. In Japan, the rising sun has already passed into the next phase of its long sunset: net population loss. 2005 was the first year since records began in which the country had more deaths than births. Japan offers the chance to observe the demographic death spiral in its purest form. It's a country with no immigration, no significant minorities, and no desire for any: just the Japanese, aging and dwindling.

At first it doesn't sound too bad: compared with the United States, most advanced societies are very crowded. If you're in a cramped apartment in a noisy, congested city, losing a couple hundred thousand seems a fine trade-off. The difficulty, in a modern social-democratic state, is managing which people to lose: already, according to the *Japan Times*, depopulation is "presenting the government with pressing challenges on the social and economic front, including ensuring provision of social security services and securing the labor force." For one thing, the shortage of children has led to a shortage of obstetricians. Why would any talented, ambitious med school student want to go into a field in such precipitous decline? As a result, if you live in certain parts of Japan, childbirth is all in the timing. On Oki Island, try to time the contractions for Monday morning. That's when the maternity ward is open—first day of the week, 10 a.m., when an obstetrician flies in to attend to any pregnant mothers who happen to be around. And at 5:30 p.m. she flies out. So if you've been careless enough to time your childbirth for Tuesday through Sunday, you'll have to climb into a helicopter and zip off to give birth alone in a strange hospital unsurrounded by tiresome loved ones.

Do Lamaze classes on Oki now teach you to time your breathing to the whirring of the chopper blades?

The last local obstetrician left the island in 2006 and the health service isn't expecting any more. Doubtless most of us can recall reading similar stories over the years from remote rural districts in America, Canada, or Australia. After all, why would a village of a few hundred people have a great medical system? But Oki has a population of 17,000, and there are still no obstetricians. Birthing is a dying business.

So what will happen? There are a couple of scenarios. Whatever Japanese feelings are on immigration, a country with great infrastructure won't empty out for long, any more than a state-of-the-art factory that goes belly up stays empty for long. At some point, someone else will move in to Japan's plant.

And the alternative? In P. D. James's *The Children of Men*, there are special dolls for women whose maternal instinct has gone unfulfilled: pretend mothers take their artificial children for walks on the street or to the swings in the park. In Japan, that's no longer the stuff of dystopian fantasy. At the beginning of the century, the country's toymakers noticed they had a problem: toys are for children and Japan doesn't have many. What to do? In 2005, Tomy began marketing a new doll called Yumel— a baby boy with a range of 1,200 phrases designed to serve as a companion for the elderly. He says not just the usual things—"I wuv you"—but also asks the questions your grandchildren would ask, if you had any: "Why do elephants have long noses?" Yumel joins his friend the Snuggling Ifbot, a toy designed to have the conversation of a five-year-old child, which its makers, with the usual Japanese efficiency, have determined is just enough chit-chat to prevent the old folks going senile. It seems an appropriate final comment on the social-democratic state: in a childish infantilized self-absorbed society where adults have been stripped of all responsibility, you need never stop playing with toys. We are the children we never had.

And why leave it at that? Is it likely an ever-smaller number of young people will want to spend their active years looking after an ever-greater

number of old people? Or will it be simpler to put all that cutting-edge
Japanese technology to good use and take a flier on Mister Roboto and
the post-human future? After all, what's easier for the governing class?
Weaning a pampered population off the good life and re-teaching them
the lost biological impulse or giving the Sony Corporation a license to
become the Cloney Corporation? If you need to justify it to yourself,
you'd grab the graphs and say, well, demographic decline is universal. It's
like industrialization a couple of centuries back; everyone will get to it
eventually, but the first to do so will have huge advantages. The relevant
comparison is not with England's early nineteenth-century population
surge but with England's industrial revolution. In the industrial age, manpower was critical. In the new technological age, manpower will be
optional—and indeed, if most of the available manpower's Muslim, it's
actually a disadvantage. As the most advanced society with the most
advanced demographic crisis, Japan seems likely to be the first jurisdiction to embrace robots and cloning and embark on the slippery slope to
transhumanism.

So perhaps the ever more elderly Japanese will go on—and on and
on, like the joke about the gnarled old rustic and the axe he's had for seventy years: he's replaced the blade seven times and the handle four times,
but it's still the same old trusty axe. We will have achieved man's victory
over death, not in the sense our ancestors meant it—the assurance of
eternal life in the unseen world—but in the here and now. Which is what
it's all about, isn't it? An eternal present tense.

Think I'm kidding? Compare the suspicion and demonization of
genetically modified foods to what's mostly either enthusiasm for or
indifference to genetically modified people. Mess with our vegetables,
we'll burn down your factory. Mess with us, and we pass you our credit
card. And by the time we wonder whether it was all such a smart idea
it'll be the clones who have the Platinum Visa cards.

If that creeps you out, there is a third option. Unlike the Europeans,
many of whom will flee their continent as Eutopia evolves into Eurabia,
the Japanese are not facing ethnic strife and civil war. They could simply
start breeding again. But will they? Fifty-one percent of all Japanese

women born in the early 1970s were still childless by their thirtieth birthday. Reporting the latest set of grim statistics, the *Japan Times* observed, almost en passant, "Japan joins Germany and Italy in the ranks of countries where a decline in population has already set in."

Japan, Germany, and Italy, eh? If the Versailles Treaty was too hard on our enemies, the World War Two settlement was kinder but lethal.

● ● ●

RED SALES IN THE SUNSET?

Japan is the most benign example of demographic decline—a problem for the Japanese but not for the rest of us. Elsewhere around the world, America is threatened by rival powers not because of their strength but because of their weakness: for one thing, a flailing, fast-declining power is less bound by maxims of prudence. Russia, for example, is in an accelerating vortex and, for Washington and other interested parties, the question is what Moscow will try to grab on to in order to slow the descent.

From a population peak in 1992 of 148 million, Russia will be down below 130 million by 2015, thereafter dropping to perhaps 50 or 60 million by the end of the century, a third of what it was at the fall of the Soviet Union. It needn't decline at a consistent rate, of course. But I'd say it's more likely to be even lower than 50 million than it is to be over 100 million. In fact, the worst projections show Russia falling to around 85 million by mid-century. The longer a country goes without arresting the death spiral, the harder it is to pull out of it. Russia has one of the lowest fertility rates in the world—1.2 children per woman—and one of the highest abortion rates. When it comes to the future, most Russian women are voting with their fetus: 70 percent of pregnancies are terminated.

Allen C. Lynch of the University of Virginia recalls visiting the country when the American pro-life film *The Silent Scream* was shown on TV there. The film is very graphic and unsparing in its examination of the effects on the fetus, its object being to prompt in the viewer revulsion and disgust at the procedure. "It turned out that more Russian women," wrote

Professor Lynch, "became more positively attuned to the idea after having watched the film." Instead of the baby's pain, Russian viewers noticed the clean hospitals, the state-of-the-art technology, the briskly professional doctors and nurses. Women marveled: "Wouldn't it be great to have an abortion in the West?" After seven decades of Communism, the physical barrenness is little more than a symptom of the spiritual barrenness.

The culture of death is having a ball at the other end too. If you're a male born in Russia in 2000, you can expect to live 58.9 years. While its womenfolk have a life expectancy comparable to their American counterparts, sickly Russian men now have a lower life expectancy than Bangladeshis—not because Bangladesh is brimming with actuarial advantages but because, if he had four legs and hung from a tree in a rain forest, the Russian male would be on the endangered species list. The decline in male longevity is unprecedented for a (relatively) advanced nation not at war, and with many attendant social and economic consequences. So far, in this first large-scale experiment on the dispensability of men, it appears that, *pace* Gloria Steinem, fish do indeed need bicycles.

Russia is the sick man of Europe, and would still look pretty sick if you moved him to Africa. There are severe outbreaks of viral hepatitis; tuberculosis is the country's leading fatal infectious disease, with a proliferating number of drug-resistant strains. It has the fastest-growing rate of HIV infection in the world. In the first five years of the new century, more people tested positive in Russia than in the previous twenty in America. The virus is said to have infected at least 1 percent of the population, the figure the World Health Organization considers the tipping point for a sub-Saharan-sized epidemic. So at a time when Russian men already have a life expectancy that doesn't make it beyond middle age, they're about to see AIDS cut them down from the other end, felling young men and women of childbearing age, and with them any hope of societal regeneration. By some projections, AIDS will soon be killing between a quarter and three-quarters of a million Russians every year. Along with those extraordinary rates of drug-fueled Hepatitis C, heart disease, and TB, HIV is just one more symptom of what happens when an entire people lacks the will to rouse itself from self-destruction.

Russia will become a nation of babushkas, unable to deploy enough young soldiers to secure its borders, enough young businessmen to secure its economy, or enough young families to secure its future. And, if its export of ideology was the biggest destabilizing factor in the history of the last century, the implosion of Russia could be a major destabilizer of this one. Iran's nuke program is merely one of the many geopolitical challenges to America in which there's a large Russian component somewhere in the background.

There are districts that are exceptions to these baleful trends, parts of Russia that have healthy fertility rates and low HIV infection. Of the country's eighty-nine federal regions, twelve are showing substantial population growth. Any ideas as to which regions they are? Once again, starts with an *I,* ends with a *slam.* The allegedly seething "Arab street" that the West's media doom-mongers have been predicting since September 11 will rise up in fury against the Anglo-American infidels remains as seething as a Westchester County cul-de-sac on a Wednesday afternoon. But the Russian Federation's Muslim street is real, and on the boil. And even its placid *quartiers* have no reason to prop up the diseased Russian bear.

So the world's largest country is dying and the question is how violent its death throes will be. Most of the big international problems operate within certain geographic constraints: Africa has AIDS, the Middle East has Islamists, North Korea has nukes. But Russia's got the lot: a potentially African-level AIDS crisis and an Islamist separatist movement sitting atop the biggest pile of nukes on the planet. Of course, the nuclear materials are all in "secure" facilities. Probably.

Russia is the bleakest example of misdirected worrying: *there are too many people and too few resources!* Exactly backward: poor old Russia is awash in resources but fatally short of Russians—and, yet again, warm bodies are the one indispensable resource. What would you do if you were the fellows in the Kremlin? What assets have you got to keep your rotting corpse of a country as some kind of player? You've got nuclear know-how—which a lot of ayatollahs and dictators are interested in. You've got an empty resource-rich eastern hinterland—which the Chinese are going to wind up with one way or the other. That was the logic

behind the sale of Alaska: in the 1850s, Grand Duke Konstantin Niko-
laevich, the brother of Alexander II, argued that the Russian Empire
couldn't hold its North American territory and that one day either
Britain or the United States would simply take it, so why not sell it to
them first? The same argument applies today to the two thousand miles
of the Russo-Chinese border. In the ever emptier Russian east there are
sixteen million people and falling. In China, there are 1.5 billion and they
need to stretch their legs. China is resource-poor; the Russian east con-
tains 80 percent of that country's resources. Given that even alcoholic
Slavs with a life expectancy of fifty-six will live to see Vladivostok return
to its old name of Haishenwei, Moscow might as well flog it to Beijing
instead of having it snaffled out from under. Facing extinction, Moscow
doesn't have much to barter with—except dangling the Chinese an offer
that could solve several of their structural problems.

In fact, Russia might offer a solution to the People's Republic's most
distinctive structural flaw: the most gender-distorted demographic cohort
in global history, the so-called *guang gun*—"bare branches." Since China
introduced its "one child" policy in 1978, the imbalance between the
sexes has increased to the point where in today's generation there are 119
boys for every 100 girls. The pioneer generation of that male surplus is
now in its twenties. Unless China's planning on becoming the first gay
superpower since Sparta, what's going to happen to those young men?
As a general rule, large numbers of excitable lads who can't get any
action are useful for manning the nuttier outposts of the jihad but not
for much else. So, given Russia's own imbalance—between sickly men of
low life expectancy and long-lived robust women—it's not hard to see
some mutual advantage in a bilateral mass hook-up for Slav women and
Chinese men, even if the boys are a bit callow and the chicks somewhat
long in the tooth.

That's not the death whimper of their Tsarist/Communist dreams most
Russian nationalists would have predicted. But then they've never been
shrewd assessors of their own defects. One reason why al Qaeda seriously
thinks it can destroy the West is because it believes that in Afghanistan,
it—and not the United States—brought about the downfall of the Soviet

Union. It will be Russia's fate to have large chunks of its turf annexed by the Islamic world, and much of what's left fall to the Chinese.

That's the danger for Washington—that most of what Russia has to trade is likely to be damaging to U.S. interests. In its death throes, it could bequeath the world several new Muslim nations, a nuclear Middle East, and a stronger China. In theory, America could do a belated follow-up to the Alaska deal and put in a bid for Siberia. But Russia's calculation is that sooner or later we'll be back in a bipolar world and that, in almost any scenario, there's more advantage in being part of the non-American pole. If a Sino-Russian strategic partnership has a certain logic to it, so, in a darker way, does a Sino-Russo-Euro-Muslim alliance of convenience. I get a surprising amount of mail from Americans who say, aw, we're too big a bunch of politically correct blue-state pussies to kick Islamobutt but fortunately the Russkies and the ChiComs have their own Muslim wackjobs and they won't be as squeamish as us wimps when it comes to sorting them out once and for all. Maybe. One day. But right now they figure the jihad is America's problem and it's in their interest to keep it that way. Hence, Russo-Chinese support for every troublemaker on the planet, from Iran's loony president to Hugo Chavez in America's backyard.

So a combination of factors is bringing about a remarkable event: the death of a great nation not through war or devastation but through its inability to rouse itself from its own suicidal tendencies. As Mrs. Thatcher likes to say, "The facts of life are conservative." The nation that tried to buck those facts of life the most thoroughly is falling the fastest. Churchill didn't know the half of it: Russia is a vacuum wrapped in a nullity inside an abyss.

● ● ●

LES FEUILLES MORTES

Demographic origin need not be the final word. In 1775, Benjamin Franklin wrote a letter to Joseph Priestley suggesting a mutual English friend might like to apply his mind to the conundrum the Crown faced:

> Britain, at the expense of three millions, has killed 150 Yankees
> this campaign, which is £20000 a head. . . . During the same time,
> 60000 children have been born in America. From these data his
> mathematical head will easily calculate the time and the expense
> necessary to kill us all.

Obviously, Franklin was oversimplifying. Not every American colonist
identified himself as a rebel. After the revolution, there were massive
population displacements: if you've ever driven along the Loyalist Park-
way east of Toronto to Kingston, you'll know that large numbers of New
Yorkers left the colony to resettle in what's now Ontario. Some American Negroes were so anxious to remain subjects of King George III they
resettled as far as Sierra Leone. For these people, their primary identity
was not as American colonists but as British subjects. For others, their
new identity as Americans had supplanted their formal allegiance to the
Crown. The question for today's Europe is whether the primary identity
of their fastest-growing demographic is Muslim or Belgian, Muslim or
Dutch, Muslim or French.

That's where civilizational confidence comes in: if "Dutchness" or
"Frenchness" seems a weak attenuated thing, then the stronger identity
will prevail. One notes other similarities between revolutionary America
and contemporary Europe: the United Empire Loyalists were older and
wealthier; the rebels were younger and poorer. In the end, the former
simply lacked the latter's strength of will.

Europe, like Japan, has catastrophic birth rates and a swollen pampered elderly class determined to live in defiance of economic reality. But
the difference is that on the Continent the successor population is already
in place and the only question is how bloody the transfer of real estate
will be.

If America's "allies" failed to grasp the significance of September 11,
it's because Europe's home-grown terrorism problems had all taken place
among notably static populations, such as Ulster and the Basque country. One could make generally safe extrapolations about the likelihood
of holding Northern Ireland to what cynical strategists in Her Majesty's

Government used to call an "acceptable level of violence." But in the same three decades as Ulster's "Troubles," the hitherto moderate Muslim populations of south Asia were radicalized by a politicized form of Islam; previously formally un-Islamic societies such as Nigeria became semi-Islamist; and large Muslim populations settled in parts of Europe that had little or no experience of mass immigration.

You can argue about what these trends mean, but surely not that they mean absolutely nothing, which is what the complaceniks assure us. On the Continent and elsewhere in the West, native populations are aging and fading and being supplanted remorselessly by a young Muslim demographic. Time for the obligatory "of courses": *Of course*, not all Muslims are terrorists—though enough are hot for jihad to provide an impressive support network of mosques from Vienna to Stockholm to Toronto to Seattle. *Of course*, not all Muslims support terrorists—though enough of them share their basic objectives (the wish to live under Islamic law in Europe and North America) to function wittingly or otherwise as the "good cop" end of an Islamic good cop/bad cop routine. But, at the very minimum, this fast-moving demographic transformation provides a huge comfort zone for the jihad to move around in. And in a more profound way it rationalizes what would otherwise be the nuttiness of the terrorists' demands. An IRA man blows up a pub in defiance of democratic reality—because he knows that at the ballot box the Ulster Loyalists win the elections and the Irish Republicans lose. When a European jihadist blows something up, that's not in defiance of democratic reality but merely a portent of democratic reality to come. He's jumping the gun, but in every respect things are moving his way.

You may vaguely remember seeing some flaming cars on the evening news toward the end of 2005. Something going on in France, apparently. Something to do with—what's the word?—"youths." When I pointed out the media's strange reluctance to use the M-word vis-à-vis the rioting "youths," I received a ton of e-mails arguing there's no Islamist component, they're not the madrassa crowd, they may be Muslim but they're secular and Westernized and into drugs and rap and meaningless sex with no emotional commitment, and rioting and looting and torching

and trashing, just like any normal healthy Western teenagers. These guys
have economic concerns, it's the lack of jobs, it's conditions peculiar to
France, etc. As one correspondent wrote, "You right-wing shit-for-brains
think everything's about jihad."

Actually, I don't think everything's about jihad. But I do think, as I
said, that a good 90 percent of everything's about demography. Take that
media characterization of those French rioters: "youths." What's the
salient point about youths? They're youthful. Very few octogenarians
want to go torching Renaults every night. It's not easy lobbing a Molo-
tov cocktail into a police station and then hobbling back with your
walker across the street before the searing heat of the explosion melts
your hip replacement. Civil disobedience is a young man's game.

Now ponder that bland statistic you heard a lot in the news reports:
"about 10 percent of France's population is Muslim." Give or take a million here, a million there, that's a broadly correct 2005 statistic as far as
it goes. But the population spread isn't even. And when it comes to those
living in France aged twenty and under, about 30 percent are said to be
Muslim, and in the major urban centers, about 45 percent. If it came
down to street-by-street fighting, as Michel Gurfinkiel, the editor of
Valeurs Actuelles, points out, "the combatant ratio in any ethnic war
may thus be one to one"—already, right now. It is not necessary, incidentally, for Islam to become a statistical majority in order to function as
one. At the height of its power in the eighth century, the "Islamic world"
stretched from Spain to India yet its population was only minority Muslim. Nonetheless, by 2010, more elderly white Catholic ethnic frogs will
have croaked and more fit healthy Muslim youths will be hitting the
streets. One day they'll even be on the beach at St. Tropez, and if you and
your infidel whore happen to be lying there wearing nothing but two
coats of Ambre Solaire when they show up, you better hope that the BBC
and CNN are right about there being no religio-ethno-cultural component to their "grievances."

In June 2006, a fifty-four-year-old Flemish train conductor called
Guido Demoor got on the number 23 bus in Antwerp to go to work.
Six—what's that word again?—"youths" boarded the bus and com-

menced intimidating the other riders. There were some forty passengers aboard. But the "youths" were youthful and the other passengers less so. Nonetheless, Mr. Demoor asked the lads to cut it out and so they turned on him, thumping and kicking him. Of those forty other passengers, none intervened to help the man under attack. Instead, at the next stop, thirty of the forty scrammed, leaving Mr. Demoor to be beaten to death. Three "youths" were arrested, and proved to be—*quelle surprise!*—of Moroccan origin. The ringleader escaped and, despite police assurances of complete confidentiality, of those forty passengers only four came forward to speak to investigators. "You see what happens if you intervene," a fellow rail worker told the Belgian newspaper *De Morgen*. "If Guido had not opened his mouth he would still be alive."

No, he wouldn't. He would be as dead as those forty passengers are, as the Belgian state is, keeping his head down, trying not to make eye contact, cowering behind his newspaper in the corner seat and hoping just to be left alone. What future in "their" country do Mr. Demoor's two children have? My mother and grandparents came from Sint-Niklaas, a town I remember well from many childhood visits. When we stayed with great-aunts and other relatives, the upstairs floors of the row houses had no bathrooms, just chamber pots. My sister and I were left to mooch around cobbled streets with our little cousin for hours on end, wandering aimlessly past smoke-wreathed bars and cafes, occasionally buying *frites* with mayonnaise. With hindsight it seemed as parochially Flemish as could be imagined. Not anymore. The week before Mr. Demoor was murdered in plain sight, bus drivers in Sint-Niklaas walked off the job to protest the thuggery of the—here it comes again—"youths." In little more than a generation, a town has been transformed.

Of the ethnic Belgian population, some 17 percent are under eighteen years old. Of the country's Turkish and Moroccan population, 35 percent are under eighteen years old. The "youths" get ever more numerous, the non-youths get older. To avoid the ruthless arithmetic posited by Benjamin Franklin, it is necessary for those "youths" to feel more Belgian. Is that likely? Colonel Gaddafi doesn't think so: "There are signs that Allah will grant Islam victory in Europe—without swords, without guns, without conquests. The fifty million Muslims of Europe will turn it into a Muslim continent within a few decades."

●　　●　　●

THE RAIN IN SPAIN

If the critical date for Americans in the new century is September 11, 2001, for Continentals it's a day two and a half years later, in March 2004. On the eleventh of the month, just before Spain's general election, a series of train bombings in Madrid killed more than two hundred people. That day, I received a ton of e-mails from American acquaintances along the lines of: "3/11 is Europe's 9/11. Even the French will be in." Friends told me: "The Europeans get it now." Doughty warriors of the blogosphere posted the Spanish flag on their home pages in solidarity with America's loyal allies in the war against terrorism. John Ellis, a Bush cousin and a savvy guy with a smart website, declared, "Every member-state of the EU understands that Madrid is Rome is Berlin is Amsterdam is Paris is London is New York."

All wrong. On Friday, March 12, hundreds of thousands of Spaniards filled Madrid's streets and stood somberly in a bleak drizzle to mourn their dead. On Sunday, election day, the voters tossed out José María Aznar's sadly misnamed Popular Party and handed the government to the Socialist Workers' Party. Aznar's party was America's principal Continental ally in Iraq; the Socialist Workers campaigned on a pledge to withdraw Spain's troops from Iraq. Throughout the campaign, polls showed the Popular Party cruising to victory. Then came the bomb.

Having invited people to choose between a strong horse and a weak horse, even Osama bin Laden might have been surprised to see the Spanish opt to make their general election an exercise in mass self-gelding. Within seventy-two hours of the carnage, voters sent a tough message to the terrorists: "We apologize for catching your eye." Whether or not Madrid is Rome and Berlin and Amsterdam and Paris, it certainly isn't New York.

To be sure, there were all kinds of Kerryesque footnoted nuances to that stark election result. One sympathized with those voters reported to be angry at the government's pathetic insistence, in the face of the emerging evidence, that the bomb attack was the work of ETA, the Basque nationalist terrorists, when it was so obviously the jihad boys. One's sympathy, however, disappeared with their decision to vote for a party committed to disengaging from the war. And no one will remember the footnotes, the qualifications—just the final score: terrorists toppled a European government.

So March 11 proved not to be a day that will live in infamy. Rather, March 14 seems likely to be the date bequeathed to posterity. That's the true equivalent to September 11, in the sense of a day that defines a people, a day to be remembered as we remember those grim markers on the road to conflagration through the 1930s, the tactical surrenders that made disaster inevitable. At least in the two and a half years between September 11 and March 11, there was always the possibility of Europe stiffening itself. Now America lives with the certainty that it won't, and can't, until it's too late. All those umbrellas in the rain at those demonstrations of defiance proved to be pretty pictures for the cameras, nothing more. The rain in Spain falls mainly on the slain. In the three days between the slaughter and the vote, it was widely reported that the atrocity had been designed to influence the election. In allowing it to do so, the Spanish knowingly made polling day a victory for appeasement and dishonored their own dead.

Why would the Spanish do what they did? Well, why wouldn't they? Who needs to show resolve when you're a country with a fertility rate of 1.1 percent? Appeasement is a vote to live in the present tense, to hold the comforts of the moment. To fight for king and country is to fight for the future. But a barren society has no future, and so what's to fight for? The terrorists would have their work cut out killing the Spanish people as fast as the Spanish are killing themselves. How can you "decimate" a population that's already halving with every generation?

On September 11, 2001, the American mainland was attacked for the first time since the War of 1812. The perpetrators were foreign—Saudis and Egyptians. Since September 11, Europe has seen the London Tube bombings, the French riots, Dutch murders of nationalist politicians. The perpetrators are their own citizens—British subjects, *citoyens de la République française*. That's the difference: America is fighting a foreign war, Eurabia is in the early stages of an undeclared civil war.

Who'll win it? In Linz, Austria, Muslims are demanding that all female teachers, believers or infidels, wear headscarves in class. The Muslim Council of Britain wants Holocaust Day abolished because it focuses "only" on the Nazis' (alleged) Holocaust of the Jews and not the Israelis' ongoing Holocaust of the Palestinians.

And how does the state react? In Seville, King Ferdinand III is no longer patron saint of the annual fiesta because his splendid record in fighting for Spanish independence from the Moors was felt to be insensitive to Muslims. In London, a judge agreed to the removal of Jews and Hindus from a trial jury because the Muslim defendant's counsel argued he couldn't get a fair verdict from them. The Church of England is considering removing St. George as the country's patron saint on the grounds that, according to various Anglican clergy, he's too "militaristic" and "offensive to Muslims." They wish to replace him with St. Alban, and replace St. George's cross on the revamped Union Flag, which would instead show St. Alban's cross as a thin yellow streak. That's a joke most satirists would reject as too crudely implausible.

In a few years, as millions of Muslim teenagers are entering its voting booths, some European countries will not be living formally under sharia, but—as have parts of Nigeria—they will have reached an accommodation with their radicalized Islamic compatriots, who like many intolerant types are expert at exploiting the "tolerance" of pluralist societies. In other Continental countries, things are likely to play out in more traditional fashion, though without a significantly different ending.

Madrid and London—along with other events such as the murder of Theo van Gogh—were the opening shots of that European civil war. You can laugh at that if you wish, but the Islamists' most oft-stated goal is not infidel withdrawal from Iraq but the re-establishment of a Muslim caliphate, living under sharia, that extends to Europe. There's a lot to be said for taking these chaps at their word and then seeing whether their behavior comports. Furthermore, given that a lot more of the world lives under sharia than did in the early seventies, as a political project radical Islam has made some headway, and continues to do so almost every day of the week: early in 2005, some 10 percent of southern Thailand's Buddhist population abandoned their homes because of Islamist violence—a far bigger disruption than the tsunami, yet all but unreported in the world press. And wherever one's sympathies lie on Islam's multiple battle fronts the fact is the jihad has held out a long time against very tough enemies. If you're not shy about taking on the Israelis and Russians, why wouldn't you fancy your chances against the Belgians and Spaniards?

In 1903, in *The Riddle of the Sands*, the first great English spy novel, Erskine Childers has his yachtsman, Davies, try to persuade the Foreign Office wallah Carruthers to take seriously the possibility of German naval marauders in the Fresian Islands:

> Follow the parallel of a war on land. People your mountains with a daring and resourceful race, who possess an intimate knowledge of every track and bridlepath, who operate in small bands, travel light, and move rapidly. See what an immense advantage such guerrillas possess over an enemy which clings to beaten tracks, moves in large bodies, slowly, and does not "know the country."

Davies wants Carruthers to apply the old principles to new forms of warfare. The Islamists are doing that. Their most effective guerrillas aren't in the Hindu Kush, where it's the work of moments to drop a daisy cutter on the mighty Pashtun warrior. They're traveling light on the bridle paths of Europe—the small cells, the opportunist imams, the ambitious lobby groups that operate in the nooks and crannies of a free society—while politicians cling to the beaten tracks of old ideas, multicultural pieties, and a general hope that things will turn out for the best.

"We're the ones who will change you," Norwegian imam Mullah Krekar told the Oslo newspaper *Dagbladet* in 2006. "Just look at the development within Europe, where the number of Muslims is expanding like mosquitoes. Every Western woman in the EU is producing an average of 1.4 children. Every Muslim woman in the same countries is producing 3.5 children." As he summed it up: "Our way of thinking will prove more powerful than yours."

Chapter Three

Men Are from Venus

PRIMARY IMPULSES
VS. SECONDARY IMPULSES

In our own time the whole of Greece has been subject to a low birth rate and a general decrease of the population, owing to which cities have become deserted and the land has ceased to yield fruit, although there have neither been continuous wars nor epidemics.... For as men had fallen into such a state of pretentiousness, avarice, and indolence that they did not wish to marry, or if they married to rear the children born to them, or at most as a rule but one or two of them, so as to leave these in affluence and bring them up to waste their substance, the evil rapidly and insensibly grew.

POLYBIUS, *THE HISTORIES*, BOOK XXXVI (CIRCA 150 BC)

How did today's demographic disaster happen? How did the wealthiest civilization in human history, the engine of global progress, opt for self-liquidation in favor of the modern world's most technologically impoverished and backward culture? Today, the typical advanced society trumpets its defects as virtues. Immigration certainly has its blessings; the provincial restaurant scene in England would be a lot duller without curry houses, etc. But it's very silly to boast about it as proof of one's moral superiority. A dependence on immigration from very limited and particular sources is not a strength but a weakness. The Continent's imams can certainly see that: they understand that Europe is the colony now.

John O'Sullivan, a former editor of *National Review*, once observed that postwar Canadian history is summed up by an old Monty Python song. "I'm a Lumberjack and I'm Okay" begins as a robust paean to the manly virtues of a rugged life in the north woods—as the intro goes, "Leaping from tree to tree! As they float down the mighty rivers of British Columbia!"—but ends with the lumberjack having gradually morphed into some sort of transvestite pick-up who sings that he likes to "wear high heels, suspenders, and a bra" and "dress in women's clothing and hang around in bars."

I know what he means. In 2005 I chanced to see a selection of images from the Miss Shemale World celebrations outside Toronto's City Hall. And what struck me was not that "shemales" should want to have a big ol' parade showing off their outsized implants—each to her own, even if in this case her own were purchased from Dow Corning. No, what seemed more pertinent was that the local government should think Miss Shemale World is an event that requires municipal approval. Of course, if they hadn't approved, they would have been guilty of being "non-inclusive." John O'Sullivan isn't saying Canadian men are literally cross-dressers—certainly no more than 35, 40 percent, and me only on weekends—but nonetheless a once manly nation has undergone a remarkable psychological makeover. In 1945, the Royal Canadian Navy had the third-largest surface fleet in the world; the Royal Canadian Air Force was one of the most effective air forces in the world; Canadian troops got the toughest beach on D-Day. But in the space of two generations, a bunch of tough hombres were transformed into a thoroughly feminized culture that prioritizes the secondary impulses of society—rights and entitlements from cradle to grave—over all the primary ones.

In that, Canada's not alone. If the O'Sullivan thesis is flawed, it's only because the Lumberjack Song could also stand as the postwar history of almost the entire developed world. To understand why the West seems so weak in the face of a laughably primitive enemy it's necessary to examine the wholesale transformation undergone by almost every advanced nation since World War Two. Today, in your typical election campaign, the political platforms of at least one party in the United States and pretty much every party in the rest of the West are all but exclusively about those secondary impulses: government health care (which America is slouching toward, incrementally but remorselessly), government day care (which was supposedly the most important issue in the 2006 Canadian election), government paternity leave (which Britain has introduced). We've elevated the secondary impulses over the primary ones: national defense, self-reliance, family, and, most basic of all, reproductive activity. If you don't "go forth and multiply" you can't afford all those secondary-impulse programs, like lifelong welfare, whose costs are multiplying a lot faster than you are. Most of the secondary-impulse stuff falls under the broad category of self-gratification issues: we want the state to take our elderly relatives off our hands not so much because it's better for them but because otherwise the old coots would cut seriously into our own time. Fair enough. But once you decide you can do without grandparents, it's not such a stretch to decide you can do without grandchildren.

I've always loved Lincoln's allusion to the "mystic chords of memory" because it conveys beautifully the layers of a healthy society: the top notes—the melody line, the tune—are the present, but the underlying harmony is critical, too; it places the present in the context of history and eternal truths, and thereby binds us not just to the past but commits us to the future, too. Yet since 1945, throughout the West, a variety of government interventions—state pensions, subsidized higher education, higher taxes to pay for everything—has so ruptured traditional patterns of inter-generational solidarity that Continentals now exist almost entirely in a present-tense culture of complete self-absorption. In the end, the primal impulses are the ones that count. Robert Kagan's observation that Americans are from Mars, Europeans are from Venus doesn't quite cover it. The Lumberjack Song and the Shemale World get closer: we're Martians who think we can cross-dress as Venusians and everything will be all right. And like some of the hotter-looking transsexuals on display at Toronto's City Hall, the modern Western democracy is perfectly feminized in every respect except its ability to reproduce.

Americans don't always appreciate how far gone down this path the rest of the developed world is: in Continental cabinets, the defense ministry is now somewhere an ambitious politician passes through on his way up to important jobs like the health department. I don't think Donald Rumsfeld would regard it as a promotion to be moved to Health and Human Services. Yet the secondary impulses are so advanced that most of America's allies no longer share the same understanding of basic words like "power." In 2002 Finnish prime minister Paavo Lipponen gave a speech in London saying that "the EU must not develop into a military superpower but must become a great power that will not take up arms at any occasion in order to defend its own interests."

No doubt it sounds better in Finnish. Nonetheless, he means it: for many Europeans, the old rules no longer apply. They've been supplanted by new measures of power, like how smoothly you fit in at the transnational yakfests (EU, UN, ICC, etc.). Yet in the long run this redefinition of the state is killing them. As Gerald Ford used to say when trying to ingratiate himself with conservative audiences, "A government big enough to give you everything you want is big enough to take away everything you have." And that's true. But there's an intermediate stage: a government big enough to give you everything you want isn't big enough to get you to give any of it back.

That's the position European governments find themselves in. Their citizens have become hooked on unaffordable levels of social programs which in the end will put those countries out of business. Just to get the Social Security debate in perspective, projected public pensions liabilities are expected to rise by 2040 to about 6.8 percent of GDP in the United States. In Greece, the figure is 25 percent—i.e., total societal collapse. So what? shrug the voters. I paid my taxes, I want my benefits.

This is the paradox of "social democracy." When you demand lower taxes and less government, you're damned by the Left as "selfish." And, to be honest, in my case that's true. I'm glad to find a town road at the bottom of my driveway in the morning, and I'm happy to pay for the Army and a new fire truck for a volunteer fire department every now and then, but, other than that, I'd like to keep everything I earn and spend it on my priorities.

The Left, for its part, offers an appeal to moral virtue: it's better to pay more in taxes and to share the burdens as a community. It's kinder, gentler, more compassionate, more equitable. Unfortunately, as recent European election results demonstrate, nothing makes a citizen more selfish than socially equitable communitarianism: once a fellow's enjoying the fruits of government health care and all the rest, he couldn't give a hoot about the general societal interest; he's got his, and if it's going to bankrupt the state a generation hence, well, as long as they can keep the checks coming till he's dead, it's fine by him. "Social democracy" is, it turns out, explicitly anti-social. To modify Polybius, it's "avarice" dressed up with "pretentiousness." And it leads, in Europe and elsewhere, to societal "indolence."

Somewhere along the way these countries redefined the relationship between government and citizen into something closer to pusher and addict. And once you've done that, it's very hard to persuade the addict to cut back his habit. Thus, the general acceptance everywhere but America is that the state should run your health care. A citizen of an advanced democracy expects to be able to choose from dozens of breakfast cereals at the supermarket, hundreds of movies at the video store, and millions of porno sites on the Internet, but when it comes to life-or-death decisions about his own body he's happy to have the choice taken out of his hands and given to the government.

The problem with this is not only fiscal but moral. Canada, according to its former foreign minister Lloyd Axworthy, wields enormous "soft power," in contrast to America with its anachronistic "hard power." If you say so. But it seems to me the real distinction is more profound—between hard culture and soft culture. That shrewd analyst of demographic and political trends Michael Barone published a book called *Hard America, Soft America: Competition vs. Coddling and the Battle for the Nation's Future*. It's hard to imagine anyone writing a book called *Hard Canada, Soft Canada* or *Hard Europe, Soft Europe*; that question got settled a generation ago. No Japanese soldier has been killed in combat since World War Two. That sounds very nice: they beat their swords into karaoke microphones and sang "Give Peace a Chance." And, as a result, their country faces a graver existential crisis than it could ever suffer in battle.

"Soft power" is wielded by soft cultures, usually because they lack the will to maintain hard power. Can you remain a soft power for long? Maybe a generation or two. But a soft culture will, by its very nature, be unlikely to find the strength to stand up to a sustained assault by blunter, cruder forces—like, say, those youths on the Antwerp bus, or the Muslim gang-rapists in France with their preferred rite of passage, the *tournante* or "take your turn." On the night of September 11 Muslim youths in northern England rampaged through the streets cheering Islam's glorious victory over the Great Satan. They pounded on the hoods—or, to use the quaintly bucolic locution of British English, the "bonnets"—of the cars, hammered the doors and demanded the drivers join them in their chants of "Osama bin Laden is a great man."

Try that in Texas, and the guy will reach into his glove box and blow your head off. Even in Vermont it's an ill-advised tactic. But in Britain you're not allowed to own a gun or even (to all intents and purposes) resist assault. So the unfortunate burghers of Bradford went home cowed and terrified, and the Muslim gangs went swaggering off with their self-esteem enormously enhanced. The bullying, intimidating side of Muslim immigration in Europe seems to be largely absent in America, in part at least because the assertiveness of the individual American citizen makes it a riskier undertaking.

New Hampshire has a high rate of firearms possession, which is why it has a low crime rate. You don't have to own a gun, and there are plenty of sissy arms-are-for-hugging granola-crunchers who don't. But they benefit from the fact that their crazy stump-toothed knuckle-dragging neighbors do. If you want to burgle a home in the Granite State, you'd have to be awfully certain it was the one-in-a-hundred we-are-the-world panty-waist's pad and not some plaid-clad gun nut who'll blow your head off before you lay a hand on his seventy-dollar TV. A North Country non–gun owner might tire of all the Second Amendment kooks with the gun racks in the pickups and move somewhere where everyone is, at least officially, a non–gun owner just like him: Washington, D.C., say, or London. And suddenly he finds that, in a wholly disarmed society, his house requires burglar alarms and window locks and security cameras.

As with state gun control, so with state God control. A hyper-rationalist can dismiss the whole God thing as a lot of applesauce, but his hyper-rationalism is a lot more vulnerable in a society without a strong Judeo-Christian culture. As the bumper sticker says, if you outlaw guns, only outlaws will have guns. Likewise, if (as Europe has done) you marginalize religion, only the marginalized will have religion. That's why France's impoverished Muslim ghettos display more cultural confidence than the wealthiest enclaves of the capital.

●　　●　　●

MORAL HEALTH

In this long twilight struggle brought into focus by September 11, the hard cultures will survive and the soft won't. In Europe, the soft culture is so pervasive—state pensions, protected jobs, six weeks of paid vacation, lavish unemployment benefits if the thirty-five-hour work week sounds too grueling—that the citizen is little more than a junkie on the state narcotic. Faced with the perfect storm of swollen pension liabilities and collapsed birth rates, even Continental politicians recognize the need to wean their citizenry off some of these entitlements. But the citizens don't. What do they care if their country will be bankrupt in twenty years and extinct in seventy? Not my problem, man. Call me when I get back from the beach.

In 2006, the *Economist* reported on the growing tendency of the state to use its power to direct your life in socially beneficial ways—to coerce you into not smoking, eating healthily, etc.—and concluded: "Its champions will say that soft paternalism should only be used for ends that are unarguably good: on the side of sobriety, prudence, and restraint. But private virtues such as these are as likely to wither as to flourish when public bodies take charge of them."

That's correct. The ends may be "unarguably good" but they lead to other ends that are unarguably bad. It's the case that in a general population some people will neglect their elderly parents and leave their children alone at home while they go off gallivanting. However, by making the government the guarantor of a comfortable old age and supervised day care, you don't end such fecklessness. Rather, by relieving the individual of the need to have "private virtues," you'll ensure that they wither away to the edges of society.

Modern social-democratic states are so corrosive of their citizens' wills and so enervating in elevating secondary priorities over primary ones that most of them would not survive even without the Islamists. That's a remarkable thought: Europe doesn't need an enemy; it's losing to its own torpor. A government big enough to give you everything you want is big enough to take away everything you have, starting with your sense of self-reliance.

There is one (partial) exception to the softening of the West: a nation that still breeds, still puts in a full work week, still maintains a vigorous military. And what's the reaction of the rest of the developed world (plus the Democratic Party, the mainstream American media, and the "international law" groupies on the Supreme Court)? It demands America quit monkeying around and sign up to the suicide pact with the rest of 'em. Take Will Hutton, former editor of the *Observer*, former Great Thinker to the prewar Tony Blair, and one of the great gasbags of the new Europe. I hasten to add I say that not as a cheap ad hominem insult—or anyway not merely as a cheap ad hominem insult—but because Mr. Hutton is the master of the dead language of statism that differentiates the modern Europhile from most Americans.

In his 2003 book *A Declaration of Interdependence: Why America Should Join the World*, Mr. Hutton is at pains to establish how much he loves the country: "I enjoy Sheryl Crow and Clint Eastwood alike, delight in Woody Allen...." I'd wager he's faking at least two of these enthusiasms, and the third, Mr. Allen, is the man the French government hired when they needed a beloved American celebrity to restore their nation's image in America. Only the French government could think an endorsement by Woody Allen would improve their standing with the American people. But, having brandished his credentials, Mr. Hutton says that it's his "affection for the best of America that makes me so angry that it has fallen so far from the standards it expects of itself." Many Americans of Left and Right could write a book like that, but, as things transpire, the great Euro-thinker is not arguing that America is betraying the Founding Fathers, but that the Founding Fathers themselves got it hopelessly wrong. This becomes explicit when he compares the American Revolution with the French Revolution of 1789, and decides the latter was better because instead of the radical individualism (boo!) of the thirteen colonies the French promoted "a new social contract" (hurrah!).

Well, you never know. It may be the defects of America's Founders that help explain why the United States has lagged so far behind France in technological innovation, economic growth, military performance, standard of living, etc. Mr. Hutton insists that "all western democracies subscribe to a broad family of ideas that are liberal or leftist." Given that New Hampshire, for example, has been a continuous democracy for two centuries longer than Germany, this seems a dubious postulation. It would be more accurate to say that almost all European nations subscribe to a broad family of ideas that are statist. Or, as Hutton has it, "the European tradition is much more mindful that men and women are social animals and that individual liberty is only one of a spectrum of values that generate a good society." Precisely. And it's the willingness to subordinate individual liberty to what Hutton calls "the primacy of society" that's blighted the Continent for over a century: statism—or "the primacy of society"—is what Fascism, Nazism, Communism, and the European Union all have in common. The curse of the Continent is big ideas, each wacky notion a response to the last flop: the prewar German middle classes put their hopes in Hitler as a bulwark against the Bolsheviks; likewise, the postwar German middle classes decided European integration was their bulwark against a resurgence of Nazism.

True, after Fascism and Communism, the European Union seems comparatively innocent—not a Blitzkrieg, just a Bitzkrieg, an accumulation of fluffy trivial pan-European directives that nevertheless takes for granted that the natural order is a world in which every itsy-bitsy activity is licensed and regulated and constitutionally defined by government. Europeans never feel obliged to defend their mystical belief in statism: though they claim to be post-Christian rationalists, it's mostly a matter of blind faith.

That's why Will Hutton feels almost physically insecure when he's in one of the few spots on the planet where the virtues of the state religion are questioned. "In a world that is wholly private," he says of America, "we lose our bearings; deprived of any public anchor, all we have are our individual subjective values to guide us." He deplores the First Amendment and misses government-regulated media, which in the EU ensures that all public expression is within approved parameters (i.e., the typical discussion panel on the Continent is comprised of representatives of the center-left, the far left, and the loony left). "Europe," he explains, "acts to ensure that television and radio conform to public interest criteria."

"Public interest criteria": keep that bland phrase in your head when you need to know everything that's wrong with Europe. It's code-speak for a kind of easy-listening tyranny.

"Public interest criteria" doesn't mean criteria that the public decides are in its interest. It means that the elite—via various appointed bodies—decide what the public's interest is for them. Which is why there are no Rush Limbaughs or James Dobsons on European radio. But you do hear a lot of Will Hutton.

The real issue, though, is not whether you like Euro-statism. Regardless of how you feel about it, it's kaput. The un-American activities in which Europe has invested its identity are deeply self-destructive. Secondary-impulse states can be very agreeable—who wouldn't want to live in a world where the burning political priorities are government-subsidized day care, the celebration of one's sexual appetites, and whether mandatory paid vacation should be six or eight weeks? But they're agreeable only for the generation or two that they last. And, as we're about to see in demographically barren, economically ossified Europe, for good or ill it's the primal impulses that count. Europe's belief that you can smooth off the rough edges of Anglo-American capitalism and still remain wealthy has trapped it in societal structures predicated on false arithmetic whose disastrous consequences can't be postponed much longer. Unchecked, government social programs are a security threat because they weaken the ultimate line of defense: the free-born citizen whose responsibilities are not subcontracted to the government.

What then would happen if America were to follow Mr. Hutton's advice and "join the world"? Well, those "40 million Americans without health insurance" would enjoy the benefit of a new government health care system and, like their 250 million neighbors, would discover the charms of the health care "waiting list"—the one year, two years, or more Britons and others wait in pain for even routine operations; the six, twelve, eighteen months Canadians wait for an MRI scan, there being more such scanners in the city of Philadelphia than in the entire Great White North. They're now pioneering the ultimate expression of government health care: the ten-month waiting list for the maternity ward.

In 2004, Debrah Cornthwaite gave birth to twin boys at the Royal Alexandra Hospital in Edmonton. That's in Alberta. Mrs. Cornthwaite had begun the big day by going to her local maternity ward at Langley Memorial Hospital. That's in British Columbia. They told her, yes, your contractions are coming every four minutes, but sorry, we don't have any beds. And, after they'd checked with the bed-availability helpline "BC Bedline," they brought her the further good news that there was not a hospital anywhere in the province in which she could deliver her babies. There followed seven hours of red tape and paperwork. Then, late in the evening, she was driven to the airport and put on a chartered twin-prop to Edmonton. In the course of the flight, the contractions increased to every two and a half minutes—and most Lamaze classes don't teach timing your breathing to turbulence over the Rockies. How many Americans would want to do that on delivery day? You pack your bag and head to your local hospital in Oakland, and they say: *Not to worry, we've got a bed for you in Denver.*

Euro-Canadian socialized health care is, in essence, subsidized by American taxpayers: since the end of World War Two, Washington has assumed the defense costs of its allies, thereby freeing up those countries to spend their tax revenues on lavish social programs. But, if America follows the Hutton plan and "joins the world," it will reduce its defense expenditures to Euro-Canadian levels. So the next time a tsunami hits Sri Lanka or Indonesia there will be no carrier groups to divert and save lives. So more people will die, waiting the weeks and weeks it took the sleepytime gals at the United Nations to arrive. Were America to "join the world," it would have to reduce its funding of the UN and other world bodies to European levels. And it might have to scale back its domestic agencies so that they're no longer able to serve in effect as international ones. Which will be tough when some kid in some village on the other side of the world comes down with some weird illness no one's seen before and they want to FedEx the test tube to the Centers for Disease Control in Atlanta to figure out what's going on. Indeed, even relatively advanced societies admired by the likes of Will Hutton take it as routine that the CDC is a kind of Health Ministry of last resort. When SARS leapt from China to infect Toronto's hospitals in 2003, the principal contribution of the WHO (World Health Organization) was to issue a travel advisory warning visitors to steer clear of Ontario, leaving it to the CDC to provide advanced and practical analysis of the problem. Toronto's mayor, Mel Lastman, had a hard time keeping track of all the acronyms, and in one press conference launched into a bitter attack on the damaging effects of the travel advisory issued by the CDC.

The doctor next to him tried to correct him: "Who," she said.

"The CDC," he repeated.

"Who," she said.

"The CDC," he repeated, wondering why she hadn't heard his answer to the question the first time. This diseased version of the Abbott and Costello routine went on a while longer, before the doc realized she had to spell it out: W-H-O, the World Health Organization.

"Oh, yeah. Them, too," said Hizzoner.

Yet under the who's-on-first shtick lay an important truth: if an infection shows up in an Atlanta hospital, no American doctor looks for guidance from a Canadian government agency. But if it shows up in a

Toronto hospital, the Ontario health system takes it for granted that the best minds of the CDC in Atlanta will be staying late at the office trying to work out what's going on.

The answer to that Canadian doctor's vaudeville feed—"Who's on first?"—is America. When something goes awry, in a Sri Lankan beach resort or a Toronto hospital, it's the hyperpower who shows up. America doesn't need to "join the world": it already provides a lot of the world's infrastructure. What Hutton means is that he wants the United States to stop being an exception and make like Europe. What would that mean? Well, it would mean more government, less religion, and a collapsed birth rate.

One should be cautious seeking correlations between social structures and fertility rates. They're falling around the world and no expert knows how to reverse them. Is it lack of religion? Whoa, steady: in Europe, the highest levels of church attendance are in those Mediterranean countries with the most wholly kaput birth rates, while Scandinavian nations with all but undetectable levels of religious observance have some of the healthiest—or, at any rate, least unhealthy—fertility rates on the Continent: 1.64 births per couple in Sweden versus 1.15 in Spain.

Likewise, of the fiercely Islamist nations causing the world so much woe, Pakistan and Saudi Arabia have birth rates of 5.08 and 4.53, while Iran's has plummeted since its long war with Iraq to 2.33.

What about economic liberty? Taking the fourteen core pre-expansion EU economies, four of the five healthiest fertility rates belong to four of the five countries that also score highest for economic freedom: Ireland, Denmark, Finland, and the Netherlands. The fifth highest fertility rate (1.89) belongs to France, which has one of the lowest rankings on economic liberty. But France is also the country with the highest Islamic population, and the evidence suggests a third of all births there are already Muslim. If one were to adjust accordingly, you could make a case for close correlation in Europe between economic freedom and fertility rates. The three lowest birth rates belong to the countries at the bottom of the economic-liberty indicators: Greece, Italy, Spain.

On the other hand, in the rest of the world, territories with high economic liberty—Hong Kong, Singapore—are nose-diving into the demographic asphalt. So how about the marriage rate?

	2002 marriage rate per 1,000 population 15–64	2005 total fertility rate
United States	11.7	2.11
Denmark	10.4	1.77
Netherlands	7.7	1.72
UK	7.3	1.6
France	7.2	1.89
Germany	7.1	1.35
Italy	6.9	1.23

That's close enough to suggest that, when your tax and social policies encourage non-traditional family models, one consequence is fewer children. Yet again, though, that doesn't apply to Japan, which still has a higher marriage rate than most European countries.

Or maybe it's speaking English. In the core "Western world," compare the Anglo-Celtic-settled Anglophone democracies with the rest of the G-8:

United States	2.11		France	1.89
New Zealand	2.01		EU average	1.38
Ireland	1.9		Germany	1.35
Australia	1.7		Japan	1.32
United Kingdom	1.6		Italy	1.23
Canada	1.48		Russia	1.14

Or maybe it's already the Muslim populations that are keeping European maternity wards going. Insofar as one can penetrate the multiculti obfuscation on the issue, the five Continental nations (excepting war-ravaged Bosnia) with the highest proportion of Muslim citizens are also the five

Continental nations with the highest fertility rates—Albania, Macedonia, France, the Netherlands, and Denmark.

But at one level this is overthinking it. Everyone writes about the differences within "the West" these days—specifically the differences between America and everybody else. In 2004, Niall Ferguson, a Brit history prof at Harvard, pronounced the Anglo-American "special relationship" doomed. "The typical British family," he wrote, "looks much more like the typical German family than the typical American family. We eat Italian food. We watch Spanish soccer. We drive German cars. We work Belgian hours. And we buy second homes in France. Above all, we bow before central government as only true Europeans can."

He has a point, though cultural similarities are not always determinative: Canadians eat American food, watch American sports, drive American cars, work American hours (more or less), and buy second homes in Florida. But they still bow down before central government as only true Europeans can.

What's more relevant surely are not the differences but the result of those differences: America's population growth is secure and Europe's is in precipitous decline. The United States and Canada make a useful study in this respect: neighboring nations that speak the same language (mostly), have an integrated economy and a shared taste in everything from Dunkin' Donuts to the Celine Dion Christmas album. But: America's marriage rate per 1,000 is 11.7; Canada's is 6.8.

Her Majesty's chilly Dominion is the land where the straights live in common-law partnerships and the gays get married. And the upshot is: America's fertility rate is 2.11; Canada's is 1.48.

And where does that lead? Canucks are aging faster than the Yanks. In 2000, oldsters formed 16.3 percent of America's population and 17 percent of Canada's—close enough. In 2040, they'll form 26 percent of America's population and 33.3 percent of Canada's.

And there'll be a lot fewer young Canadians to stick with the bill for increased geriatric care. Take the "aged dependency ratio"—the number of elderly people receiving state benefits relative to the working-age adults slogging away each day to pay for them. In 2000, America, Australia, and Canada all had 0.26 seniors for every working stiff. In 2040, America will have 0.47 seniors for every worker, Australia 0.56, Canada 0.63.

Across the developed world, we're at the beginning of the end of the social-democratic state. The surest way to be in the demographic death spiral is to be a former Communist country in Europe: the five lowest birth rates in the world are Latvia, Bulgaria, Slovenia, Russia, and Ukraine. But the next surest way is just to be in Europe: nineteen of the lowest twenty birth rates in the world are on the Continent (the twentieth is Japan). Conversely, the only advanced nation with a sizeable population reproducing at replacement rate is the United States. True, there are significant variations from red state to blue state, immigrant to native-born, and in other areas: Mormons in Utah have one of the highest fertility rates on the planet, while the city of San Francisco could easily be mistaken for an EU capital, though in fairness to the good burghers of that town they had to embrace homosexuality to achieve levels of childlessness the Continentals have managed to achieve through ostensibly conventional sexual expression.

But the fact remains: Europe is dying and America isn't. Europe's system doesn't work and America's does, just about.

So here's a radical thought for Will Hutton and the Europeans: instead of calling for America to "join the world," why not try calling on Europe to rejoin the real world? Otherwise, you'll be joining what we used to call "the unseen world."

Or here's an even more radical thought: why doesn't "the world" try joining America?

That sound you hear is Will Hutton, Jacques Chirac, and the Belgian cabinet rolling on the floor howling with laughter.

Part II

Arabian Night

BELIEVERS, CONVERTS, SUBJECTS

Chapter Four

Flying the Coop

BIG MO VS. BIG MAC

People in Najd at that time lived in a condition that could not be approved by any believer. Polytheism had spread widely; people worshiped domes, trees, rocks, caves, or any persons who claimed to be Awliya (saints). Magic and soothsaying also had spread. When the Shaikh saw that polytheism was dominating the people and that no one showed any disapproval of it or no one was ready to call people back to Allah, he decided to labor singly and patiently in the field. He knew that nothing could be achieved without Jihad, patience and suffering.

SHAIKH ABDUL AZIZ IBN ABDULLAH IBN BAZ, *IMAAM MUHAMMAD IBN ABDUL WAHHAB—HIS LIFE AND MISSION* (1996)

n 2005, I had lunch with someone who'd just bought a photograph of Abraham Lincoln's second inaugural. "There they all are," he said. "Look." And he pointed to a vaguely familiar figure in the crowd just a few feet from the president: John Wilkes Booth. And then his finger zipped over the photo, picking out the other conspirators standing around Lincoln and already well advanced in what was then a plot merely to kidnap him. March 4, 1865, a rainy Saturday in Washington, and the chief of state is giving his speech unaware that he's in the last six weeks of his life and that he's surrounded by the group of men who will end it.

Proximity is all. If they can't get to you, they can't get you. Most of us locate our fears on the far horizon—like the old maps where the known world dribbles away and the cartographer scrawls "Here be dragons." Sometimes, as Lincoln learned, the problem's right there standing next to you.

A couple of weeks after seeing that photograph, I was passing through London and discovered that Britain was in the grip of bird flu fever: any minute now there would be toxic cockatoos over the white cliffs of Dover, and the East End would be reeling under a blitzkrieg of sneezing parakeets. Those less easily panicked argued it was nutty and way out of proportion, *One Flu Over the Cuckoo's Nest* stuff—business as usual from a government that spent the years after September 11 warning of chemical attacks on the Underground and Saddam nuking the British bases on Cyprus. Avian flu? Just the usual Tony Blairy phony-scary rigmarole.

But then again, the Tube did eventually get bombed: just because the government says something will happen doesn't mean it won't. In rural China pigs are valued possessions and sleep in the living room. That's why hundreds of members of a Catholic charismatic group from New York state had to go into isolation for a hitherto unknown respiratory disease in April 2003. A doctor from SARS-riddled Guangdong province went to a wedding at the Metropole Hotel in Hong Kong, where he managed to infect sixteen other guests with rooms on the same floor, including Kwan Sui Chu, an elderly lady staying there for one night. She flew home to Toronto and died, her death being attributed to a "chest infection." Her son Tse Chi Kwai went to Scarborough Grace Hospital and, as is traditional in Canada, was left on a gurney in Emergency for twelve hours exposed to hundreds of people. Lying next to him was Joe Pollack, who was being treated for an irregular heartbeat and whose wife wandered around the wards and came across an eighty-two-year-old man from a Catholic charismatic group. Mr. Pollack, Mrs. Pollack, the octogenarian charismatic, and his wife all died, and their sons infected at least thirty other members of their religious group plus a Filipina nurse, who flew back to Manila and before her death introduced SARS to a whole new country.

The fellow with the irregular heartbeat, the Catholic charismatics, the Filipina nurse: none of these people went anywhere near rural China. They didn't have to. They were like Lincoln in that photograph: they didn't know the infected doctor from Guangdong was, metaphorically, standing next to them.

In a globalized economy, the anti-glob mob and the eco-warriors want us to worry about rapacious First World capitalism imposing its ways on bucolic, pastoral, primitive Third World backwaters. But globalization cuts both ways, and the peculiarities of the backwaters can leap instantly to the metropolis just because someone got on a plane. The African mosquito who hitched a ride on a U.S.-bound flight and all by himself introduced West Nile virus to North America is merely the high-altitude heir to those flea-bitten rats on the Italian ships homebound from the Orient who brought the Black Death to Europe in the 1340s. That too was a globalization quid pro quo: the Continent's success in opening up trade with the East also opened it up to disease from the East.

That's the lesson of September 11: the dragons are no longer on the edge of the map. When you look at it that way, the biggest globalization success story of recent years is not McDonald's or Microsoft but Islamism: the Saudis took what was not so long ago a severe but peripheral strain of Islam practiced by Bedouins in the middle of a desert miles from anywhere and successfully exported it to Jakarta and Singapore and Alma-Ata and Grozny and Sarajevo and Lyons and Bergen and Manchester and Ottawa and Dearborn and Falls Church. It was a strictly local virus, but the bird flew the coop. And now, instead of the quaintly parochial terrorist movements of yore, we have the first globalized insurgency. In 2006, Danes reeling from the Muslim world's cartoon-provoked commercial boycott could only dream of boycotting Islam's products half so effectively.

As a bleary Dean Martin liked to say, in mock bewilderment, at the start of his stage act: "How did all these people get in my room?" How did all these jihadists get rooms in Miami and Portland and Montreal? How did we come to breed suicide bombers not just in Gaza but in

Yorkshire? In the globalized pre–September 11 world, we in the West thought in terms of nations—the Americans, the French, the Chinese—and, insofar as we considered transnational groups, were obsessed mostly with race—whites, blacks, Hispanics. Religion wasn't really on the radar. So an insurgency that lurks within a religion automatically has a global network. You don't need "deep cover" as a "fifth columnist": you can hang your shingle on Main Street and we won't even notice it. And when we do—as we did on September 11—we still won't do anything about it, because, well, it's a religion, and modern man is disinclined to go after any faith except perhaps his own.

But Islam is not just a religion. Those lefties who bemoan what America is doing to provoke "the Muslim world" would go bananas if any Western politician started referring to "the Christian world." When such sensitive guardians of the separation of church and state endorse the first formulation but not the second, they implicitly accept that Islam has a political sovereignty too. There is an "Organization of the Islamic Conference": it's like the EU and the Commonwealth and the G-8—that is, an organization of nation states whose heads of government hold regular meetings. It's the largest bloc on the new UN Human Rights Council, which explains why that pitiful joke of a council does nothing for human rights. Imagine if someone proposed an "Organization of the Christian Conference" that would hold summits attended by prime ministers and presidents and voted as a bloc in transnational bodies. And Islam is also a legal code. There is no "Christian law": indeed, English Common Law and France's Napoleonic Code are very different philosophically.

So it's not merely that there's a global jihad lurking within this religion, but that the religion itself is a political project—and, in fact, an imperial project—in a way that modern Christianity, Judaism, Hinduism, and Buddhism are not. Furthermore, this particular religion is historically a somewhat bloodthirsty faith in which whatever's your bag violence-wise can almost certainly be justified. And, yes, Christianity has had its blood-drenched moments, but the Spanish Inquisition, which remains a byword for theocratic violence, killed fewer people in a century and a half than the jihad does in a typical year.

So we have a global terrorist movement insulated within a global political project insulated within a severely self-segregating religion whose adherents are the fastest-growing demographic in the developed world. The jihad thus has a very potent brand inside a highly dispersed and very decentralized network much more efficient than anything the CIA can muster. And these fellows can hide in plain sight. As the *Times* of London reported in 2006:

> An American al Qaeda operative who was a close associate of the leader of the July 7 bombers was recruited at a New York mosque that British militants helped to run. British radicals regularly travelled to the Masjid Fatima Islamic Centre, in Queens, to organise sending American volunteers to jihadi training camps in Pakistan. Investigators reportedly found that Mohammad Sidique Khan had made calls to the mosque last year in the months before he led the terrorist attack on London that killed 52 innocent people.
>
> Mohammad Junaid Babar, one recruit from the Masjid Fatima Islamic Centre, has told US intelligence officials that he met Khan in a jihadi training camp in Pakistan in July 2003. He claims that the pair became friends as they studied how to assemble explosive devices. Babar, 31, a computer programmer, says that it was at the Masjid Fatima centre that he became a radical.

And so it goes. The mosques are recruiters for the jihad and play an important role in ideological subordination and cell discipline. In globalization terms, that's a perfect model. Unlike the Soviets, it's a franchise business rather than owner-operated; the Commies had "deep sleepers" who had to be "controlled" in a very hierarchical chain. But who needs that with Islam? Not long after September 11, I said, just as an aside, that these days whenever something goofy turns up on the news chances are it involves some fellow called Mohammed. It was a throwaway line, but if you want to compile chapter and verse, you can add to the list every week.

A plane flies into the World Trade Center? Mohammed Atta.

A sniper starts killing gas station customers around Washington, D.C.? John Allen Muhammed.

A guy fatally stabs a Dutch movie director? Mohammed Bouyeri.

A gunman shoots up the El Al counter at Los Angeles airport? Hesham Mohamed Hedayet.

A terrorist slaughters dozens in Bali? Noordin Mohamed.

A British subject self-detonates in a Tel Aviv bar? Asif Mohammed Hanif.

A terrorist cell bombs the U.S. embassies in Kenya and Tanzania? Ali Mohamed.

A gang rapist preys on the women of Sydney? Mohammed Skaf.

A group of Dearborn, Michigan, men charged with cigarette racketeering in order to fund Hezbollah? Fadi Mohamad-Musbah Hammoud, Mohammed Fawzi Zeidan, and Imad Mohamad-Musbah Hammoud.

A Canadian terror cell is arrested for plotting to bomb Ottawa and behead the prime minister? Mohammed Dirie, Amin Mohamed Durrani, and Yasim Abdi Mohamed.

These last three represent a "broad strata" of Canadian society, according to Mike McDonnell, assistant commissioner of the Royal Canadian Mounted Police and a man who must have aced Sensitivity Training class. To the casual observer, the broad strata would seem to be a very singular stratum: in their first appearance in court, all twelve men arrested in that Ontario plot requested the Koran.

When I made my observation about multiple Mohammeds in the news, Merle Ricklefs, a professor at the National University of Singapore and South-East Asian editor of the sixteen-volume *Encyclopedia of Islam*, remarked sarcastically, "Deep thinking, indeed." Well, gosh, maybe it's not terribly sophisticated. But then again, when you're dealing with fellows who decapitate female aid workers in Iraq and engage in mass slaughter of Russian schoolchildren, maybe sophistication isn't always helpful. Particularly when sophistication seems mostly to be a form of obfuscation by experts wedded to the notion that Islam is something that simply can't be understood unless you've read all sixteen volumes of their Encyclopedia, or, better yet, written them. For those of us who aren't professors of Islamic studies, the obvious course is to step back and try to work from first principles: What's happening? Who's doing it? The five-thousand-guys-named-Mo routine meets the "reasonable man" test: it's the first thing an averagely well-informed person who's not a multiculti apologist notices—here's the evening news and here comes another Mohammed.

Sophisticates object that very few of the Mohammeds on the list above are formal agents of al Qaeda. But so what? There are no "card-carrying members" of this enemy: that's what makes them an ever bigger threat. You don't need to plant sleepers. The September 11 fellows were an official al Qaeda cell, Richard Reid the shoe-bomber had some loose al Qaeda connections, the Washington snipers and the LAX murderer were just ideological sympathizers who woke up one morning and decided to take a crack at freelance jihadism. If you've got a big pool of manpower and a big idea that's just out there all the time—24/7, flickering away invitingly like a neon sign in the Western darkness—that's enough to cause a big heap of trouble. As I mentioned earlier, Mohammed is the most popular boy's name in Brussels and Amsterdam and many other places, so evidently only a tiny proportion of Mohammeds kill and bomb and fly planes into skyscrapers. Nonetheless, as a point of fact, Mohammed is:

(a) the most popular baby boy's name in much of the Western world

(b) the most common name for terrorists and murderers

(c) the name of the revered Prophet of the West's fastest-growing religion

It's at the intersection of these statistics—religious, demographic, terrorist—that a dark future awaits.

One further point: there are minimal degrees of separation between all these Mohammeds and the most eminent figures in the Muslim world and the critical institutions at the heart of the West. For example, in 2003, Abdurahman Alamoudi was jailed for attempting to launder money from a Libyan terror-front "charity" into Syria via London. Who's Abdurahman Alamoudi? He's the guy who until 1998 certified Muslim chaplains for the United States military, under the aegis of his

Saudi-funded American Muslim Armed Forces and Veterans Affairs Council. In 1993, at an American military base, at a ceremony to install the first imam in the nation's armed forces, it was Mr. Alamoudi who presented him with his new insignia of a silver crescent star.

He's also the fellow who helped devise the three-week Islamic awareness course in California public schools, in the course of which students adopt Muslim names, wear Islamic garb, give up candy and TV for Ramadan, memorize suras from the Koran, learn that "jihad" means "internal personal struggle," profess the Muslim faith, and recite prayers that begin "In the name of Allah," etc. The Ninth Circuit Court of Appeals—the same court that ruled the Pledge of Allegiance unconstitutional because of the words "under God"—decided in this case that making seventh graders play Muslim for two weeks was perfectly fine, just an interesting exposure to a fascinating "culture" from which every pupil can benefit. Separation of church and state? That may be, but nobody said nuthin' about separation of mosque and state.

Oh, and, aside from his sterling efforts on behalf of multicultural education, Mr. Alamoudi was also an adviser on Islamic matters to Hillary Rodham Clinton.

And it turns out he's a bagman for terrorists.

Infiltration-wise, I would say that's pretty good. The arthritic desk jockeys at the CIA insist, oh no, it would be impossible for them to get any of their boys inside al Qaeda. Can't be done. But the other side has no difficulty setting their chaps up in the heart of the U.S. military, and the U.S. education system, and the U.S. political establishment, and the offices of U.S. senators and former First Ladies.

Richard Reid, the shoe-bomber, was converted to radical Islamism while in prison by a chaplain who came to Britain under a fast-track immigration program for imams set up by Her Majesty's Government. They felt they had a shortage of Muslim chaplains, and not knowing much about the mullah business or where to look for 'em, felt it easiest to put up a big sign at Heathrow saying, "Hey, imams, come on down." It all seemed to be working well until they noticed that these guys appeared to be the spiritual mentors of a lot of the wackiest terrorists.

The jihad's marketing strategists singled out the prison populations of North America, Australia, and Western Europe as a ripe target demographic. Granted, a lot of religions seek to convert the fallen, but, to be honest, a wimp church like the Congregational crowd doesn't have much appeal to the average jailbird. The salient feature about Islamism is that, if you're a violent thug, embracing this particular religion doesn't mean having to do anything icky like help with the church bazaar or be nice to gay people. As an Islamist, you can pretty much carry on doing all the things you like doing and the only difference is you'll be doing them for your new religion: you can lie, cheat, steal, rape, kill women and children, and as long as you're doing it for Allah and his victory over the infidels, it's cool. So we have not just a global terrorist movement and a global political project but a global gang culture insulated within the West's fastest-growing demographic.

If you're thinking of profiling dodgy-looking fellows with beards and robes when you're next on the subway, how are you going to spot Assem Hammoud? Arrested for plotting to blow up the Holland Tunnel, Mr. Hammoud said he had been ordered by Osama bin Laden to "live the life of a playboy...live a life of fun and indulgence." That way he would avoid detection. Cunning, eh? Just to show how seriously he took his assignment, there was a picture of Assem with a trio of burqa-less hotties on a "mission" in Canada, looking like a traveling man who's decided to blow the last night of expenses on the three-girl special. What a master of disguise. "I was proud," declared Mr. Hammoud, "to carry out my orders"—even though they required him to booze it up and bed beautiful infidels all week long. But it's okay, because he was nailing chicks for Allah. So he gamely put on a brave show of partying like it's 1999 even though, as a devout Muslim, he'd obviously much rather party like it's 799.

As religious fanaticism goes, that doesn't sound to me like a movement that's going to have recruitment problems.

In globalized terms, Islam is a unitary ideology with multiple appeals. For the likes of Zac Moussaoui and Richard Reid, it's the ultimate global gang; for many European females, it's a refuge from the slatternly image of post-feminist Western womanhood; for Assem Hammoud, it's a great way to meet slatternly Western women; for impressionable types from John Walker Lindh to the Prince of Wales, its eastern exoticism has more appeal than the dreary occidental faiths; for a particular strain of old-school bigotry, it's the current home for up-to-the-minute thinking about the international Jewish conspiracy; for Abu Musab al-Zarqawi and the slaughterers of the Beslan schoolchildren and the death cultists of Hamas, it's the ultimate in nihilist depravity. A while back I took my little girl to a science exhibition in Vermont and we spent a fun half-hour flipping balls into one of those big mechanical contraptions full of levels and runways and elevators. But no matter which corner of the table you tossed the ball in, eventually it dropped into a little bucket and was deposited in the hole in the center. That's the way it is with the ideology du jour: you come at it from the Richard Reid or the John Walker Lindh or the Taliban end, but you all drop down the same big hole in the center.

We still have no strategy for dealing with the ideology. Indeed, for the first few years of the war on "terror," our leaders declined to acknowledge there was an ideology. And, as the years roll on, groups with terrorist ties are still able to insert their recruiters into America's military bases, prisons, and pretty much anywhere else they get a yen to go. How come? What gives the jihad its global reach? It's not difficult to figure out: Wahhabism is the most militant form of Islam, the one followed by all nineteen of the September 11 terrorists and by Osama bin Laden. The Saudis, whose state religion is Wahhabism, export their faith and affiliated local strains in lavishly endowed schools and mosques all over the world and, as a result, traditionally moderate Muslim populations from the Balkans to South Asia have been dramatically radicalized.

That kind of operation doesn't come cheap. So who pays for it?

You do. After September 11, George W. Bush told the world, "You're either with us or with the terrorists." In fact, much of the world is with neither, and much of the rest is with both. And why should anyone take the president's demand to choose sides seriously when America itself refuses to: the United States is both "with us" and "with the terrorists." American taxpayers are in the onerous position of funding both sides in this war. In the five years after September 11, the price of oil rose from $12 per barrel to hit an all-time high of $70—so, if you sell oil, your revenues are five times what they were. And there's nothing like bigger oil windfalls to drive powerful despots down ever crazier paths. "Looking at it another way," wrote Frank Gaffney in his book *War Footing*, "Saudi Arabia—which currently exports about ten mbd [million barrels of oil a day]—receives an extra half billion dollars every day." Where does that extra half-bil go? It goes to the mosques and madrassas that the Saudis fund in every corner of the planet. Oil isn't the principal Saudi export, ideology is—petroleum merely bankrolls it.

How could the federal government be so complacent as to subcontract the certification of chaplains in U.S. military bases to Wahhabist institutions?

Well, because they didn't notice it until it was too late—like SARS in that Toronto hospital. If your idea of globalization is a McDonald's in Belgrade or a Kentucky Fried Chicken in Lahore, who's running the imams in British and American jails doesn't seem terribly important. The Saudis fund mosques that radicalize distant Muslim populations from Indonesia to Oregon, and schools that turn out terrorists on every continent on the face of the Earth. They set up Islamic lobby groups that put spies in our military bases and terror recruiters in our prisons. They endow think tanks that buy up and neuter the massed ranks of retired diplomats, and assistant secretaries of state, and national security advisers: as the journalist Matt Welch remarked, if you close your eyes, America's ex-ambassadors to Saudi Arabia sound like they're Saudi.

Oh, and the wife of the Saudi ambassador to America "accidentally" funded the September 11 killers: Princess Haifa makes monthly payments of several thousand dollars by cashier's check from the Riggs Bank in Washington to Majeda Ibrahim, an allegedly financially strapped woman in Virginia she supposedly doesn't know, and Majeda Ibrahim signs at least some of those checks over to a friend of hers who's married to a guy in San Diego who's paying the rent for Khalid Almidhar and Nawaf Alhamzi, who subsequently fly Flight 77 into the Pentagon. Pure coincidence, say the smooth-talking Saudi princelings put up on the talk-show circuit when the story breaks. Could happen to any kind-hearted princess. And Barbara Bush, wife of the first President Bush, and Alma Powell, wife of Colin, call the princess to commiserate at all this unnecessary publicity.

For a bunch of ramshackle Bedouin, the Saudis got the hang of global networking quicker than the Canadians and Scandinavians.

●   ●   ●

GLOBAL TAKE-OUT

Which globalization is shaping the world? The movies or the madrassas? Burger King or Burqa King? Big Macs or Big Mo? A friend of mine recalled a Londoner asking him, a few weeks before the first McDonald's opened in Britain, what exactly one of these American "fast-food restaurants" was. So my chum explained. "You eat the hamburger out of a polystyrene carton?" marveled the Englishman. "Good grief, they'll lose their shirts. That's never going to catch on." Americans think nothing of changing the world's dining habits or entertainment tastes but recoil at the notion that cultural imperialism might cut a little deeper, and extend to, say, theories of government and liberty. Whether or not you can "give" people freedom, all over the world Middle Eastern Islamists have given millions of Asians and Africans and Europeans (and, yes, North Americans) an ideology and identity that hitherto they never knew they wanted. And it's hard to argue it kinda snuck up on us. In 1871, John Norman, the acting chief justice of India, was stabbed to death by a Wahhabi called Abdullah. The following year, the viceroy, Lord Mayo, was also fatally stabbed, by a Wahhabi named Shere Ali. He declared that Allah was his "*shereek*" (accomplice) and, at the gallows, was reciting verses from the Koran as the trap fell.

After the Sepoy Mutiny of 1857, William Tayler wrote:

> With the Soonnees the Wahabees are on terms of tolerable agreement, though differing on certain points, but from the Sheahs, they differ radically, and their hatred, like all religious hatred, is

bitter and intolerant. But the most striking characteristic of the
Wahabee sect, and that which principally concerns this narrative,
is the entire subservience which they yield to the Peer, or spiritual guide.

Mr. Tayler, a minor civil servant in Bengal, was a genuine "multicultur-
alist." Although he regarded his own culture as superior, he was engaged
enough by the ways of others to study the differences between them. By
contrast, contemporary multiculturalism absolves one from knowing
anything about other cultures as long as one feels warm and fluffy
toward them. After all, if it's grossly judgmental to say one culture's better than another, why bother learning about the differences? "Celebrate
diversity" with a uniformity of ignorance. Had William Tayler been
around when the Islamification of the West got under way and you'd said
to him there was a mosque opening down the street, he'd have wanted
to know: What kind of mosque? Who's the imam? What branch of
Islam? Old-school imperialists could never get away with the feel-good
condescension of PC progressives.

Here's Tayler again: "The tenets originally professed by the Wahabees
have been described as a Mahomedan Puritanism joined to a Bedouin
Phylarchy, in which the great chief is both the political and religious
leader of the nation."

Too right. In 1946, Colonel William Eddy, the first United States minister to Saudi Arabia, was told by the country's founder, Ibn Saud, "We
will use your iron, but you will leave our faith alone."

Had William Tayler been on hand, he might have questioned whether
that was such a great deal. American "iron"—money and technology
invested in the oil industry—transformed Saudi Arabia's financial fortunes while leaving its faith and everything else alone. In 1974, the oil
industry accounted for 91 percent of Saudi exports. In 2000, it accounted
for 91.4 percent. Two trillion dollars poured into the House of Saud's
treasury, and what did they do with it? Diversify the economy? Launch
new industries? Open up the tourism sector? Not a thing. The country
remained the same desert, literally and psychologically, it was a quarter

century earlier. So where did all that money go? From the seventies onward, Saudi Arabia used their Yanqui dollars to export their faith even more widely than the oil. Instead of diversifying their industrial exports, they honed their ideological one, financing Islamic centers, mosques, and schools in Morocco, Uzbekistan, Indonesia, Bosnia, Nigeria, Britain, and America. In 2005, a twenty-three-year-old American citizen named Ahmed Omar Abu Ali was charged with plotting to assassinate the president. Like that photograph of Lincoln and Booth, Mr. Abu Ali was closer than you might think: according to the Associated Press report in the *New York Times*, he "was born in Houston and moved to Falls Church, Va., where he was valedictorian of his high school class."

High school valedictorian from northern Virginia, huh? Was he in that year's production of *Bye Bye Birdie*? Not exactly. Neither the *Times* nor the AP had space to mention that the typical Virginia high school Mr. Abu Ali attended was the Islamic Saudi Academy, funded by the Kingdom of Saudi Arabia. It's on American soil but it describes itself as "subject to the government of the Kingdom of Saudi Arabia" and its classes are based on "the curriculum, syllabus, and materials established by the Saudi Ministry of Education." So what does it teach? No room for American history, but that's not so unusual in Virginia high schools these days. Instead, the school concentrates on Wahhabi history and "Islamic values and the Arabic language and culture," plus "the superiority of jihad." By the eleventh grade, students are taught that on the Day of Judgment Muslims will fight and kill the Jews, who will find that the very trees they're hiding behind will betray them by saying, "Oh Muslim, oh servant of God, here is a Jew hiding behind me. Come here and kill him." Beats climate change and gay outreach, or whatever they do in the regular Falls Church high school.

Here is a standard Saudi Ministry of Education exercise, as taught in the first grade at that Virginia academy and at other Saudi-funded schools in the Western world:

> Fill in the blanks with the appropriate words:
> Every religion other than _____ is false.
> Whoever dies outside of Islam enters _____.

Correct answers: Islam, hellfire.

And what do America's president and the secretary of state and the deputy secretary of this and the undersecretary of that say in return?

The Saudis are our _____.

Fiends? Whoops, sorry, friends. The Saudis are our friends. No matter how many of us they kill.

The Germans and Japanese had to make do with Lord Haw-Haw and Tokyo Rose. If only they could have had Third Reich Academies in every English city and Hirohito Highs from Alaska to Florida and St. Adolf's Parish Church in every medium-sized town around the world. Of all the many examples of how our multiculti mainstream ushers the extremists from the dark fringe to the center of Western life, there is no more emblematic tale than a famous 2004 court victory won by an adolescent schoolgirl called Shabina Begum. Had the verdict not been overturned on appeal in 2006, all British schools would have had to permit students to wear the full "jilbab"—Muslim garb that covers the entire body except the eyes and hands. This triumph over the school dress code was achieved with the professional support of both Cherie Booth, the wife of Tony Blair, and of Hizb ut-Tahrir, a group that advocates violence in support of a worldwide caliphate and which (according to the BBC) "urges Muslims to kill Jewish people." What does an "extremist" have to do to be too extreme for the wife of the British prime minister?

Ms. Booth hailed her initial court win as "a victory for all Muslims who wish to preserve their identity and values despite prejudice and bigotry." It seems almost too banal to observe that such an extreme preservation of young Shabina Begum's Muslim identity must perforce be at the expense of any British identity. Is it "bigoted" to argue that the jilbab is a barrier to acquiring the common culture necessary to any functioning society? Is it "prejudiced" to suggest that in Britain a Muslim woman ought to reach the same sartorial compromise as, say, a female doctor in Bahrain?

Nor, incidentally, was Miss Begum "preserving" any identity: she's of Bangladeshi origin, and her belated adoption of the jilbab is a symbol of the Arabization of South Asian (and African and European and North American) Islam that's at the root of so many current problems. Even as an honored Arab tradition, it dates all the way back to the seventies. Not the 1070s or 1570s but the 1970s. There is no evidence that any Muslim woman anywhere ever wore the jilbab before the disco era, when it was taken up by the Muslim Brotherhood and others in the Arab world. It is no more ancient and traditional than platform shoes, bell bottoms, and cheesecloth shirts. It's no more part of Shabina Begum's inherited identity than my little boy dressing up in his head-to-toe Darth Vader costume, to which at a casual glance it's not dissimilar. So it's a wholly invented and consciously chosen identity. It's not part of her Bangladeshi heritage, it's not part of British custom. It is equally alien in both the Indian subcontinent and the British Isles, and its appearance in both places is, in point of fact, political rather than spiritual: it's part of a movement explicitly hostile to what Tony Blair calls "our way of life." If it's too unreasonable to expect young Shabina Begum to choose a British identity, couldn't Mr. and Mrs. Blair at least encourage her to preserve her authentic Bangladeshi one?

During the cartoon jihad, a Muslim demonstrator in Toronto spelled it out: "We won't stop the protests until the world obeys Islamic law."

Or as Kofi Annan framed it, rather more soothingly, "The offensive caricatures of the Prophet Muhammad were first published in a European country which has recently acquired a significant Muslim population, and is not yet sure how to adjust to it."

If you've also "recently acquired" a significant Muslim population and you're not sure how to "adjust" to it, well, here's the difference: back when my Belgian grandparents emigrated to Canada, the idea was that the immigrants assimilated with the host country. As Kofi and Co. see it, today the host country has to assimilate with the immigrants. But it goes beyond that—because the immigrant populations themselves are adjusting, developing an Islamic identity far more intense than anything practiced by their forbears. Take Nada Farooq, a student at Meadowvale Secondary School in Mississauga, Ontario. In 2004 she started an Internet forum for Muslim teens in the area. One poster thought it would be fun if they had a thread explaining what made Canada unique, but Nada nixed that one in nothing flat: "Who cares? We hate Canada."

So what does grab her interest? Well, she wasn't too thrilled to hear that Abdel Aziz al-Rantissi, a Hamas honcho, had been killed by an Israeli missile. "May Allah crush these jews," she declared, "bring them down to their knees, humiliate them. Ya Allah make their women widows and their children orphans." But she and her fellow Meadowvale students were extremely partial to a very bloody video showing the beheading of an American hostage in Iraq.

Oh, well. Excitable teens often pass through a somewhat turbulent phase. But two years later Miss Farooq's husband and sixteen other men were arrested in a terrorist plot that included wide-ranging plans to blow up the Toronto Stock Exchange, seize Parliament in Ottawa, and kidnap and behead the prime minister.

I'm often damned as a "self-loathing Canadian" because I'm opposed to socialized health care and government-funded multiculturalism and whatnot. But in the self-loathing stakes I've got nothing on Nada Farooq. "We hate Canada." Yet no one calls her a self-loathing Canadian. Perhaps that's because she's not a gal you'd want to tangle with; when she married, she gave serious thought to getting a prenup that would dissolve the union if her husband failed to partake in jihad. Or perhaps it's because, at heart, no one expects her to feel "Canadian," whatever that means these days. Miss Farooq's father is a pharmacist who fills prescriptions at a military base in Wainwright, Alberta, and says he supports the Princess Patricia's Canadian Light Infantry on their mission in Afghanistan. After the terror cell was cracked, Mohammed Umer Farooq told the press that his daughter's views—hating Canada, in favor of shipping homosexuals to Saudi Arabia to be executed or crushed, etc.—were new to him, but that she's always been "more religious" than he is. He described her as "100 percent religious" and himself as "30 percent religious."

Nada Farooq is typical of a significant minority of young Muslims: raised in the West by "moderate Muslim" parents, she is, unlike them, ferociously Muslim, Islamist, jihadist. Her father's generation brought to the West the Indian subcontinent's traditional moderate Sufi Islam. In

Pakistan, Britain, and Canada, that Sufism is yielding to a hard-line strain of Deobandi Islam—essentially a local subsidiary of Wahhabism. Unlike her parents, Nada Farooq has no natural Pakistani identity and she rejects her thin, reedy multicultural Canadian identity, choosing instead a pan-Islamic consciousness that transcends nationality: she planned to name her son Khattab, after the Chechen mujahadeen commander killed in 2002. Growing up in a Toronto suburb, she found recent Chechen history more inspiring than Canadian history, assuming she was taught any.

How many Nada Farooqs are there? On the first anniversary of the July 7, 2005, Tube bombings, the *Times* of London commissioned a poll of British Muslims. Among the findings:

- 16 percent say that while the attacks may have been wrong, the cause was right.
- 13 percent think that the four men who carried out the bombings should be regarded as "martyrs."
- 7 percent agree that suicide attacks on civilians in the United Kingdom can be justified in some circumstances, rising to 16 percent for a military target.
- 2 percent would be proud if a family member decided to join al Qaeda. 16 percent would be "indifferent."

If this is a war, then that is a substantial fifth column. There are, officially, one million Muslims in London, half of them under twenty-five. If 7 percent think suicide attacks on civilians are justified, that's 70,000 potential supporters in Britain's capital city. Most of them will never bomb a bus or even provide shelter or a bank account to someone who does. But some of them will. As September 11 demonstrated, you only have to find nineteen stout-hearted men, and from a talent pool of 70,000 that's not bad odds.

Besides, a large majority of Western Muslims support almost all the terrorists' strategic goals: according to one poll, over 60 percent of British Muslims want to live under sharia in the United Kingdom.

Another poll places the percentage favoring "hard-line" sharia at a mere 40 percent. So there's one definition of a "moderate Muslim": he's a Muslim who wants stoning for adultery to be introduced in Liverpool, but he's a "moderate" because he can't be bothered flying a plane into a skyscraper to get it. Another poll found that 20 percent of British Muslims sympathized with the "feelings and motives" of the July 7 London Tube bombers. Or, more accurately, 20 percent were prepared to admit to a pollster they felt sympathy, which suggests the real figure might be somewhat higher. Huge numbers of Muslims—many of them British subjects born and bred—see their fellow Britons blown apart on trains and buses and are willing to rationalize the actions of the mass murderers.

The Islamic lobby groups pressure governments to make concessions to them rather than to the terrorists—even though both share the same aims. In fact, sharing the same aims as the terrorists is what gives the Islamic lobby groups their credibility. If there were a "moderate Muslim" lobby—one that, say, believed that suicide bombing is always wrong, even against Israelis, or that supported the liberation of Iraq on the grounds that the Iraqi people are in favor of it—your average Western government would immediately be suspicious that such a group was not "authentically" Muslim. Whereas, if you oppose the occupation of Iraq and seek to justify the depravity of Hamas, you have instant credibility. And so government ministers in Western nations spend most of their time taking advice on the jihad from men who agree with its aims. You can pluck out news items at random: in London, a religious "hate crimes" law that makes honest discussion of Islam even more difficult; in Ottawa, a government report that recommends legalizing polygamy; in Seattle, the introduction of gender-separate Muslim-only swimming sessions in municipal pools. . . . The September 11 terrorists were in favor of all these ends. The disagreement is only on the means.

A while back, I found myself behind a car in Vermont that had a one-word bumper sticker containing the injunction "CO-EXIST." It's one of those sentiments beloved of Western progressives, one designed principally to flatter their sense of moral superiority, part of the multiculti mood music that makes lefty pieties one long soothing express elevator to cloud-cuckoo land. On this "CO-EXIST" sticker, the "C" was the Islamic crescent, the "O" was the hippy peace sign, the "X" was the Star of David and the "T" was the Christian cross. Very nice, hard to argue with. But the reality is that it's the first of those symbols that has a problem with "co-existence." Take the crescent out of the equation and you wouldn't need a bumper sticker at all. Indeed, co-existence is what the Islamists are at war with—or, if you prefer, pluralism; the idea that different groups can rub along together within the same general neighborhood. And even those who nominally respect the idea tend, on closer examination, to mean by "pluralism" something closer to "subjugation." Take one of those famous "moderate Muslims": Imam Zaid Shakir, the subject of a flattering profile in the *New York Times* under the headline "U.S. Muslim Clerics Seek a Modern Middle Ground." Good for them, but what does a "modern middle ground" mean? As Imam Shakir—who grew up as Ricky Mitchell in Georgia and Connecticut—says, "Every Muslim who is honest would say, I would like to see America become a Muslim country. I think it would help people, and if I didn't believe that, I wouldn't be a Muslim."

I think he's right when he says honest Muslims want America to be a Muslim country. But they don't mean it in quite the same sense Christians do when they speak of America as a Christian country. By a "Muslim country," they don't just foresee a country with a majority of Muslim inhabitants but a country whose civil institutions are Muslim.

The Islamists incite jihad from American, Canadian, British, European, and Australian mosques, and they get away with it. The West's elites lapse reflexively into twittering over insufficient "respect" and entirely fictional outbreaks of "Islamophobia." The Mounties, the FBI, Scotland Yard, and others are reasonably efficient at breaking up cells and plots, but they're the symptoms, not the disease. It's the ideological pipeline that needs to be dismantled. Through their network of schools and mosques, the Saudis are attempting to make themselves into a Muslim Vatican—if not infallible, at any rate the most authoritative voice in the Islamic world. We might have responded to the Wahhabist challenge by distinguishing, as William Tayler did, between Sunni and Shia, Sufi and Salafi, and all the rest, and attempting to exploit the divisions. But, as proper Western multiculturalists, we celebrate diversity by lumping them all together as "Islam."

So if the jihad has its war aims, maybe we should start thinking about ours. What would victory look like? As Fascism and Communism were in their day, Islamism is now the ideology of choice for the world's grievance-mongers. That means we have to destroy the ideology, or at least its potency—not Islam per se, but at the very minimum the toxic strain of Wahhabism, which thanks to Saudi oil money has been transformed from a fetish of isolated desert derelicts into the most influential radicalizing force of our time. If the implausible mantra of Western politicians that Islam is a "religion of peace" had any strategic value against the head hackers and suicide bombers, it would be as a prelude to pointing out that, sadly, Wahhabism is an exception to this otherwise saintly character, that Wahhabism is a religion of pieces. But our lack of curiosity about which particular school of imam is setting up shop on Main Street is greatly facilitating the cause of pan-Islamism, a much better example of globalization than McDonald's. In Bangladesh and Bosnia, it's put indigenous localized Islams out of business and imposed a one-size-fits-all Wahhab-Mart version cooked up by some guy at head office in Riyadh. One way to reverse its gains would be with a kind of anti-trust approach designed to restore all the less threatening mom n' pop Islams run out of town by the Saudis' Burqa King version of global homogeneity.

By contrast, the much reviled yet mostly mythical "American imperialism" is up on bricks and rusting in the back of the garage. Wearying of what he regards as the deluded idealism of the liberty-touting Bush doctrine, *National Review*'s John Derbyshire began promoting the slogan "Rubble Doesn't Cause Trouble." Cute, and I wish him well with the T-shirt sales. But, in arguing for a "realist" foreign policy of long-range bombing as necessary, he overlooks the very obvious point that rubble causes quite a lot of trouble: the rubble of Bosnia is directly responsible for radicalizing a generation of European Muslims, including Daniel Pearl's executioner; the rubble of Afghanistan became an international terrorist training camp, whose alumni include the shoe-bomber Richard

Reid, the millennium bomber Ahmed Ressam, and the September 11 plotters; the rubble of Grozny turned Chechen nationalists into pan-Islamist jihadi. Those correspondents of mine who send me e-mails headed "Nuke Mecca!" might like to ponder the bigger strategic impact on a billion Muslims from Indonesia to Yorkshire, for whom any fallout will be psychological rather than carcinogenic. Rubble is an insufficient solution, unless you're also going to attend to the Muslim world's real problem: its intellectual rubble.

Arab Muslims fought in Afghanistan, British Muslims took up arms in Bosnia, Pakistani Muslims have been killed in Chechnya. When you're up against a globalized ideology, you need to globalize your own, not hunker down in Fortress America.

What's the bigger threat? A globalization that exports cheeseburgers or a globalization that exports the harshest and most oppressive features of its culture? Far too many American conservatives still think the dragons are at the far fringes of the map—that in the twenty-first century the United States can be a nineteenth-century republic untroubled by the world's pathogens because of its sheer distance from them. But, in an age of globalized proximity all of us in the modern multicultural West are like Lincoln on the steps of the Capitol that Saturday morning: the world is in the room with us. At the dawn of the twenty-first century, Marshall McLuhan's global village is finally within reach: the Yanks run the diner, the Chinese the health clinic, and the Saudis the church. From America's point of view, that doesn't seem the best deal.

Chapter Five

The Anything They'll Believe In

CHURCH VS. STATE

Islam is not only a religion, it is a complete way of life. Islam guides Muslims from birth to grave. The Quran and prophet Muhammad's words and practical application of Quran in life cannot be changed.

Islam is a guide for humanity, for all times, until the day of judgment. It is forbidden in Islam to convert to any other religion. The penalty is death. There is no disagreement about it.

Islam is being embraced by people of other faiths all the time. They should know they can embrace Islam, but cannot get out. This rule is not made by Muslims; it is the supreme law of God.

Please do not ask us Muslims to pick some rules and disregard other rules. Muslims are supposed to embrace Islam in its totality.

NAZRA QURAISHI, KINDERGARTEN TEACHER, IN THE *LANSING STATE JOURNAL* (MICHIGAN), JULY 5, 2006

What we still don't know, as the years drift by since September 11, is how deep the psychoses of jihadism reach within Islam in general, and the West's Muslim populations in particular. How many are revolted by the slaughter of those Beslan schoolchildren or the beheading of Daniel Pearl and other hostages, and how many are willing to rationalize it? More to the point, of those Muslims who are affronted by what is done in the name of their religion, what percentage are prepared to do anything about it? How many Western Muslims have formed "Not In Our Name" groups and marched to protest the bombings of their fellow citizens in New York, Madrid, and London? How many have joined "Islam Against Suicide Bombing" or banded together to force jihadist imams out of their mosques? How many are prepared to stand up and say they didn't come to America or Europe to raise their children as Saudis?

Hello? Anyone out there?

We—the befuddled infidels—talk airily about "reforming" Islam. But what if the reform has already taken place and jihadism is it? What if the long percolation of Islam through Wahhabism, the Muslim Brotherhood, the Iranian revolution, and contemporary Western-promoted whining over grievances such as "colonialism" *is* the reform?

We chatter breezily about "assimilating" Western Muslims. But compare a gathering of mainstream Muslim politicians and religious leaders in Baghdad with any similar get-together in London or Detroit or Sydney, and you realize the Iraqis sound a lot more reasonable and amenable than most Western Muslim lobby groups. What if the problem is not that Muslims in the West are unfamiliar with the customs of their new land but rather that they are all too familiar with them—and explicitly reject them? And that the result is a mutated form of Islam uniquely well informed in its hostility to the infidel—and one furthermore in which ancient tribal hostilities between Sunni and Shia, Arab and non-Arab have been subsumed within a new pan-Islamic identity.

Muslims have assimilated brilliantly, at least when it comes to mastering the principal discourse of the advanced democratic state—the legalisms, victimology, and entitlement culture. Here are two small foot-of-the-page news items: first, a decision by the Massachusetts Supreme Court as reported by the *Boston Herald*: "The state's highest court has ruled that the state prison system has failed to justify denying a Muslim inmate special feast-day meats, such as oxen and camel."

The Third Infantry Division has to make do with MREs, but a Muslim prisoner can sue because they're not serving him camel. Meanwhile, in Britain they're rebuilding half the bathrooms in Her Majesty's prisons because Muslim inmates have complained that the toilets face Mecca and that therefore they're obliged to ride sidesaddle, which can be very uncomfortable.

And, if you're looking for "root causes" of terrorism, why not start with Euro-Canadian welfare systems? While it's not true that every immigrant on welfare is an Islamic terrorist, the vast majority of Islamic terrorists in Europe are on welfare, living in radicalized ghetto cultures with nothing to do but sit around the flat plotting the jihad all day at taxpayers' expense. Muhammed Metin Kaplan used his time on welfare in Germany to set up his Islamist group, Caliphate State; the so-called "caliph of Cologne" was subsequently extradited to Turkey for planning to fly a plane into the mausoleum of Kemal Ataturk. Ahmed Ressam, arrested in Washington state en route to blow up Los Angeles International Airport, hatched his plot while on welfare in Montreal. Abdul Nacer Benbrika, leader of a group of Australian Islamists, lived in Melbourne for ten years and never did a day's work; now he's been jailed for terrorism-related activities, and taxpayers are ponying up $50,000 a year in benefits to his wife. Abu Hamza became Britain's most famous fire-breathing imam while on welfare in London and, after being charged with incitement to murder and sent to jail, sued the government for extra benefits on top of the £1,000 a week his family already received. Abu Qatada, a leading al Qaeda recruiter, became an Islamist big shot while on welfare in Britain, and only when he was discovered to have £150,000 in his bank account did the Department for Work and Pensions turn off the spigot. Oh, and here's another Welfare Megabucks bonanza, from the *Times* of London: "Police are investigating allegations that the four suspected July 21 bombers collected more than £500,000 in benefits payments in Britain."

No-hoper jihadists in their twenties have a quarter-million dollars in welfare cash in their checking accounts. I'm not saying every benefit recipient is a terrorist welfare queen, only that the best hope of reforming bloated European welfare systems is if America declares them a national security threat.

A terrorist wakes up in Baghdad early Monday morning, straps on the old explosives, and toddles off to blow up some infidels at the gate to the

Green Zone, dreaming of getting at least a couple of the virgins in before lunch. But the belt jams and U.S. troops arrest him and he's stuck on a plane to Gitmo and forty-eight hours later he's whining to his D.C. lawyer about the quality of the chicken chasseur and plotting his Supreme Court case. When they want to, Islamists can assimilate at impressive speed. So we have fire-breathing imams milking Euro-welfare and litigious lobby groups with high-rent legal teams. Neither of these are features of Arab life. Rather, they illustrate how adept Islam is at picking and choosing what aspects of Westernization are useful to it. Whatever the arguments for and against "gay marriage," there are never going to be many takers for it. But the justifications for same-sex marriage are already being used to advance the cause of polygamy, and there are far more takers for that. It's already practiced de facto if not de jure in France, Ontario, and many other Western jurisdictions, and government agencies, such as the United Kingdom's pensions ministry, have already begun according polygamy piecemeal legal recognition for the purposes of inheritance law. Neither feminists nor homosexuals seem obvious allies for Islam, but lobby groups have effortlessly mastered the lingo, techniques, and pseudo-grievances of both.

For example, Iqbal Sacranie is a Muslim of such exemplary "moderation" he's been knighted by the Queen. Around the time *Brokeback Mountain* opened, Sir Iqbal, head of the Muslim Council of Britain, was on the BBC and expressed the view that homosexuality was "immoral," "not acceptable," "spreads disease," and "damaged the very foundations of society." A gay group complained and Sir Iqbal was investigated by Scotland Yard's "community safety unit" which deals with "hate crimes" and "homophobia."

Independently but simultaneously, the magazine of GALHA (the Gay And Lesbian Humanist Association) called Islam a "barmy doctrine" growing "like a canker" and deeply "homophobic." In return, the London Race Hate Crime Forum asked Scotland Yard to investigate GALHA for "Islamophobia."

Got that? If a Muslim says that Islam is opposed to homosexuality, he can be investigated for homophobia; but if a gay says that Islam is opposed to homosexuality, he can be investigated for Islamophobia.

As someone who's called Islamophobic and homophobic every day of the week, I can't help marveling at the speed and skill with which Muslim lobby groups have mastered the language of victimhood so adroitly used by the gay lobby. If I were the latter, I'd be a little miffed at these Ahmed-come-latelys. "Homophobia" was always absurd: people who are antipathetic to gays are not afraid of them in any real sense. The invention of a phony-baloney "phobia" was a way of casting opposition to the gay political agenda as a kind of mental illness: don't worry, you're not really against same-sex marriage; with a bit of treatment and some medication, you'll soon be feeling okay.

On the other hand, "Islamophobia" is not phony or even psychological but very literal—if you're a Dutch member of parliament or British novelist or Danish cartoonist in hiding under threat of death or a French schoolgirl in certain suburbs getting jeered at as an infidel whore, your Islamophobia is highly justified. But Islam's appropriation of the gay lobby's framing of the debate is very artful. It's the most explicit example of how Islam uses politically correct self-indulgent victimology as a cover. You'll recall that most Western media outlets declined to publish those Danish cartoons showing the Prophet Mohammed. Thus, even as they were piously warning of a rise in bogus "Islamophobia"—i.e., entirely justified concerns over Islamic terrorism and related issues—they were themselves suffering from genuine Islamophobia—i.e., a very real fear that, if they published those cartoons, an angry mob would storm their offices. It was a fine example of how the progressive mind's invented psychoses leave it without any words to describe real dangers.

● ● ●

THE NON-VISIBLE MINORITY

Still, as we always say, the "vast majority" of Muslims oppose "extremism." These are the so-called "moderate Muslims." One is tempted to update the old joke: a ten-dollar bill is in the center of the crossroads. To the north, there's Santa Claus. To the west, the Tooth Fairy. To the east, a radical Muslim. To the south, a moderate Muslim. Who reaches the ten-dollar bill first?

Answer: the radical Muslim. All the others are mythical creatures.

The "moderate Muslim" is not entirely fictional. But it would be more accurate to call them quiescent Muslims. In the 1930s, there were plenty of "moderate Germans," and a fat lot of good they did us or them. Today, the "moderate Muslim" is a unique contributor to cultural diversity: unlike all the visible minorities, he's a non-visible one—or, at any rate, non-audible. But that doesn't mean we can't speak up on his behalf. So, for example, EU officials have produced new "guidelines" for discussing the, ah, current unpleasantness. The phrase "Islamic terrorism" is out. Instead, the EU bureaucrats have replaced it with the expression "terrorists who abusively invoke Islam."

Who's some white-bread Belgian to say whether Johnny bin Jihad is "abusively" invoking Islam? There seem to be plenty of Muslim scholars and imams who would disagree. We know, because Western politicians and religious leaders tell us so incessantly, that the "vast majority" of Muslims do not support terrorism? Yet how vast is the minority that does? One percent? Ten percent? Here are a couple of examples that suggest it might be rather more. Dr. Mahfooz Kanwar, a sociology professor at Mount Royal College in Calgary, went along to a funeral at the city's largest mosque and was discombobulated when the man who led the prayers—in Urdu—said, "Oh, God, protect us from the infidels, who pollute us with their vile ways." Dr. Kanwar said, "How dare you attack my country," and pointed out to the crowd that he'd known this man for thirty years, most of which time he'd been living on welfare and thus the food on his table came courtesy of the taxes of the hardworking infidels.

As Licia Corbella wrote in the *Calgary Sun*: "Guess which of the two men is no longer welcome at the Sarcee Trail mosque?"

Final score: Radical Islam 1, Moderate Muslims 0.

Here's another example: Souleiman Ghali was born in Palestine and, as he put it, raised to hate "Shiites, Christians—and especially Jews." After emigrating to America, he found himself rethinking these old prejudices and in 1993 helped found a mosque in San Francisco. As Mr. Ghali's website states: "Our vision is the emergence of an American Muslim identity founded on compassion, respect, dignity, and love." That's hard work, especially given the supply of imams. In 2002, Mr. Ghali fired an imam who urged California Muslims to follow the sterling example of Palestinian suicide bombers. Safwat Morsy is Egyptian and speaks barely any English, but he knew enough to sue Mr. Ghali's mosque for wrongful dismissal and was awarded $400,000.

So far, so typical. But the part of the story that matters is that the firebrand imams had a popular following, and Mr. Morsy's firing was the final straw. Mr. Ghali was forced off the board and out of any role in the mosque he founded. And, as the *Wall Street Journal* reported, Safwat Morsy—a man who thinks American Muslims should be waddling around in Semtex belts—is doing a roaring trade: "His mosque is looking to buy a building to accommodate the capacity crowds coming these days for Friday prayers."

That's Radical Islam 2, Moderate Muslims 0.

What proportion of mosques is "extreme"? And what proportion of "worshippers" is jihadist? Twenty percent? Two percent? Point-two percent? Nobody knows—because we (and most Western legal systems) see them as analogous to Catholic churches or Congregationalist meeting-houses.

At this point it's time to throw in another round of "of courses": *of course* most Western Muslims aren't terrorists and *of course* most have no desire to be terrorists. One gathers anecdotally that they're secure enough in their Muslim identity to dismiss the fire-breathing imam down the street as a kind of vulgar novelty act for the kids—in the same way that middle-class suburban white parents sigh and roll their eyes when Junior comes home with "Slap Up My Bitch" or "I'm Gonna Shoot That Cop Right After I F— His Ho" or whatever the latest popular vocal ditty is. But, aside from the few brave but marginalized men like Mr. Ghali, one can't help noticing that the most prominent "moderate Muslims" would seem to be more accurately designated as apostate or ex-Muslims,

like the feminist lesbian Canadian Irshad Manji and the California aca-
demic Wafa Sultan. It seems likely that the beliefs of Mohammed Atta
are closer to the thinking of most Muslims than those of Ms. Manji are.

The pseudonymous apostate Ibn Warraq makes an important distinction: there are moderate Muslims, but no moderate Islam. Millions of
Muslims just want to get on with their lives, and there are—or were—
remote corners of the world where, far from Mecca, Muslim practices
reached accommodation with local customs. But all of the official
schools of Islamic jurisprudence commend sharia and violent jihad. So a
"moderate Muslim" can find no formal authority to support his moderation. And to be a "moderate Muslim" publicly means standing up to
the leaders of your community, to men like Shaker Elsayed, leader of the
Dar al Hijrah, one of America's largest mosques, who has told his core-
ligionists in blunt terms: "The call to reform Islam is an alien call."

And even if you're truly a "moderate" Muslim, why should you be
expected to take on the most powerful men in Islam when the West's
media and political class merely pander to them? What kind of support
does the culture give to those who speak out against the Islamists? The
Iranians declared a fatwa on Salman Rushdie and he had to go into hiding for more than a decade while his government and others continued
fawning on the regime that issued the death sentence. The Dutch filmmaker Theo van Gogh spoke out and was murdered, and the poseur dis-
senters of Hollywood were too busy congratulating themselves on their
courage and bravery in standing up to Bush even to mention their poor
dead colleague in the weepy Oscar montage of the year's deceased. To
speak out against the Islamists means to live in hiding and under armed
security in the heart of the so-called "free world."

Meanwhile, Yale offers a place on its campus to a former ambassador-
at-large for the murderous Taliban regime.

When you look at the syncretist forms of Islam that endured for
many years in Mecca's remoter outposts—from the Balkans to Central
Asia to Indonesia—they derived their "moderate" nature not from any
particular school of Islam itself but from the character of the surround-
ing culture; Soviet regimes, a Chinese mercantile class, European impe-

rialism all successfully tempered the more extreme forms of Islam. It's no surprise that, with the loss of Western confidence, the free world's Muslim populations are growing more radical with each generation.

So within the ever larger Muslim population is an ever larger Western Muslim population and within that ever larger Western Muslim population is an ever more radicalized Western Muslim population. And when you penetrate through all the various layers, there is a very profound challenge at the heart of the Islamic question. It was embodied by Abdul Rahman, a man on trial for his life in post-Taliban Afghanistan because he had committed the crime of converting to Christianity. "We will not allow God to be humiliated. This man must die," said Abdul Raoulf of the nation's principal Muslim body, the Afghan Ulama Council. "Cut off his head! We will call on the people to pull him into pieces so there's nothing left." Needless to say, Imam Raoulf is one of Afghanistan's leading "moderate" clerics. "Even if the government does not sentence him to death, then the people of Afghanistan will kill him," declared Maulavi Enayatullah Baligh, a lecturer in Islamic "law" at Kabul University, but evidently one who likes to take his work home with him and practice it ad hoc with the local lynch mob.

Eventually, after a word in Hamid Karzai's ear from various Western prime ministers and Condi Rice and Co., the issue was finessed through back channels and poor Mr. Rahman was bundled onto a plane out of Kabul and dropped off in Rome. But Condi and Co. won't be there for every Abdul Rahman, and so the question at the heart of his struggle remains unresolved: if Nazra Quraishi, quoted above, is correct that one "can embrace Islam but cannot get out," that Islam is a religion one can only convert to, not from, then in the long run it is a threat to every free person on the planet. It cuts to the heart of what the multicultural state is, or believes itself to be. "Radical Islamism," wrote Fouad Ajami, "has come to mock the very principle of nationality and citizenship."

But is that really so hard to do? Contemporary Canadian, British, Dutch, and Swedish nationality is to a large extent self-mocking. Alleged "conservatives" like the former prime minister Joe Clark spoke favorably of Canada being a "nation of nations," meaning Indian nations, Inuit nations, the Quebec nation, the Ukrainian-Canadian nation, etc., with nary a thought for what other forces might set up shop in such a waste-land of a concept. The jihad is a functioning version of everything the multicultists have promoted for years. The Left talked up sappy Benetton-ad one-worldism, while the pan-Islamists got on with their own particu-lar strain of one-worldism—strong, unyielding, and slipping across borders with ease.

Anjem Choudary, a thirty-nine-year-old British Muslim leader, hailed September 11 as "magnificent" and its perpetrators "heroes"; he mocked the victims of the London Tube bombings, calls on Muslims to refuse to cooperate with the British police, and advocates sharia for the United Kingdom. He and his wife are welfare recipients, but nevertheless he's able to rack up impressive frequent-flyer mileage jetting off to liaise with like-minded Muslims in other countries. On the BBC, he was asked why he didn't simply move to a state that already has sharia. "Who says you own Britain, anyway?" he replied. "Britain belongs to Allah. The whole world belongs to Allah." Warming to his theme, he added, "If I go to the jungle, I'm not going to live like the animals, I'm going to propagate a superior way of life. Islam is a superior way of life."

But Britain is a jungle of declawed lions, its leadership divided between outright appeasers and dismal fatalists. And those who call for a Muslim Reformation in the spirit of the Christian Reformation ignore the obvious flaw in the analogy—that Muslims have the advantage of knowing (unlike Luther and Calvin) where reform in Europe ultimately led: the banishment of God to the margins of society.

Muslims are less likely to fall for that than to exploit the obvious opportunities it presents. What will be the next phase of the Islamist advance in the West? If you're a teenager in most European cities these days, you've a choice between two competing identities—a robust confi-dent Islamic identity or a tentative post-nationalist cringingly apologetic European identity. It would be a mistake to assume the former is attrac-tive only to Arabs and North Africans.

• • •

THE POST-CHRISTIAN WEST

In the run-up to Christmas not so long ago, I was in a store in Vermont buying a last-minute gift when the owner's twenty-something daughter walked in. "Thanks for the sweater, Mom," she said. "Kevin really liked his present too."

"But it's only the twenty-third," said the bewildered lady.

"Mom," sighed the kid, wearily. "How many times do I have to tell you? We always open our presents on the solstice."

A couple of weeks later, a neighbor of mine in New Hampshire got married. He's a biker and a tattooist, and he's deeply spiritual. So he and his bride were married in the middle of a field in a service filled with imprecations to Odin, Thor, and sundry other Norse gods. The congregation of bikers rolled their eyes, which may or may not be a traditional Norse mark of respect.

It is, indeed, the case that when men cease to believe in God they'll believe in anything. But the anything they'll believe in is at least in part environmentally determined. In 2006, Alice Thomson of the *Daily Telegraph* was granted an interview with the Dalai Lama at Dharmsala, in northern India, where he lives in exile. En route to his pad, she encountered both a native Tibetan bearing the brutal marks of Chinese torture and, at one of the luxury hotels that have sprung up for moneyed pilgrims, a "rotund Austrian biscuit heiress" who turned to Buddhism after her stomach staple failed to take. Not all my North Country neighbors can afford air tickets and a suite in Dharmsala. So, given those constraints, solstice worship and Norse deities seem a reasonable fit with the landscape of northern New England. But they'd be a tougher sell in, say, Glasgow or Rotterdam. So what would work in the densely populated parts of Western Europe? At the risk of piling too many doomsday scenarios atop one another, it's worth noting that throughout the Western world Islam is advancing not just by outbreeding but also by conversion.

Herbert Asquith is not the most famous British prime minister to American ears, but he's the one who took his country into the Great War, which is the one that ended the Caliphate and delivered the Arab world into British hands. His great-granddaughter, Emma Clark, is now a Muslim. She's a landscape artist and has designed an "Islamic garden" at the home of the Prince of Wales. The Honorable Jonathan Birt, son of Lord Birt, the former director-general of the BBC, is also a Muslim and is known as Yahya Birt. The Earl of Yarborough is a Muslim, and goes by the name Abdul Mateen, though whether he can get served in the House of Lords tea room under that moniker is unclear.

The above "reverts"—as Islam calls converts (as they see it, everyone is born a Muslim, it's just that some of us don't know it yet)—are not merely the Muslim equivalents of the Richard Gere Buddhists and Tom Cruise Scientologists but the vanguard of something bigger. As English and Belgian and Scandinavian cities Islamify, their inhabitants will face a choice between living as a minority and joining the majority. Many will opt for the latter. At the very minimum, Islam will meet the same test as the hippy-dippy solstice worship does in Vermont: it will seem environmentally appropriate. For many young men, it already provides the sense of identity that the happy-face nothingness of multiculturalism declines to offer. In Britain, a white supremacist neo-Nazi whose writings inspired a 1999 Soho nail bombing that killed three people has since converted to Islam. David Myatt, a founder of the British National Socialist Movement, is now Abdul-Aziz ibn Myatt. Formerly opposed to non-white immigration into the United Kingdom, he now says that "the pure authentic Islam of the revival, which recognizes practical jihad (holy war) as a duty, is the only force that is capable of fighting and destroying the dishonor, the arrogance, the materialism of the West.... For the West, nothing is sacred, except perhaps Zionists, Zionism, the hoax of the so-called Holocaust, and the idols which the West and its lackeys worship, or pretend to worship, such as democracy." It's hard to imagine him ever changing back, and not just because he's on record as supporting the killing of those who leave Islam: a lot of his fellow "white supremacists" will find it's not the "white" but the "supremacist" bit they really like.

Islam already has a certain cachet: another revert, Omar Brooks, marked the first anniversary of the Tube bombings by doing some Islamostand-up at the Small Heath Youth and Community Centre in Birmingham. As the *Times* of London reported: "At one point he announces dramatically that the September 11 attacks on the World Trade Center 'changed many people's lives.' After a pause, he brings the house down by adding: 'Especially those inside.'"

He didn't literally bring the house down. He leaves that to Mohammed Atta. Nonetheless, even an Islamist lounge act is doing his part to provide a bigger pool for the jihadists to swim in.

In 2005, a reader in Asia sent me an e-mail link: "Canadian Converts to Islam Being Recruited by al Qaeda." It was from the Press Trust of India. If it appeared in any Canadian paper, I didn't see it. But lo and behold, a year later there were "Canadian converts to Islam" among the seventeen Torontonians arrested for plotting to blow up the Stock Exchange. They're not the only reverts in the news in the post–September 11 period:

- The Miami cell plotting to take down the Sears Tower in Chicago
- The shoe-bomber, Richard Reid
- The July 7 London Tube bomber, Germaine Lindsay
- The Washington sniper, John Allen Muhammad
- The Belgian lady Muriel Degauque, who blew herself up in a sui-cide attack on U.S. troops in Baghdad
- The Australian factory worker Jack Roche, sentenced in Perth for plotting to blow up the Israeli embassy in Canberra
- The founder and members of the Rajah Solaiman Movement, a Fil-ipino Muslim group believed to be responsible for a ferry bombing that killed more than a hundred people in 2004
- Abdul Wahid, born Don Stewart-Whyte, son of a British Conserv-ative Party official, half-brother of a top model, and former brother-in-law of French tennis star Yannick Noah, who was arrested in August 2006 for planning to blow himself up on a flight from Heathrow to New York

And on, and on. It would seem obvious that the use of reverts is a conscious strategy. The only question I have about that Press Trust of India headline—"Canadian Converts to Islam Being Recruited by al Qaeda"—is the implication that their Muslim conversion predates and is separate from their jihadist recruitment. It's more likely that the two processes are simultaneous—that they are converted precisely in order to be jihadists. That's just plain operational good sense: the most gung-ho Pushtun yakherd may be hot for martyrdom but he's going to stand out at the U.S. Air check-in in a way that a third-generation Canadian Muslim isn't or—better yet—a revert of non-Arab appearance and a name that isn't going to set off any flags in the computer—"Steven Chand," "Richard Reid," "Jack Roche." By some accounts, 80 percent of the imams in Canadian mosques are said to be "extreme." So what kind of converts would they be looking for, and what kind would be likely to respond to their rhetoric?

In 2002, I asked a Muslim in Paris why Islam was the fastest-growing religion in the West. He said four out of five converts in Europe were women, positing therefrom that, aside from spousal conversions, significant numbers of Western females found the feminist notion of womanhood degrading and unworthy. Whether or not that's true, I was startled in successive weeks to hear from Dutch and English acquaintances that they've begun going out "covered." The Dutch lady lives in a rough part of Amsterdam and says when you're on the street in Islamic garb, the Muslim men smile at you respectfully instead of jeering at you as an infidel whore. The English lady lives in a swank part of London but says pretty much the same thing. Both felt there was not just a physical but a psychological security in being dressed Muslim. They're not "reverts," but, at least for the purposes of padding the public space, they're passing for Muslim. And as more of the public space becomes Muslim it will seem more and more comfortable to do that.

How quickly will that happen? In late 2005, the *Observer* ran the following story: "Olympic Costs Set to Double: Londoners Face Huge Tax Rise."

Oh, come on. Only double? Surely you can do better than that. Well, it was early days for 2012 Olympic overspend, and proud Britons were no doubt certain that by the time the Queen opens the Games there'll be a few more zeroes added to their tax bills. Meanwhile, the same week as that *Observer* story, Tablighi Jamaat, an Islamic missionary group, announced plans to build a mosque in the East End—right next door to the new Olympic stadium. The London Markaz will be the biggest house of worship in the United Kingdom: it will hold 70,000 people—only 10,000 fewer than the Olympic stadium, and 67,000 more than the largest Christian facility (Liverpool's Anglican cathedral). Tablighi Jamaat plans to raise the necessary £100 million through donations from Britain and "abroad."

And I'll bet they do. Tablighi Jamaat is an openly Islamist organization of global reach and, according to the FBI, an al Qaeda recruiting front for terrorists. But, watching these two construction projects go up side by side in Newham, I don't think there'll be any doubt which has the tighter grip on fiscal sanity. A tax bill or two down the line and Londoners may be wishing they could subcontract the entire Olympics to Tablighi Jamaat.

No doubt it would have been heartening if the archbishop of Canterbury had announced plans to mark the 2012 Olympics by constructing a 70,000-seat state-of-the-art Anglican cathedral, but what would you put in it? Even an all-star double bill comprising a joint Service of Apology to Saddam Hussein followed by Ordination of Multiple Gay Bishops in Long-Term Committed Relationships (Non-Practicing or Otherwise, According to Taste) seems unlikely to fill the pews. Whatever one feels about it, the London Markaz will be a more accurate symbol of Britain in 2012 than Her Majesty pulling up next door with the Household Cavalry.

● ● ●

THE POTEMKIN CHURCH

The Saddam Apology is not a joke, by the way. In 2005, a "working group" of Anglican bishops produced a 101-page document called (with no discernible sense of irony) *Countering Terrorism*. Its central proposal was that Western Christians should show "institutional repentance" for the Iraq war by having their bishops and cardinals make a formal apology for the wrong they did at a gathering of "mainly Muslim" leaders. Aside from its comedic value, the mooted prostration would in itself have provided confirmation to Muslims of the widespread belief that Christianity has embarked on a new Crusade: why would these bishops be apologizing for the war if they weren't the ones who'd launched it?

If only. The last thing any Muslim needs to worry about is an Anglican bishop coming after him. The bishop of Lichfield, at Evensong, on the night of the London Tube bombings, was at pains to assure his congregants that "just as the IRA has nothing to do with Christianity, so this kind of terror has nothing to do with any of the world faiths." Father Paul Hawkins of St. Pancras parish church, a few hundred yards from the scene of the atrocities, told his own congregation that Sunday, "There are no Muslim terrorists. There are terrorists."

It's not the explicit fatuousness of the assertion so much as the meta-message it conveys: we're the defeatist wimps; bomb us and we'll apologize to you. Even in America, the interim pastor at my local church in New Hampshire on the Sunday morning of September 16, 2001, was principally concerned to warn us not to attack any Muslims, even though in that notably undiverse corner of America finding any Muslims to attack would have involved a three-hour drive. That's why the Church of England and the Episcopal Church and the Congregational Church and the United Church of Canada and many others are sinking beneath the bog of their own relativist mush, while Islam is the West's fastest-growing religion. There's no market for a faith that has no faith in itself.

One reason why the developed world has a difficult job grappling with the Islamist threat is that it doesn't take religion seriously. It condescends to it. In Europe's wholly secularized environment, the enduring religiosity of America is not just odd, but primitive. It puts Americans in the same category as remote tribes in Africa or cargo culters in the Pacific—anthropologically fascinating, but nonetheless backward. Hence, British novelist Martin Amis on the eve of the Iraq war:

One of the exhibits at the Umm Al-Maarik Mosque in central Baghdad is a copy of the Koran written in Saddam Hussein's own blood (he donated twenty-four litres over three years). Yet this is merely the most spectacular of Saddam's periodic sops to the mullahs. He is, in reality, a career-long secularist—indeed an "infidel," according to bin Laden. Although there is no Bible on Capitol Hill written in the blood of George Bush, we are obliged to accept the fact that Bush is more religious than Saddam: of the two presidents, he is, in this respect, the more psychologically primitive. We hear about the successful "Texanisation" of the Republican Party. And doesn't Texas sometimes seem to resemble a country like Saudi Arabia, with its great heat, its oil wealth, its brimming houses of worship, and its weekly executions?

Clever. After the long post–Cold War drought, the Europeans have finally found a new "moral equivalence." "It's nonsense to say, 'We're the force of good,'" scoffed Pierre Hassner of the Center for International Studies and Research in Paris. "We're living through the battle of the born-agains: Bush the born-again Christian, bin Laden the born-again Muslim."

In 1944, at a terrible moment of the most terrible century, Henri de Lubac wrote a reflection on Europe's civilizational crisis, *Le drame de l'humanisme athée*. By "atheistic humanism" he meant the organized rejection of God—not the freelance atheism of individual skeptics but atheism as an ideology and political project in its own right. As de Lubac wrote, "It is not true, as is sometimes said, that man cannot organize the world without God. What is true is that, without God, he can only organize it against man." Reviewing the film *The Lion, the Witch, and the Wardrobe*, Polly Toynbee, the queen of progressivist pieties in Britain, wrote that Aslan "is an emblem for everything an atheist objects to in religion. His divine presence is a way to avoid humans taking responsibility for everything here and now on earth, where no one is watching, no one is guiding, no one is judging, and there is no other place yet to come. Without an Aslan, there is no one here but ourselves to suffer for our sins, no one to redeem us but ourselves: we are obliged to settle our own disputes and do what we can."

Sounds very nice. But in practice the lack of belief in divine presence is just as likely to lead to humans avoiding responsibility: if there's nothing other than the here and now, who needs to settle disputes at all? All you have to do is manage to defer them till after you're dead—which is the European electorates' approach to their unaffordable social programs. The meek's prospects of inheriting the earth are considerably diminished in a post-Christian society: chances are they'll just get steamrollered by more motivated types. You don't have to look far to get the cut of my jib.

And yet even those who understand very clearly the nature of Islam are complacent about Europe's own structural defects. Olivier Roy, one of the most respected Islamic experts in France, nevertheless insists "secularism is the future." Almost by definition, secularism cannot be a future: it's a present-tense culture that over time disconnects a society from cross-generational purpose. Which is why there are no examples of sustained atheist civilizations. "Atheistic humanism" became inhumanism in the hands of the Fascists and Communists and, in its less malign form in today's European Union, a kind of dehumanism in which a present-tense culture amuses itself to extinction. Post-Christian European culture is already post-cultural and, with its surging Muslim populations, will soon be post-European.

If ever there were a time for a strong voice from the heart of Christianity, this would be it. And yet most mainline Protestant churches are as wedded to the platitudes du jour as the laziest politician. These days, if it weren't for homosexuality, the "mainstream" Christian churches would get barely any press at all. In 2005, the big story in America was the Episcopal Church's first openly gay bishop; in Britain, the nomination of a celibate gay bishop; in Canada, New Westminster's decision to become the first diocese in the Anglican communion to perform same-sex ceremonies. In Nigeria, where on any Sunday the Anglicans in the pews outnumber those in America, Britain, and Canada combined, the archbishop is understandably miffed that the only news he gets from head office revolves around various permutations of gayness. Getting a reputation as a cult for upscale Western sodomites and a few attendant fetishists doesn't help when half your country's in the grip of sharia and the local Islamoheavies are just itching to torch your churches.

Whatever one's views of homosexuality, it would seem in the greater scheme of things to be marginal, and thus the preoccupation with minority sexuality is best understood as an example of mainstream Protestantism's retreat to the periphery. It's the difference between the Broadway of Rodgers and Hammerstein and the Broadway of Stephen Sondheim. The former was the great central thruway of American popular culture; the latter may be, as its admirers claim, better, sharper, more sophisticated, but it's also underattended. The bishop of Maryland, making a painful attempt to get with the program, tried to square the awkward Biblical strictures on homosexuality with the vigorous sex life of Gene Robinson, the Anglican Communion's first openly gay bishop. His line is that God isn't against gay sex per se, just gay sex practiced by heterosexual men. Really.

"We might say about the Sodom passage," he elaborated, "that it is not really about a group of gay men behaving badly, but a group of heterosexual men behaving atrociously." Similarly, in Romans, Paul isn't objecting to homosexual men having sex with each other, just heterosexual men having sex with each other.

Who knew? So God's cool with practicing straights, He's cool with practicing gays; it's just bi-guys He's got a problem with. Or have I misunderstood the bishop's argument?

Anything to say on non-gay issues? Well, the archbishop of Canterbury, Dr. Rowan Williams, declared during the Afghan campaign that the United States Air Force pilot and the suicide bomber are morally equivalent—both "can only see from a distance: the sort of distance from which you can't see a face, meet the eyes of someone, hear who they are, imagine who and what they love. All violence works with that sort of distance."

That doesn't even work as glib lefty equivalence. The distinguishing feature of the suicide bomber is that he doesn't see at a distance. He looks into your face, meets your eyes—and he still blows you up, because even face to face he can't imagine who you are or what you love. He can't see anything about you, other than that you're the Other. So, like the Beslan schoolhouse slaughterers and Daniel Pearl's decapitators, he looks into the eyes—and then he kills. The United States Air Force pilot is running on GPS technology—that blip's a mosque, that one's a nursery—and from hundreds of miles and thousands of feet he can still see the common humanity more clearly. And, most perplexing of all, he can see more clearly than the archbishop of Canterbury, insulated by the distance of his own assumptions.

Most mainline Protestant churches are, to one degree or another, post-Christian. If they no longer seem disposed to converting the unbelieving to Christ, they can at least convert them to the boggiest of soft-left political clichés, on the grounds that if Jesus were alive today he'd most likely be a gay Anglican bishop in a committed relationship driving around in an environmentally friendly car with an "Arms Are for Hugging" sticker on the way to an interfaith dialogue with a Wiccan and a couple of Wahhabi imams.

Yet if the purpose of the modern church is to be a cutting-edge political pacesetter, Islam is doing the better job. It's easy to look at gold-toothed Punjabi yobs in northern England or Berber pseudo-rappers in French suburbs and think, oh well, their Muslim identity is clearly pretty residual. But that's to apply Westernized notions of piety. Most of us have known that moment when we realize we're in the presence of someone good, or at least goody-goody: the clean-cut Christian youth group that boards the plane and takes the seats around you, and whose very *niceness* makes you feel awkward. But the mosque is a meetinghouse, and throughout the West what it meets to discuss is, even when not explicitly jihadist, always political. The mosque or madrassa is not the place to go for spiritual contemplation as much as political motivation. The Muslim identity of those French rioters or English jailbirds may seem spiritually vestigial but it's politically potent. Pre-modern Islam beats post-modern Christianity.

In 2006, a dozen intellectuals published a manifesto against Islamism and in defense of "secular values for all." The signatories included Ayaan

Hirsi Ali, the Dutch parliamentarian; Irshad Manji, the Canadian writer; and Salman Rushdie, the British novelist. All three are brave figures and important allies in the campaign against the Islamist tide. But they're making a mistake: secular humanism is an insufficient rallying cry. As another Canadian, Kathy Shaidle, wrote in response: "It is secularism itself which is part of the problem, not the solution, since secularism is precisely what created the Euro spiritual/moral vacuum into which Islamism has rushed headlong."

It's not an unprecedented arc: Hitler followed Weimar—or, for fans of *Cabaret*, prison camps followed transvestites in cutaway buttocks. There's an extremely fine line between "boldly transgressive" and spiritually barren, and it's foolish of secular Western elites to assume their own populations are immune to the strong-horse pitch. There's a reason that Islam is winning reverts in Europe and North America. *Prayers for the Assassin*, a portrait of the Islamic Republic of America in the year 2040, is an inventive piece of "what if?" fiction by Robert Ferrigno, hitherto an efficient writer of lurid Californian crime novels full of porno stars, druggies, and a decadent elite: a slice of everyday life in the Golden State. In its way, Ferrigno's imagined Islamic future is a corrective to that present:

> Jill Stanton's proclamation of faith while accepting her second Academy Award would have been enough to interest tens of millions of Americans in the truth of Islam, but she had also chosen that moment in the international spotlight to announce her betrothal to Assan Rachman, power forward and MVP of the world champion Los Angeles Lakers. Celebrity conversions cascaded in the weeks after that Oscars night.

They're the American equivalents of Emma Clark and Britain's Muslim soccer players. Absent some transformative catastrophe—as in Ferrigno's novel—the United States has a strain of evangelical Protestantism strong enough to grow in the years ahead. Unfortunately, there is no such surging evangelicalism in Europe. In search of the guiding hand of God, some Europeans will return to Pope Benedict's church, some will accept Islam, but there will be no takers for the archbishop of Canterbury's watery obsolescent soft-left pap. In "Dover Beach," Matthew Arnold wrote:

> The Sea of Faith
> Was once, too, at the full, and round earth's shore
> Lay like the folds of a bright girdle furl'd.
> But now I only hear
> Its melancholy, long, withdrawing roar,
> Retreating, to the breath
> Of the night-wind, down the vast edges drear
> And naked shingles of the world.

The "melancholy, long, withdrawing roar" has been so long withdrawing in Europe that they don't yet understand the sound they hear is a new roar, not withdrawing but gradually advancing, a new Sea of Faith that one day will be at the full and round Europe's shore like the folds of a bright girdle furl'd.

By the time that Olympic mega-mosque is open for business in the London of 2012, you'll be surprised how well it fits in.

Chapter Six

The Four Horsemen
of the Eupocalpyse

EUTOPIA VS. EURABIA

The decline of the French monarchy invited the attack of these insatiate fanatics. The descendants of Clovis had lost the inheritance of his martial and ferocious spirit; and their misfortune or demerit has affixed the epithet of "lazy" to the last kings of the Merovingian race. They ascended the throne without power, and sunk into the grave without a name.... The vineyards of Gascony and the city of Bourdeaux were possessed by the sovereign of Damascus and Samarcand; and the south of France, from the mouth of the Garonne to that of the Rhone, assumed the manners and religion of Arabia. But these narrow limits were scorned by the spirit of Abdalraman, or Abderame, who had been restored by the caliph Hashem to the wishes of the soldiers and people of Spain. That veteran and daring commander adjudged to the obedience of the prophet whatever yet remained of France or of Europe; and prepared to execute the sentence, at the head of a formidable host, in the full confidence of surmounting all opposition either of nature or of man.

EDWARD GIBBON, *THE DECLINE*
AND FALL OF THE ROMAN EMPIRE (1776–1788)

To mark the Fourth of July 2006, the *Los Angeles Times* published an essay by Mark Kurlansky, author of *The Big Oyster: History on the Half Shell*. It began thus:

Someone has to say it or we are never going to get out of this rut: I am sick and tired of the founding fathers and all their intents. The real American question of our times is how our country in a little over two hundred years sank from the great hope to the most backward democracy in the West. The U.S. offers the worst health care program, one of the worst public school systems, and the worst benefits for workers. The margin between rich and poor has been growing precipitously while it has been decreasing in Europe. Among the great democracies, we use military might less cautiously, show less respect for international law, and are the stumbling block in international environmental cooperation. Few informed people look to the United States anymore for progressive ideas.

We ought to do something. Instead, we keep worrying about the vision of a bunch of sexist, slave-owning eighteenth-century white men in wigs and breeches.

Etc. The assumptions behind Kurlansky's piece are widely held, and not just by the Left—the assumption, for example, that Scandinavia is the natural destination of the fully evolved Western democracy and America's just taking a little longer to get there than the Dutch and the Canadians. That's what "the most backward democracy" means: the least like Europe. But it ought to be clear by now that Europe is ahead of America mainly in the sense that its canoe is already halfway over the falls. There may be many things wrong with the United States but only a blind fool who hasn't been paying attention for the last twenty years would hold Europe up as the alternative. The U.S. has the "worst benefits for workers"? Maybe. But it also has the lowest unemployment rate—about half the rate in France and Germany, where it hovers permanently at around 10 percent. As for being "the stumbling block in international environmental cooperation," European countries signed Kyoto and failed to meet its emission reduction targets, whereas the United States didn't sign it but reduced its emissions anyway—through that traditional American virtue of innovation. Self-loathing Americans are in danger of sounding like self-loathing squares if they pin their hopes on a decayed Eutopia a quarter century past its sell-by date.

Two forces are facing off on the European continent: on the one side, the modern social-democratic state that the American Left thinks should be our model; on the other, the resurgent Islam that the American Left insists is just a scam cooked up by Karl Rove. We now have an excellent opportunity to test both propositions. How bad is it going to get in Europe? As bad as it can get—as in societal collapse, fascist revivalism, and then the long Eurabian night, not over the entire Continent but over significant parts of it. And those countries that manage to escape the darkness will do so only after violent convulsions of their own.

You could avoid some of the bloodshed if European leaders were more responsive. Instead, they've spent so long peddling Eutopian illusions most of the political class is determined to stick with them come what may. The construction of a pan-continental Eutopia was meant to ensure that Europe would never again succumb to militant nationalism of one form or another. Instead, the European Union's governing class has become as obnoxiously post-nationalist as it was once nationalist: its post-nationalism has become merely the latest and most militant form of militant nationalism—which, aside from anything else, makes America, as the leading "nation state" in the traditional sense, the prime target of European ire.

It's true that there are many European populations reluctant to go happily into the long Eurabian night. But, alas for them, modern Europe is constructed so as to insulate almost entirely the political class from populist pressures. As the computer types say, that's not a bug, it's a feature: the European Union is a 1970s solution to a 1940s problem, and one of the problems it was designed to solve is that fellows like Hitler and Mussolini were way too popular with the masses. Just as the House of Saud, Mubarak, and the other Arab autocracies sell themselves to the West as necessary brakes on the baser urges of their peoples, so the European leadership deludes itself on the same basis: why, without the EU, we'd be back to Auschwitz. Thus, on the eve of the 2005 referendum on the European "constitution," the Dutch prime minister, Jan Peter Balkenende, warned his people where things would be headed if they were reactionary enough to vote no. "I've been in Auschwitz and Yad Vashem," he said. "The images haunt me every day. It is supremely important for us to avoid such things in Europe."

Golly. So the choice for voters on the Euro-ballot was apparently: yes to the European Constitution or yes to a new Holocaust. If there was a neither-of-the-above box, the EU's rulers were keeping quiet about it. The notion that the Continent's peoples are basically a bunch of genocidal wackos champing at the bit for a new bloodbath is one I'm not unsympathetic to. But it's a curious rationale to pitch to one's electorate: vote for us; we're the straitjacket on your own worst instincts. In the end, the French and Dutch electorates voted no to the new constitution. One recalls the T-shirt slogan popular among American feminists: "What part of 'No' don't you understand?" In the chancelleries of Europe, pretty much every part. At the time of the constitution referenda, the rotating European "presidency" was held by Luxembourg, a country slightly larger than your rec room. Jean-Claude Juncker, its rhetorically deranged prime minister and European "president," staggered around like a collegiate date-rape defendant, insisting that all reasonable persons understand that "Non" really means "Oui." As he put it before the big vote: "If it's a yes, we will say 'on we go,' and if it's a no we will say 'we continue.'"

And if it's a neither of the above, he will say "we move forward." You get the idea. Confronted by the voice of the people, "President" Juncker covers his ears and says, "Nya, nya, nya, can't hear you!"

Only in totalitarian dictatorships does the ballot come with a preordained correct answer. Yet "President" Juncker distilled the great flaw at the heart of the EU constitution into one disarmingly straightforward expression of contempt for the will of the people. For his part, the architect of the constitution—the former French president Valéry Giscard d'Estaing—was happy to pile on: why, even if the French and Dutch had been boorish enough to want to vote no to the constitution, they would have been incapable of so doing, as the whole thing was designed to be way above their pretty little heads. "It is not possible for anyone to understand the full text," declared M. Giscard. During his labors on the constitution, he'd told me he saw himself as "Europe's Jefferson." By referendum night he'd apparently become Europe's Jefferson Airplane, boasting about the impenetrability of his hallucinogenic lyrics. The point is that his ingrate subjects had no need to read beyond the opening sentence: "We the people agree to leave it to you the people who know better than the people."

After that, the rest doesn't matter: you can't do trickle-down nation-building. That's another feature of the paternalistic welfare state—that the paternalists, the rulers, come to regard the electorate as children, to be seen but not heard. Hence Europe's ever-widening gulf between a remote disconnected political establishment and a population with a growing list of concerns its leaders refuse to discuss. To carry on supporting the Euroconsensus of the Junckers and Giscards is not so much a vote to commit suicide but a vote to take as many people over the ledge with you as possible.

The transatlantic "split" has nothing to do with disagreements over Iraq, and can't be repaired by a more Europhile president in Washington: you can't "mend bridges" when the opposite bank is sinking into the river. If Americans think that the post-bombing 2004 Spanish election result was a disgrace, look down the road to the next election cycle, in France, Belgium, the Netherlands, and beyond. In the United States, psephologists speculate on the impact of Ralph Nader's 2 or 3 percent in swing states. Think about an election in which 20 percent of the voters are a self-segregating Muslim bloc. If Washington had a hard time getting any useful contribution to the war from Europe in 2001 or 2003, you do the math ten or fifteen years hence.

If there is a ten or fifteen years hence. The U.S. government's National Intelligence Council is predicting the EU will collapse by 2020. I think that's rather a cautious estimate myself. Ever since September 11, I've been gloomily predicting that the European powder keg's about to go up, and that within the next couple of election cycles the internal contradictions of the EU will manifest themselves in the usual way. If you were one of those "redneck Christian fundamentalists" the world's media are always warning about apropos America, you might think the Continent's in for what looks awfully like the Four Horsemen of the Eupocalypse— although in tribute to Euro-perversity they're showing up in reverse order: Death—the demise of European races too self-absorbed to breed; Famine—the end of the lavishly funded statist good times; War—the decline into bloody civil unrest that these economic and demographic factors will bring; and Conquest—the recolonization of Europe by Islam.

Happily, most Europeans are far too "rational" and "enlightened" and "post-Christian" to believe in such outmoded notions as apocalyptic equestrians. Nonetheless, in some still barely articulated way, many of them understand that their continent is dying, and it's only a question of whether it goes peacefully or through convulsions of violence.

On that point, I bet on form.

●　　●　　●

DEATH

There are many agreeable aspects of old Europe—old buildings, good food, foxy-looking women who dress to show themselves off. Compared to a strip mall in Jersey, the Continent is "sophisticated." But it's sophisticated in the sense that a *belle époque* Parisian boulevardier is sophisticated—outwardly dapper and worldly, inwardly eaten away by syphilis and gonorrhea. It's only a question of how many others the clapped-out *bon vivant* infects before his final collapse. The seventeen nations that have slipped below the "lowest-low" fertility rate of 1.3 and remained there are embarking on a historically unprecedented exercise in self-extinction. I certainly hope some countries can summon the will to change: I don't believe the Poles and Hungarians saw off the Soviets only to be consumed by a disaster from the Western end of the Continent a generation later. But the logic of the European Union is to ensnare the least decayed polities in the problems of the Euro-core—the Germans and the French—and the latter's problems are not something anybody else should willingly yoke himself to.

By 2050, there will be 100 million more Americans, 100 million fewer Europeans. In 1970, there were 4.6 million Italians under five years old. By 2004, there were 2.6 million. And the fewer babies you have today, the fewer grown-ups are around to have babies in twenty years. What do you figure the 2020 numbers will look like? If you think that a nation is no more than a "great hotel" (as Canadian novelist Yann Martel approvingly described his own country), you can always slash rates and fill the empty rooms—for as long as there are any would-be lodgers left out there to move in. But if you believe a nation is the collective, accumulated wisdom of a shared past, then a dependence on immigration alone for population replenishment will leave you lost and diminished.

Americans take for granted all the "it's about the future of our children" hooey that would ring so hollow in a European election. In the 2005 German campaign, voters were offered what would be regarded in the United States as a statistically improbable choice: a childless man (Herr Schröder) vs. a childless woman (Frau Merkel). Statist Europe signed on to Hillary Rodham Clinton's alleged African proverb—"It takes a village to raise a child"—only to discover they got it backward: on the Continent, the lack of children will raze the village. And most of the villagers still refuse to recognize the contradictions: you can't breed at the lethargic rate of most Europeans and then bitch and whine about letting the Turks into the European Union. Demographically, they're the kids you couldn't be bothered to have.

One would assume a demographic disaster is the sort of thing that sneaks up on you because you're having a grand old time: you stayed in university till you were thirty-eight, you took early retirement at forty-five, you had two months a year on the Côte d'Azur, you drank wine, you ate foie gras and truffles, you marched in the street for a twenty-eight-hour work week.... It was all such great fun there was no time to have children. You thought the couple in the next street would, or the next town, or in all those bucolic villages you pass through on the way to your weekend home.

But the strange thing is that Europeans aren't happy. The Germans are so slumped in despond that in 2005 the government began running a Teutonic feel-good marketing campaign in which old people are posed against pastoral vistas, fetching gays mooch around the Holocaust memorial, Katarina Witt stands in front of some photogenic moppets, etc., and then they all point their fingers at the camera and shout "*Du bist Deutschland!"*—"You are Germany!"—which is meant somehow to pep up glum Hun couch potatoes. Can't see it working myself. The European Union got rid of all the supposed obstacles to happiness—war, politics, the burden of work, insufficient leisure time, tiresome dependents— and yet their people are strikingly gloomy. They especially got rid of that oppressive Christianity. In the words of the official slogan of John Lennon International Airport at Liverpool: "Above us only sky." In Europe, they embraced the sappy nihilism of "Imagine" wholeheartedly:

- "Imagine there's no heaven." No problem. Large majorities of Scandinavians and Dutchmen and Belgians are among the first peoples in human history to be unable to imagine there's any possibility of heaven: no free people have ever been so voluntarily secular.
- "Imagine all the people/Living for today." Check.
- "Imagine there's no countries." Check. The EU is a post-nationalist pseudo-state.
- "Nothing to kill or die for/And no religion, too." You got it.

And yet somehow "all the people/Living life in peace" doesn't seem to be working out.

You can't help noticing that since abandoning its faith in the unseen world Europe seems also to have lost faith in the seen one. Consider this poll taken in 2002 for the first anniversary of September 11: 61 percent of Americans said they were optimistic about the future, as opposed to 43 percent of Canadians, 42 percent of Britons, 29 percent of the French, 23 percent of Russians, and 15 percent of Germans. I wouldn't reckon those numbers will get any cheerier over the years.

What's the most laughable article published in a major American newspaper in the last decade? A strong contender would be a column published in the *New York Times* in July 2005 by the august Princeton economist Paul Krugman. The headline is "French Family Values," and the thesis is that, while parochial American conservatives drone on about "family values," the Europeans live it, enacting policies that are more "family friendly." On the Continent, claims Professor Krugman, "government regulations actually allow people to make a desirable tradeoff—to modestly lower income in return for more time with friends and family."

How can an economist make that claim without noticing that the upshot of all these "family friendly" policies is that nobody has any families? Isn't the first test of a pro-family regime its impact on families?

As for all that extra time, what happened? Europeans work fewer hours than Americans, they don't have to pay for their own health care, they don't go to church and they don't contribute to other civic groups, they don't marry and they don't have kids to take to school and basketball and the 4-H stand at the county fair.

So what do they do with all the time?

Forget for the moment Europe's lack of world-beating companies: they regard capitalism red in tooth and claw as an Anglo-American fetish, and they mostly despise it. And in fairness some of their quasi-state corporations are very pleasant: I'd much rather fly Air France than United or Continental. But what about the things Europeans supposedly value? With so much free time, where is the great European art? Assuredly Gershwin and Bernstein aren't Bach and Mozart, but what have the Continentals got? Their pop culture is more American than it's ever been. Fifty years ago, before European welfarism had them in its vise-like death grip, the French had better pop songs and the Italians made better movies. Where are Europe's men of science? At American universities. Meanwhile, Continental governments pour fortunes into prestigious white elephants of Euro-identity, like the Airbus 380, the QE2 of the skies, capable of carrying five hundred, eight hundred, a thousand passengers at a time, if only somebody somewhere would order the damn thing, which they might consider doing once all the airports have built new runways to handle it. Don't get me wrong, I'm sure it's a swell idea. It'll come in very useful for large-scale evacuation operations circa 2015.

"When life becomes an extended picnic, with nothing of importance to do," writes Charles Murray in *In Our Hands*, "ideas of greatness become an irritant. Such is the nature of the Europe syndrome." The Continent has embraced a spiritual death long before the demographic one. In those seventeen European countries that have fallen into "lowest-low fertility," where are the children? In a way, you're looking at them: the guy sipping espresso at a sidewalk café listening to his iPod, the eternal adolescent charges of the paternalistic state. The government makes the grown-up decisions and we spend our pocket money on our record collection. Hilaire Belloc, incidentally, foresaw this very clearly in his book *The Servile State* in 1912—before record collections, or even teenagers, had been invented. He understood that the long-term cost of welfare is the infantilization of the population. The populations of wealthy democratic societies expect to have total choice over their satellite TV packages, yet think it perfectly normal to allow the state to make all the choices in respect of their health care. It's a curious inversion of citizenship to demand control over peripheral leisure activities but to contract out the big life-changing stuff to the government. And it's hard to come up with a wake-up call for a society as dedicated as latter-day Europe to the belief that life is about sleeping in.

● ● ●

FAMINE

In 2005, responding to Islamist terrorism in Britain and elsewhere, Germany was reported to be considering the introduction of a Muslim public holiday. As Mathias Döpfner, chief executive of the media group Axel Springer, put it: "A substantial fraction of Germany's government—and, if polls are to be believed, the German people—believe that creating an official state Muslim holiday will somehow spare us from the wrath of fanatical Islamists."

Great. At least the appeasers of the 1930s did it on their own time. But, in recasting appeasement as yet another paid day off, the new proposal cunningly manages to combine the worst instincts of the old Europe and the new. If you want the state of the Continent in a nutshell, consider this news item from the south of France, 2005: A fellow in Marseilles was charged with fraud because he lived with the dead body of his mother for five years in order to continue receiving her pension of 700 euros a month. She was ninety-four when she croaked, so she'd presumably been enjoying the old government check for a good three decades or so, but her son figured he might as well keep the money rolling in until her second century and, with her corpse tucked away under a pile of rubbish in the living room, the female telephone voice he put on for the benefit of the social services office was apparently convincing enough. As the Reuters headline put it: "Frenchman Lived with Dead Mother to Keep Pension."

That's the perfect summation of Europe: welfare addiction over demographic reality.

Think of the European Union as that flat in Marseilles, and the Eutopian political consensus as the stiff, and lavish government largesse as that French guy's dead mom's benefits. Take the one-time economic powerhouse of the Continent—Germany—and pick any of the usual indicators of a healthy advanced industrial democracy: Unemployment? The highest since the 1930s. House prices? Down. New car registration? Nearly 15 percent lower in 2005 than in 1999. General nuttiness? A third of Germans under thirty think the United States government was responsible for the terrorist attacks of September 11.

While the unemployment, real estate, and car sales may be reversible, that last number suggests the German electorate isn't necessarily the group you'd want to pitch a rational argument to, especially about the urgent need either to give up the unsustainable welfare state or to produce a population capable of sustaining it—whether by immigration, trans-human science, or the old-fashioned method of a box of chocolates, the lights down low, and Johnny Mathis on the hi-fi. Here's another statistic: 30 percent of German women are now childless. Among German university graduates, it's over 40 percent.

Yet according to polls taken before the inconclusive 2005 German elections, 70 percent of people want no further cuts in the welfare state and prefer increasing taxation on the very rich (whoever he is), and only 45 percent of Germans agreed that competition is good for economic growth and employment. It seems things are going to have to get a lot worse before European voters will seriously consider "necessary reforms" and "painful changes." And the longer European countries postpone the "painful" reforms, the more painful they're going to be.

Almost every issue facing the European Union—from immigration rates to crippling state pension liabilities—has at its heart the same root cause: a huge lack of babies. Every day you get ever more poignant glimpses of the Euro-future, such as it is. One can talk airily about being flushed down the toilet of history, but even that's easier said than done. In eastern Germany, rural communities are dying, and one consequence is that village sewer systems are having a tough time adjusting to the lack of use. Populations have fallen so dramatically that there are too few people flushing to keep the flow of waste moving. Traditionally, government infrastructure expenditure arises from increased demand. In this case, the sewer lines are having to be narrowed at great cost in order to cope with dramatically decreased demand.

There's no precedent for managed decline in societies as advanced as Europe's, but the early indications are that it's going to be expensive. One notes again that the environmentalists got it exactly backward: it's not a question of "sustainable growth" but of sustainable lack of growth. And no advanced society has attempted that experiment till now. For purposes of comparison, by 2050 public pensions expenditures are expected to be 6.5 percent of GDP in the United States, 16.9 percent in Germany, 17.3 percent in Spain, and 24.8 percent in Greece. In Europe, we're talking not about the prospect of having to reduce benefits but about so long, farewell, auf wiedersehn, adieu, adieu, adieu to yieu and yieu and yieu. American reformers like to say that Social Security is a Ponzi scheme. The EU has a vastly greater problem: the entire modern European edifice is a Ponzi scheme. And the political establishments in Paris, Berlin, Brussels, et al. show no sign of producing leaders willing to confront it.

Germany has a shrinking economy, a shrinking and aging population, and potentially catastrophic welfare liabilities. Yet the average German worker now puts in 22 percent fewer hours per year than his American counterpart, and no politician who wishes to remain electorally viable would suggest closing the gap. The Dutch and the Norwegians are even bigger slackers.

This isn't a deep-rooted cultural difference between the Old World and the New. It dates back all the way to, oh, the 1970s. It's a product of the U.S. military presence, a security guarantee that liberated European budgets; instead of having to spend money on guns, they could concentrate on butter, and buttering up the voters. But even with reduced defense expenditure, the European welfare state depends on economic growth and population growth. The former is now barely detectable and the latter is already in reverse.

After the rejection of the European Constitution, Jacques Chirac reacted to his impertinent electorate's appalling lèse-majesté by appointing as French prime minister a man who was the very embodiment of the ruling elite's serene insulation from popular opinion—Dominique de Villepin, the magnificently obstructionist big-haired foreign minister in the run-up to the Iraq war. Aside from his Byronic locks, M. de Villepin also writes sub-sub-sub-Byronic doggerel. Whenever he turns up on CNN, starry-eyed Democrat viewers send cooing e-mails to Wolf Blitzer and Jack Cafferty, wondering why their own vulgar republic can't produce a political leader who speaks English with such suave erudition—a veritable Rimbaud to Bush's Rambo. So, in his first big speech in the gig, Monsieur Sophisticate was at pains to reassure French voters that the internal tensions of a pampered lethargic over-regulated welfare society could all be resolved through "Gallic genius": "In a modern democracy, the debate is not between the liberal and the social, it is between immobilism and action. Solidarity and initiative, protection and daring: that is the French genius."

Ooh-la-la! C'est magnifique! C'est formidable, n'est-ce pas? All those elegant nouns just waiting for a stylishly coiffed French genius to steer the appropriate course between the Scylla of solidarity and the Charybdis of initiative, between protection and daring, immobilism and action, inertia and panic, stylish insouciance and meaningless gestures, abstract nouns and street riots, etc, etc. The French electorate has relatively down-to-earth concerns: crime, jobs, immigration. But for a man of letters that's all too dreary and prosaic compared with an open-ended debate between solidarity and initiative stretching lazily into the future.

Across half a century, Continental politics evolved to the point where almost any issue worth talking about was ruled beyond the bounds of polite society. Austria was the classic example: year in, year out, whether you voted for the center-left party or the center-right party, you wound up with the same center-left/center-right coalition presiding over what was in essence a two-party one-party state. In France, M. Chirac isn't really "center-right" so much as ever so slightly left-of-right-of-left-of-center—and even that distinction only applies when he's standing next to his former prime minister, the right-of-left-of-right-of-left-of center Lionel Jospin. Though supposedly from opposite ends of the political spectrum, in the 2002 presidential election they wound up running against each other on identical platforms, both passionately committed to high taxes, high unemployment, and high crime.

Americans often make the same criticism of their own system—the "Republicrats," etc.—but the United States still has a more genuinely responsive politics with more ideological diversity than anywhere in Western Europe. On the Continent, the Eurodee and Eurodum mainstream parties are boxed into a consensus politics that's no longer viable. The people are weary of certain aspects of this postwar settlement—permanent double-digit unemployment and the Islamization of their cities—but they're not yet ready to give up the social programs, the short work weeks, long vacations, and jobs for life. Europe's structural problems would require immense cultural change to correct. Is it likely that Europe will muster the will for "painful economic reforms"? It was always a political project masquerading as an economic one, and thus the ruling class's investment in it is largely emotive and ideological. Hence the *Guardian*'s attack on the British prime minister for demanding reform of the Common Agricultural Policy:

> It is unreasonable of Mr. Blair to repeatedly flourish as if self-evidently outrageous the simple arithmetic of 40 percent of spending on 4 percent of the European workforce, when rural life is of such social, psychological and aesthetic importance to a vastly larger proportion of the continent's population.

I think "aesthetic importance" means "we have to drive past a lot of French farms to get to our holiday homes." Rural life was central to France's sense of itself. But so was the Catholic Church, and it's empty now. And so were Catholic-size families, and they're down to one designer kid. So the character of those quaint villages is utterly changed. Why should the British taxpayer subsidize an ersatz French heritage park about as authentic as Disney's *Hunchback of Notre Dame*? If Pierre's given up the church and the family, what's the big deal about giving up the farm?

Ah, well, it won't be a problem much longer. Under its present economic arrangements, it's Europe that's bought the farm.

• • •

WAR

According to its Office du Tourisme, the big event in Évreux the first weekend of November 2005 was supposed to be the annual *fête de la pomme, du cidre et du fromage* at the Place de la Mairie. Instead, in this charmingly smoldering cathedral town in Normandy, a shopping mall, a post office, two schools, upwards of fifty vehicles and, oh yes, the police station were destroyed by—what's that word again?—"youths."

Over at the Place de la Mairie, M. le Maire himself, Jean-Louis Debré, seemed affronted by the very idea that *un soupçon de* carnage should be allowed to distract from the cheese-tasting. "A hundred people have smashed everything and strewn desolation," he told reporters. "Well, they don't form part of our universe."

Maybe not, but, unfortunately, you form part of theirs.

M. Debré, a close pal of President Chirac's, was a little off on the numbers. There were an estimated two hundred "youths" rampaging through Évreux. With baseball bats. They injured, among others, a dozen firemen. "To those responsible for the violence, I want to say: Be serious!" M. Debré told France Info radio. "If you want to live in a fairer, more fraternal society, this is not how to go about it."

Oh, dear. Who's not "being serious" here? In Normandy, it's not just the cheese that's soft and runny. Granted that France's over-regulated economy severely obstructs the social mobility of Muslim immigrants, even M. Debris—whoops, sorry—even M. Debré cannot be so out of touch as to think "seriously" that the rioters were rioting for "a fairer, more fraternal society." But maybe he does. The political class and the media seem to serve as mutual reinforcers of their own obsolete illusions.

In December 2002, I was asked to take part in a symposium on Europe and began with the observation that "I find it easier to be optimistic about the futures of Iraq and Pakistan than, say, Holland or Denmark." At the time, this was taken by the Left as confirmation of my descent into insanity: Europe was still regarded as a bastion of progress. By 2006, the Right was querying the thesis, arguing that the Bush Doctrine is a crock: how can liberty save the Muslim world when Muslims are jeopardizing liberty in Europe?

Well, they're not contradictory positions. In the Middle East, it may well be that, as the gnarled old Yankees tell tourists, you can't get there from here. But I'd argue there's a sporting chance of being able to get at least partway there from the here and now of the present Muslim world. Whatever their problems, most Islamic countries will be embarking on their evolution into free states as reasonably homogenous societies. European nations face the trickier job of retaining their freedoms at a time of increasing societal incoherence: they're getting there from here in the one-way express lane, and they're not going to like where they end up. About six months after September 11, I went on a grand tour of the Continent's Muslim ghettos and then flew on to the Middle East. The Muslims I met in Europe were, almost to a man, more alienated and angrier than the ones back in Araby. Don't take my word for it. It was a Hamburg cell that pulled off September 11, a British subject who was the shoe-bomber, a London School of Economics graduate who had Daniel Pearl executed...

True, America and Australia grew the institutions of their democracy with relatively homogeneous populations and then evolved into successful "multicultural" societies. But the Continent isn't multicultural so much as bicultural. You have hitherto homogeneous Scandinavian soci-

eties whose cities have become 40 percent Muslim in the space of a generation. Imagine colonial New England when it was still the Mayflower
crowd and one day they woke up and noticed that all the Aldens and
Standishes, Cookes and Winslows were in their fifties and sixties and all
the young guys were called Ahmed and Mohammed. That's what's happened in Rotterdam and Malmö. There are aging native populations and
young Muslim populations and that's it: "two solitudes," as they say in
my beloved Quebec. If there's three, four, or more cultures, you can all
hold hands and sing "We Are the World." But if there's just two—you
and the Other—that's generally more fractious. Bicultural societies are
among the least stable in the world, especially once it's no longer quite
clear who's the majority and who's the minority—a situation that much
of Europe is fast approaching, as you can see by visiting any French, Austrian, Belgian, or Dutch maternity ward.

Take Fiji—not a comparison France would be flattered by, although
until the late 1980s the Fijians enjoyed a century of peaceful, stable, constitutional evolution the French were never able to manage. At any rate,
Fiji is comprised of native Fijians and ethnic Indians brought in as inden-
tured workers by the British. If memory serves, 46.2 percent are native
Fijians and 48.6 percent are Indo-Fijians. Fifty-fifty, give or take, with no
intermarrying. In 1987, the first Indian-majority government came to
power. A month later, Colonel Sitiveni Rabuka, officer of the Order of
the British Empire, staged the first of his two coups.

Is it that difficult to sketch a similar situation for France? Even in relatively peaceful bicultural societies, politics becomes tribal: loyalists vs.
nationalists in Northern Ireland, separatists vs. federalists in Quebec. Picture a French election circa 2020: the Islamic Republican Coalition wins
the most seats in the National Assembly. The Chiraquiste crowd give a
fatalistic shrug and M. de Villepin starts including crowd-pleasing suras
from the Koran at his poetry recitals. But would Jean-Marie Le Pen or
(by then) his daughter take it so well? Or would the temptation to be
France's Colonel Rabuka prove too much?

And the Fijian scenario—a succession of bloodless coups—is the optimistic one, and not just when measured against such notable bicultural

societies as Rwanda. After all, the differences between Fijian natives and Indians are nothing compared to those between the French and *les beurs*. All those Bush Doctrine naysayers who argue that Iraq is an artificial entity that can never be a functioning state ought to take a look at the Netherlands. You think Kurds and Arabs, Sunni and Shia are incompatible? What do you call a jurisdiction split between post-Christian secular gay potheads and anti-whoring anti-sodomite anti-everything-you-dig Islamists? If Kurdistan's an awkward fit in Iraq, how well does Pornostan fit in the Islamic Republic of Holland? Europe's problems don't nullify the Bush Doctrine so much as present a more urgent case for it.

As to the "French" "youth," a gentleman in Antibes cautioned me against characterizing the disaffected as "Islamist" and advised me to examine them more closely. "They look like L.A. gangsters," he said, "not beturbaned prophet-monkeys."

Leaving aside more than a few cries of "Allahu Akhbar!" on the streets, my friend is correct. But that's the point. The theoretical virtue of "multiculturalism" is that it's a form of mellifluous cultural cross-pollination: the best of all worlds. But just as often it gives us the worst of all worlds: the worst attributes of Muslim culture—the subjugation of women—combined with the worst attributes of Western culture—license and self-gratification. Tattooed, pierced Pakistani skinhead gangs swaggering down the streets of northern England are as much a product of multiculturalism as the turban-wearing Sikh Mountie in the royal escort. Islamofascism itself is what it says: a fusion of Islamic identity with old-school European totalitarianism. But, whether in turbans or gangsta threads, just as Communism was in its day, so Islam is today's identity of choice for the world's disaffected.

In 2001, Paris elected its first openly homosexual mayor, Bertrand Delanoë, and, as always, this was taken as evidence of how cool and relaxed everyone is about the whole gay thing nowadays. M. le Maire certainly worked hard to put the gay in gay Paree—potted palms and parasols along the Seine all summer long, etc. His big idea was the *Nuit Blanche*—the "Sleepless Night"—of October 5, 2002, when the city's landmarks would be open for one big all-night party. Come to the Louvre, the Arc de Triomphe, the Eiffel Tower, and if you make it through till dawn there'll be free coffee and croissants. City Hall itself was done up like a stylish 'tween-wars nightclub—and no state security metal detectors on the doors, because, after all, what genuine jazz *boîte* would have such things?

And that's where M. Delanoë was, in the thick of the festive throng, when he got stabbed. His assailant missed his aorta by less than an inch, but gamely the mayor insisted that the party go on while he was taken to the Pitié-Salpêtrière hospital for a three-hour operation that saved his life.

His would-be killer was a Muslim immigrant, Azedine Berkane. But, as the establishment was at pains to emphasize, the good news is that he wasn't a terrorist. No, he's just a Muslim who hates homosexuals.

And that's good news how, exactly?

Le Monde reported from M. Berkane's wretched riot-prone ghetto the views of his neighbors: "He was a bit like us," said one. "We're all homophobic here, because it's not natural."

"It's against Islam," said another. "Muslim fags don't exist."

A traditional terrorist has demands which are in most cases subject to circumstances: He doesn't want your troops on his soil? Okay, we don't really need them there anyway.

But a Muslim who hates you just cuz? That's all but impervious to external pressure.

The old joke about British Palestine was that it was the twice-promised land: hence today a Western democracy and a disaffected Muslim population exist in (for the most part) two solitudes on the same piece of real estate. But doesn't that sum up Europe too? The jihadists understand that the Continent is up for grabs in a way that America isn't. And as their numbers grow it seems likely that wily Islamic leaders in the Middle East will embrace the cause of the rights of European Muslims in the same way that they claim solidarity with the Palestinians. When France began contemplating its headscarf ban in schools, it dispatched government ministers to seek the advice of Egyptian imams, implicitly accepting the view of Islamic scholars that the Fifth Republic is now an outlying province of the Dar al-Islam. As the Zionist Entity can testify, that's not a club you necessarily want to be signed up for (though it helps explain why the Quai d'Orsay can live with Iran becoming the second Muslim nuclear power. As things stand, France is on course to be the third).

And what happens when, say, Iran starts spreading a little terror start-up money through France and the Netherlands the way the ayatollahs have done in Lebanon and Gaza? What would it take to persuade a European Muslim to blow himself up in an Amsterdam gay bar?

Few EU leaders have a clue what to do about this, but, as France's headscarf law and Britain's Incitement to Racial Hatred bill underline, mediation between what Tony Blair called (in the wake of the Tube bombing) "our way of life" and Muslim values has already become a central dynamic of European political culture—a remarkable achievement for a minority few Europeans were more than vaguely conscious of before September 11. Meanwhile, across the borders pour not primarily suicide bombers or suitcase nukes, though they will come in the end, but ideology—fierce, glamorous, and implacable. Here's the final irony, and perhaps the most distressing of all to European anti-Semites: in one of history's better jests, in this scenario they're the Jews.

● ● ●

CONQUEST

As the *Guardian* reported in London in 2005; "French youths fired at police and burned over 300 cars last night as towns around Paris experienced their worst night of violence in a week of urban unrest."

Ah, those "French youths." You mean Pierre and Jacques and Marcel and Alphonse? Granted that most of the "youths" are technically citizens of the French Republic, it doesn't take much time in *les banlieues* of Paris to discover that the rioters do not think of their primary identity as "French," and likely never will. Four years after September 11, it turned out there really is an explosive "Arab street," but it's in Clichy-sous-Bois. Since the beginning of this century, French Muslims have been carrying on a low-level intifada against synagogues, kosher butchers,

Jewish schools, etc. The concern of the political class has been to prevent the spread of these attacks to targets of more, ah, general interest. They're losing that battle. Unlike America's Europhiles, France's Arab street correctly identified Chirac's opposition to the Iraq war for what it was: a sign of weakness.

The French have been here before, of course. Seven-thirty-two. Not 7:32 Paris time, which is when the nightly Citroen-torching begins in the 'burbs, but 732 AD—as in one and a third millennia ago. By then, the Muslims had advanced a thousand miles north of Gibraltar to control Spain and southern France up to the banks of the Loire. In October 732, the Moorish general Abd al-Rahman and his Muslim army were not exactly at the gates of Paris, but they were within two hundred miles, just south of the great Frankish shrine of St. Martin of Tours. Somewhere on the road between Poitiers and Tours, they met a Frankish force and, unlike other Christian armies in Europe, this one held its ground "like a wall . . . a firm glacial mass," as *The Chronicle of Isidore* puts it. A week later, Abd al-Rahman was dead, the Muslims were heading south, and the French general, Charles, had earned himself the surname "Martel"— "the Hammer."

Poitiers was the high-water point of the Muslim tide in Western Europe. It was an opportunistic raid by the Moors, but if they'd won, they'd have found it hard to resist pushing on to Paris, to the Rhine and beyond. "Perhaps," wrote Edward Gibbon in *The Decline and Fall of the Roman Empire*, "the interpretation of the Koran would now be taught in the schools of Oxford, and her pulpits might demonstrate to a circumcised people the sanctity and truth of the revelation of Mahomet." There would be no Christian Europe. The Anglo-Celts who settled North America would have been Muslim. Poitiers, said Gibbon, was "an encounter which would change the history of the whole world."

Battles are very straightforward: Side A wins, Side B loses. But Europe is way beyond anything so clarifying. Today, a fearless Muslim advance has penetrated far deeper into Europe than Abd al-Rahman. They're in Brussels, where Belgian police officers are advised not to be seen drinking coffee in public during Ramadan, and in Malmö, where

Swedish ambulance drivers will not go without police escort. It's way too late to re-run the Battle of Poitiers. When Martine Aubry, the mayor of Lille, daughter of former prime minister and EU bigwig Jacques Delors and likely presidential candidate in the post-Chirac era, held a meeting with an imam in Roubaix, the gentleman demanded that it take place on the edge of the neighborhood—in recognition that his turf was Muslim territory which she was bound not to enter. Mme. Aubry conceded the point, as more and more politicians will in the years ahead.

The peoples of Europe may not be willing to go as far down the appeasement path as their rulers, but Europe is a top-down construct, so the rulers will get quite a long way down before the masses start to drag them back. One observes, for example, that brave figures who draw attention to these trends—men and women such as Theo van Gogh, Bat Ye'or, and Oriana Fallaci—are either murdered, forced to live under armed guard, driven into exile overseas, or sued under specious hate-crimes laws. Dismissed by the European establishment, they're banished to the fringe. Ayaan Hirsi Ali, the Somali-born Dutch parliamentarian, spoke out against the ill-treatment of Muslim women, a subject she knows about firsthand, and found herself under threat of death. Her neighbors, the justice system, and the Dutch government reacted to this by taking her to court, getting her evicted from her home, and announcing plans to revoke her citizenship. Boundlessly tolerant Europe, which finds it so hard to expel openly treasonous jihad-inciting imams, finally found one Muslim it's willing to kick out.

Meanwhile, the complaceniks hold down prestigious chairs at European universities and think tanks and assure us there's no problem. Timothy Garton Ash is an Oxford professor who directs its European Studies Center, the sort of chap National Public Radio calls in when they need an "expert" on the EU. Very reasonable fellow, so reasonable that in 2003 he was attacking yours truly in every leading European newspaper for promoting "anti-Europeanism in the United States." Yet after scoffing at my Euro-predictions for many years, he seems to have accepted them. The only difference between us is that he thinks it's a good thing:

The populations of Europe are aging fast, so more immigrants will be needed to support the pensioners, and these will largely be Muslim immigrants. For this increasingly Muslim Europe to define itself against Islam would be ridiculous and suicidal.... Let's imagine, for a moment, Europe in 2025 at its possible best. A political, economic, and security community of some forty free countries and 650 million people, embracing all the lands in which the two world wars began, and producing, still, a large part of the wealth of the world. A further 650 million people, born in the most explosive parts of the early twenty-first-century globe, but now living in a great arc of partnership with this European Union, from Marrakesh, via Cairo, Jerusalem, Baghdad, and Tbilisi, all the way to Vladivostok. That would not be nothing.

No, indeed. It would certainly be something, but quite what he declines to say. And that's what Garton Ash sees as the Continent's "possible best"—a giant Euro-Muslim "arc of partnership." Faced with a choice between correcting course or drifting irrevocably into Eurabia, Garton Ash has chosen consciously to embrace the latter. He will not be the last.

And so those Continental demographic trends will accelerate, as they did during the decline of the Roman Empire, when the imperial capital's population fell at one point as low as five hundred. Some French natives will figure they don't have the stomach for the fight and opt for retirement elsewhere. The ones who don't will increasingly be drawn down the old road to the neo-nationalist strongmen promising to solve the problem. That's why I call it the Eurabian civil war. The de Villepin-Chiraquiste tendency will be to accommodate and capitulate, but an unreconstructed minority will not be so obliging and will eventually act. Meanwhile, it will be the Muslims who develop a pan-European identity, if only because many have no particular attachment to France or Belgium or Denmark, and they'll quickly grasp that cross-border parties and lobby groups will further enhance their status. The European Union's already the walking dead, but the Eurabian Union might well be a runner.

If Chirac, de Villepin, and Co. aren't exactly Charles Martel, the rioters aren't doing a bad impression of the Muslim armies of thirteen centuries ago. They're seizing their opportunities, testing their foe, probing
his weak spots. If burning the 'burbs gets you more "respect," they'll
burn 'em again and again. In defiance of traditional immigration patterns, these young men are less assimilated than their grandparents. And
why should they be? On present demographic trends, it will be for ethnic Europeans to assimilate with them. In *City Journal*, Theodore Dal-
rymple concluded a piece on British suicide bombers with this grim
summation of the new Europe: "The sweet dream of universal cultural
compatibility has been replaced by the nightmare of permanent conflict."

Which sounds an awful lot like a new Dark Ages—or the future
implicit in Cardinal Ratzinger's choice of name for his papacy: Benedict
XVI. Born in Umbria in 480, St. Benedict was the man who ensured during the Dark Ages that the critical elements of Roman and Greek civilization were preserved and that, by infusing them with Christianity, they
would emerge in a new and stronger form: the basis for Europe and
Western Civilization. Referring to his namesake, Pope Benedict XVI once
quoted a Benedictine motto: "*Succisa virescit.*" Pruned, it grows again.

That may prove true for Christianity: it's a growing faith in Africa
and China, and could yet be so again in Europe. Whether there will be
any Spaniards or Italians left to re-enlist is more questionable. In the
course of the twenty-first century, Germany's population will fall by over
50 percent to some thirty-eight million or lower—killed not by disease
or war but by the Eutopia to which the German people are wedded. And
every time they're asked to vote on the issue they decide that, like that
Frenchman, they can live with the stench of death as long as the state
benefits keep coming. The trouble with the social-democratic state is
that, when government does too much, nobody else does much of anything.

After September 11, I wondered rhetorically midway through a column what we in the West are prepared to die for, and got a convoluted
e-mail back from a French professor explaining that the fact that Europeans weren't prepared to die for anything was the best evidence of their

superiority: they were building a post-historical utopia—a Europe it would not be necessary to die for.

But sometimes you die anyway.

Part III

The New Dark Ages

...AND HOW TO LIGHTEN UP

Chapter Seven

The State-of-the-Art Primitive

THE KNOWN UNKNOWNS VS.
THE KNOWINGLY UNKNOWING

Pale Ebenezer thought it wrong to fight
But Roaring Bill (who killed him) thought it right.

HILAIRE BELLOC, "THE PACIFIST" (1938)

Every so often, I find myself, for the umpteenth time, driving behind a Vermont granolamobile whose bumper not only proclaims the driver's enduring post-2004 support for Kerry/Edwards but also bears the slogan "FREE TIBET."

It must be great to be the guy with the printing contract for the "FREE TIBET" stickers. Not so good to be the guy back in Tibet wondering when the freeing thereof will actually get under way. Are you in favor of a Free Tibet? It's hard to find anyone who isn't. Every college in America is. There's the Indiana University Students for a Free Tibet, and the University of Wisconsin–Madison Students for a Free Tibet, and the Students for a Free Tibet University of Michigan chapter, and the University of Montana Students for a Free Tibet in Missoula, which is where they might as well relocate the last three Tibetans by the time it is freed.

Everyone's for a free Tibet, but no one's for freeing Tibet. So Tibet will stay unfree—as unfree now as it was when the first Free Tibet campaigner slapped the very first "FREE TIBET" sticker onto the back of his Edsel. Idealism as inertia is the hallmark of the movement. Well, not entirely inert: it must be a pain in the neck when you trade in the Volvo for a Subaru and have to bend down and paste on a new "FREE TIBET" sticker. For a while, my otherwise not terribly political wife got extremely irritated by the Free Tibet shtick, demanding to know at a pancake breakfast at the local church what precisely some harmless hippy-dippy old neighbor of ours meant by the sticker he'd been proudly displaying decade in, decade out: "But what exactly are you doing to free Tibet?" she insisted. "You're not doing anything, are you?"

"Give the guy a break," I said when we got back home. "He's advertising his moral superiority, not calling for action. If Rumsfeld were to say, 'Free Tibet? Jiminy, what a swell idea! The Third Infantry Division goes in on Thursday,' the bumper-sticker crowd would be aghast. They'd have to bend down and peel off the 'FREE TIBET' stickers and replace them with 'WAR IS NOT THE ANSWER.'"

But there'll never be a Free Tibet—because, through all the decades Americans were driving around with the bumper stickers, the Chinese were moving populations, torturing Tibetans, imposing inter-marriage until Tibet was altered beyond recognition. By the time the guys with the Free Tibet stickers get around to freeing Tibet there'll be no Tibet left to free.

That's "stability."

As President Reagan liked to say, "status quo" is Latin for "the mess we're in." When Amr Moussa, secretary-general of the Arab League, warns (as he did before the Iraq war) that America is threatening "the whole stability of the Middle East," it's important to remember that "stability" is Arabic for "the mess we're in."

Yet just as the environmentalists believe in ongoing dramatic "climate change," so the foreign policy establishment believes equally in ongoing, undramatic geopolitical non-change. And, just as there's minimal evidence for "climate change," so there's minimal evidence for "stability." The geopolitical scene is never stable; it's always dynamic. If the Western world decides in 2005 that it can "contain" President Sy Kottik of Wackistan indefinitely, that doesn't mean the relationship between the two parties is set in aspic. Wackistan has a higher birth rate than the West, so after forty years of "stability" there are a lot more Wackistanis and a lot fewer Frenchmen. And Wackistan has immense oil reserves, and President Kottik has used the wealth of those oil reserves to fund radical schools and mosques in hitherto moderate parts of the Muslim world. And large numbers of Wackistanis have emigrated to the European Union, obliging opportunist politicians in marginal constituencies to pitch for their vote. And cheap air travel and the Internet and bank machines that take every card on the planet and the freelancing of nuclear technology mean that Wackistan's problems are no longer confined to Wackistan; for a few hundred bucks, they can be outside the Empire State Building within eight or nine hours.

"Stability" is a surface illusion, like a frozen river; underneath, the currents are moving, and to the casual observer the ice looks equally "stable" whether there's a foot of it or just two inches. There is no status quo in world affairs. "Stability" is a fancy term to dignify inertia and complacency as sophistication. If America and its allies defer to their foreign policy stability fetishists in the years ahead and continue to place their faith in September 10 institutions like the UN, then in the long run we'll all go the way of Tibet: there'll be nothing left to free.

"Containment" is another overvalued commodity: it's an expensive dictator-management program that, in the case of Iraq after the first Gulf War, required the United States Air Force and the RAF to bomb the country ineffectually every other week for twelve years, in return for which the Americans and British were blamed for UN sanctions and systematically starving to death a million Iraqi kids—or two million, according to which "humanitarian" agency you believe. Of course, the minute the war started and these genocidal sanctions came to an end, the Left decided this UN "containment" had after all been a marvelous and desirable thing. Even what's regarded as a successful example of the strategy—the West's decision to "contain" the Warsaw Pact—was in practice no such thing, not for those on the receiving end. Aside from the fact that telling the other fellow he has to spend fifty years under Communism is easy for you to say, the toll taken on those nations with every passing decade was grisly. On the hit parade of nations with the unhealthiest demographic profile, the top five are all former provinces of European Communism: Latvia, Bulgaria, Slovenia, Russia, and Ukraine. Of the top ten, nine are ex-Commie (the exception is Spain). Of the top twenty, sixteen are. Communism was so loathed by its subjects they gave up even breeding. And every year we allowed the Warsaw Pact to remain in place we weakened further the viability of any post-Communist societies that might emerge from the rubble.

"Stability" and "containment" pose the opposite challenge in the Muslim world. Those countries are mostly in the upper reaches of the fertility hit parade. Whatever they loathe about their regimes, they don't loathe Islam: in many cases, the mosques provide the only political space in those lands. So they breed with gusto, and thus every year we remain committed to "stability" increases the Islamists' principal advantage: it strengthens the religion—the vehicle for their political project—and multiplies the raw material.

So another decade or two of "stability" and the world will be well on its way to a new Dark Ages. Now, as then, Europe has its do-nothing kings—*les rois fainéants*—though these days we call them European commissioners and chancellors and prime ministers. Now, as then, we have a Great Plague—the virus of Islamism—and the great migrations—the continent-wide version of "white flight" already under way in Holland, as the beleaguered Dutch leave their native land for Canada, Australia, and New Zealand. Now, as then, we must all bow before the "edict of toleration"—as laws and customs are rearranged to abase themselves before the gods of boundless multicultural tolerance.

But the central fact of a new Dark Ages is this: it would be not a world in which the American superpower is succeeded by other powers but a world with no dominant powers at all. Today, lots of experts crank out analyses positing China as the unstoppable hegemon of the twenty-first century. Yet the real threat is not the strengths of your enemies but their weaknesses. China is a weak power: its demographic and other structural defects are already hobbling its long-term ambitions. Russia is a weak power, a kind of greatest-hits medley of all the planet's worst pathologies—disease-wise, nuke-wise, Islamist-wise. Europe is a weak power, a supposed Greater France remorselessly evolving month by month into Greater Bosnia.

Islam is a weak power: in the words of Dr. Mahathir bin Mohammed, the former prime minister of Malaysia, one of the least worst Muslim nations in the world, "We produce practically nothing on our own, we can do almost nothing for ourselves, we cannot even manage our wealth." Yet in Iran they're working full-speed on nukes that will be able to hit every European city.

North Korea is the weakest power of all. But on the Fourth of July 2006 its dictator gamely got in the spirit and held a fireworks display. Impressive stuff: the rockets' red glare, the bombs bursting in air—though, as sometimes happens with your highest-price firecracker, it was over sooner than expected. Kim Jong-il has No Dong. Please, no giggling. It's not a side effect of that counterfeit Viagra that North Korea manufactures (seriously). No Dong is the name of his missile system. "Dong" is Korean for "dong," and "no" is Korean for "big swinging," and that's how Kim Jong-il sees himself on the freelance nuke scene. Anyway, on the Glorious Fourth, he decided to test the latest version of his No Dong. That's a "test" in the sense that I test my new shotgun by firing it through your kitchen window and seeing if it penetrates to the living room. Kim's Dong went up and came straight down again forty seconds later. From the trajectory, experts calculated that it was headed to Hawaii. Instead, it fell in the Sea of Japan.

And everyone had a big laugh. What a loser, what a bozo. Mister Nukes R Us talks the talk but he can't nuke the nuke. Ha ha, what a joke.

But no, that's the point. That's why he's dangerous. He's not the United States, not the Soviet Union, not India, he's not even France. He's an incompetent but he's got nuclear weapons. In 2006, he aimed for Hawaii and just about cleared his perimeter fence. Next time, he might aim for Hawaii and hit San Diego. Or Oakland. Or Calgary, or Presque-Isle, Maine. Or Beijing, Addis Ababa, Salzburg, or Dublin. He's a self-taught nuclear madman and he hasn't quite gotten the hang of it. If you're on the New Jersey Turnpike and there's a confused ninety-three-year-old granny behind the wheel of a Toyota Corolla, that's mostly a problem for her. If she's in an eighteen-wheeler and coming across the median, that's a problem for you. North Korea has millions of starving people; it has one of the lowest GDPs per capita on the planet, lower than Ghana, lower than Zimbabwe, lower than Mongolia.

But it's a nuclear power.

The danger we face is not a Chinese superpower or an Islamist super-power: if there's a new boss, you learn the new rules and adjust as best you can. But the greater likelihood is of a world with no superpower at all, in which unipolar geopolitics gives way to non-polar geopolitics, a world without order in which pipsqueak thug states who can't feed their own people globalize their psychoses.

Take the subject of, say, decapitation—not something most of us had given a thought to since, oh, the French Revolution. But there's a lot of it about. In 2006, a Taliban-like Islamist regime took control of Soma-lia, and, in the course of their seizure of Mogadishu, captured troops from the warlords' side and beheaded them. The so-called emir of al Qaeda in Iraq, Abu Musab al-Zarqawi, made beheading his signature act, cutting the throats of American hostage Nick Berg and British hostage Ken Bigley and then releasing the footage as boffo snuff videos over the Internet.

And it's not just guerrillas and insurgents who are hot for decapita-tion. The Saudis, who are famously "our friends," behead folks on a daily basis. In 2005, the kingdom beheaded six Somalis. What for? Mur-der? Rape? Homosexuality? No, it was worse than that: auto theft. They'd been convicted and served five-year sentences but at the end thereof the Saudi courts decided to upgrade their crime to a capital offense. Some two-thirds of those beheaded in Saudi Arabia are foreign nationals, which would be an unlikely criminal profile in any civilized state and suggests that the justice "system" is driven by the Saudis' contempt for non-Saudis as much as anything else.

The decapitators are getting closer. In an Ontario courtroom in 2006, it was alleged that a terrorist cell planned to storm the Canadian parliament and behead the prime minister. On the face of it, that sounds ridiculous. As ridiculous as it must have seemed to Ken Bigley, a British contractor in Iraq with no illusions about the world. He'd spent most of his adult life grubbing around the seedier outposts of empire and thought he knew the way the native chappies did things. He never imagined the last sounds he'd ever hear were delirious cries of "Allahu Akhbar" and the man behind him reaching for the blade to saw his head off.

And why would an act of such awesome symbolic power remain confined to Islamists? A week or two after the revelation of that Toronto plot, there was a flurry of beheadings on America's southern border: the heads of three decapitated policemen were found in the Tijuana River; a fourth turned up in Acapulco a week later. It's wishful thinking to assume hip depravity won't migrate beyond the Islamist world. But no doubt Al Gore will carry on talking about global warming and Nancy Pelosi about college tuition costs and Hillary Clinton about prescription drug plans as the world sinks into economic decline, arbitrary bombings and kidnappings, the occasional nuking—and a million small concessions to Muslim sensitivities that will nudge Western society ever further down a bleaker path. Writing about the collapse of nations such as Somalia, the *Atlantic Monthly*'s Robert D. Kaplan referred to the "citizens" of such "states" as "re-primitivized man." When lifelong Torontonians are hot for decapitation, when Yorkshiremen born and bred into fish n' chips and cricket and lousy English pop music self-detonate on the London Tube, it would seem that the phenomenon of "re-primitivized man" is being successfully exported around the planet.

In 1998, Thomas Friedman of the *New York Times* unveiled his Golden Arches theory—that no two countries with a McDonald's franchise ever went to war. The ink was barely dry when America and NATO began bombing Serbia. So much for the civilizing effects of Big

Macs in Belgrade. The Yugoslav meltdown of the nineties suggests the opposite of Friedman's thesis. In the eighties, the federation was on its way to a comfortable, prosperous, post-Communist future: Croatia was a popular holiday destination with Britons, Germans, and other wealthy Westerners. But, invited to choose between a booming economy and ancient hatreds, the people of Yugoslavia preferred to reduce their country to rubble. How many other bits of the map, under pressure from predatory forces and with a leading power unable to lead, might opt for "re-primitivization"?

A couple of weeks after September 11, Edward Said, the New York-based America disparager and author of the bestselling *Orientalism*, made some remarks about the "interconnectedness" of the West and Islam. The professor deplored the tendency of commentators to separate cultures into what he called "sealed-off entities," when in reality Western Civilization and the Muslim world are so "intertwined" that it was impossible to "draw the line" between them.

Rich Lowry, the editor of *National Review*, wasn't impressed by this notion. "The line seems pretty clear," he said. "Developing mass commercial aviation and soaring skyscrapers was the West's idea; slashing the throats of stewardesses and flying the planes into the skyscrapers was radical Islam's idea."

True. But, as a form of cross-civilization intertwining, that's not to be disdained, at least from one party's point of view. Indeed, Mr. Lowry has identified the only "interconnectedness" a significant chunk of Islam is interested in. Islamism is a twenty-first-century political project driven by seventh-century ideology. That's a potent combination of ancient and modern. In Europe and North America, incendiary imams—uneducated and knowing barely a word of the language spoken by the society in which they live—have nevertheless done a grand job at re-primitivizing second- and third-generation Western Muslims. Not all of them, of course, but how many does it have to be to become a problem?

There are three strategies Islam deploys against a dying West: first, demography; second, conversion; and third, the murky "intertwining" of modern technology and ancient hatreds.

For example, I hadn't really followed Sudanese current events closely since, oh, General Kitchener's victory at the Battle of Omdurman in 1898, but in 2003 a story from that benighted land happened to catch my eye. In the fall of that year mass hysteria apparently swept the capital city, Khartoum, after reports that foreigners were shaking hands with Sudanese men and causing their penises to disappear. One victim, a fabric merchant, told his story to the London Arabic newspaper *Al-Quds Al-Arabi*: a man from West Africa came into the shop and "shook the store owner's hand powerfully until the owner felt his penis melt into his body."

I know the feeling. The same thing happened to me after shaking hands with Senator Clinton. Anyway, as *Al-Quds* reported, "The store owner became hysterical, and was taken to the hospital." The country's chief criminal attorney general, Yasser Ahmad Muhammad, told the Sudanese daily *Al-Rai Al-A'am* that "the rumor broke out when one merchant went to another merchant to buy some Karkady [a Sudanese beverage]. Suddenly, the seller felt his penis shriveling." The invaluable Middle East Media Research Institute, in its exhaustive coverage, noted that the penises of Khartoum were vulnerable not merely to handshaking: "Another victim, who refused to give his name, said that while he was at the market, a man approached him, gave him a comb, and asked him to comb his hair. When he did so, within seconds, he said, he felt a strange sensation and discovered that he had lost his penis."

Tales of the vanishing penises ran rampant through the city. Sudan's attorney general, Salah Abu Zayed, declared that all complaints about missing dangly bits would be brought before a special investigative committee, though doctors had determined that the first plaintiff was "perfectly healthy." The health minister, Ahmad Bilal Othman, said that the epidemic was "scientifically groundless," and that it was "sorcery, magic, or an emotional problem."

Whatever it is, it's the perfect tale of Islamic victimhood: the foreigners have made us impotent! It doesn't matter that the foreigners didn't do anything except shake hands. It doesn't matter whether you are, in fact, impotent. You feel impotent, just as (so we're told constantly) millions of

Muslims from Algerian Islamists to the Bali bombers on the other side of the world feel "humiliated" by the Palestinian situation. Whether there is a rational basis for their sense of humiliation or impotence is irrelevant.

But here's the telling detail: the vanishing-penis hysteria was spread by cell phones and text messaging.

Think about that: you can own a cell phone, yet still believe that shaking hands with an infidel will cause you to lose your penis. That's a state-of-the-art primitive.

Aside from its doubts in its collective manhood, Sudan is no laughing matter. Two million people were slaughtered there in the nineties. That's one-third of the victims of the Holocaust—and the world barely noticed. So much for "never again." The Christian minority is vanishing a lot faster than that fabric merchant's privates. Among the, er, non-Christian majority, Osama certainly found the country fertile ground for his ideology: Sudanese mujahideen have been captured as far afield as Algeria, Bosnia, Chechnya, and Afghanistan. Sudan is an economic basket case with a 27 percent literacy rate that nevertheless has managed to find enough spare cash to export revolutionary Islam to many other countries. And they've got half a billion dollars' worth of top Chinese weaponry imported via Iran.

What else might Sudan get from Tehran in the years ahead? In April 2006, Iran's Supreme Leader, Ayatollah Khamenei, announced that his government was ready to share its nuclear technology with other interested parties. "Iran's nuclear capability is one example of various scientific capabilities in the country," said the ayatollah. "The Islamic Republic of Iran is prepared to transfer the experience, knowledge, and technology of its scientists."

He made this offer at a meeting with the president of Sudan, Omar al-Bashir.

A handshake-fearing guy with a cell phone is one thing; what happens when the handshake-fearers have cell phones and a suitcase nuke? It's at the meeting of apparently indestructible ancient ignorance and cheap, widely available modern technology that the dark imponderables of the future lie.

How far does that techno-primitive hybrid reach? In 2004, there was another story about cell phones in the paper. Not Khartoum this time. The *Times* of London reported that "mobile phones are being used by young Muslims living in Britain to watch videos of hostages being beheaded by militants in Iraq." "This is the best use of this phone," the paper was told by "an Algerian in his thirties who has lived in London for almost ten years" and has collected the entire set of snuff videos on his cell. "Most of the people in this country are using it to download pictures of naked women. For us the jihad is alive in our hands as we watch American infidels get their heads chopped off.... Within a few minutes of the Americans dying last week I was watching them on my phone. The Englishman should not have been there," he added, referring to then hostage Ken Bigley. "He will be beheaded and I can tell you I will see it here on my phone."

He was and that Muslim Londoner undoubtedly did.

In 1898, after Kitchener slaughtered the dervishes at Omdurman, Hilaire Belloc wrote a characteristically pithy summation of the British technological advantage:

> Whatever happens
> We have got
> The Maxim gun
> And they have not.

But the dervishes have cell phones now, and there are plenty of people out there willing to help them get cheap knock-offs of the twenty-first century's Maxim gun. And, Maxim guns aside, we're bound by "maxims of prudence" (in Kant's phrase), and they're not. As Lee Harris wrote, "The liberal world system has collapsed internally." We no longer know the limits of behavior. When the president of Iran threatens to wipe Israel off the face of the map, we cannot reliably assure ourselves that this is just a bit of rhetorical red meat, a little playing to the gallery for the Saturday-night jihad crowd.

Nonetheless, many foolish experts do. We persist in seeing Iran's President Ahmadinejad as the equivalent of the Sudanese crazy raving about his vanished manhood, except that in this case he's raving about having No Dong, which, like a nuclear K-Mart, Kim Jong-il is happily dispersing around the planet. (One could foresee certain problems if the president of Sudan goes on TV and announces, "I am proud to tell the people I have No Dong." Oh no—the epidemic's spread to the palace! Mass panic, etc.) Confronted by the minimal degrees of separation between the loonies and many of their leaders, we look away and pretend that President Ahmadinejad is no different from the Politburo of yore. The Reds could have nuked us but they had compelling reasons not to. They had the capability but we were able to make a rational assessment of their intent by considering what we would do in their situation. It's the other way around with Iran. They have the intent and the only question mark is over their capability.

President Ahmaddamatree is the globalized version of those Khartoum men who own cell phones and yet believe a handshake can make one's manhood disappear. He owns nukes and he believes he can make the West's manhood disappear. Indeed, his wish to obliterate Israel is one of his less nutty aspects. That can be seen as a slightly overheated version of politics-as-usual in the Middle East. What's more significant is that he believes in the return of the Twelfth Imam—the so-called "hidden imam"—and quite possibly that he personally is the fellow's designated deputy. The president, as mayor of Tehran, wanted the city's boulevards widened so that the hidden imam wouldn't be insulted by having to ride in triumph through narrow streets. He's also claimed that when he addressed the United Nations General Assembly in 2005 a mystical halo appeared and bathed him in its aura. (It wasn't the "Exit" sign—or, if it was, it didn't endow the prime minister of Canada with any similar beatific aura.) Shortly afterwards, he told Natwar Singh, the Indian foreign minister, that everything would be hunky-dory in two years' time, which Mr. Singh took to mean when Iran's nukes would be ready but which turned out to be the Twelfth Imam's ETA. Human history has never wanted for millennial cultists of one form or another, but ours is the first age in which such men have the means to pull off the apocalypse. In medieval Europe, the apocalyptics had intent; President Ahmageddo-nouttahere is an apocalyptic with a delivery system. "The end is nigh" is an old slogan. Now the means are nigh.

●   ●   ●

THE LOOK

One of the most enduring vignettes of the Great War comes from its first Christmas: December 1914. The Germans and British, separated by a few yards of mud on the western front, put up banners to wish each other season's greetings, sang "Silent Night" in the dark in both languages, and eventually scrambled up from their opposing trenches to play a Christmas Day football match in No Man's Land and share some German beer and English plum jam. After this Yuletide interlude, they went back to killing each other.

The many films, books, and plays inspired by that No Man's Land truce all take for granted the story's central truth: that our common humanity transcends the temporary hell of war. When the politicians and generals have done with us, those who are left will live in peace, playing footie (i.e., soccer), singing songs, as they did for a moment in the midst of carnage.

Now cross to Israel, to Haifa on a Saturday night in 2003: nineteen diners were killed in a packed restaurant by a twenty-something female suicide bomber, her hair attractively tied in a Western-style ponytail, to judge from the detached head she left as her calling card. Try to find the common humanity between the participants in that war. Try to imagine the two sides ever kicking a ball around, swapping songs. The only place in the modern Middle East where Arabs and Jews coexist is in Israel, especially in Haifa. The restaurant young Hanadi Jaradat blew apart had been jointly owned by an Arab family and a Jewish family for forty years. It would be interesting to know whether it was targeted for that very reason, in the same way that, in Northern Ireland, the IRA took to killing the Catholic caterers and cleaners who worked at army bases. But the intifada is too primal for anything that thought out. It's more likely that once Miss Jaradat had slipped into Israel proper—through a gap in the unfinished security fence the European Union and the State Department so deplore— she decided that any target would do. She was busting to blow.

The Palestinian death cult negates all the assumptions of Western sentimental pacifism—not least that war is a board game played by old men with young men as their chess pieces: if only the vengeful aged generals got out of the way, there'd be no conflict. But such common humanity as one can find on the West Bank resides, if only in their cynicism, in the leadership. Old Arafat may have showered glory and honor on his youthful martyrs but he was human enough to keep his own kid in Paris, well away from the suicide-bomber belts. It's hard to picture Saeb Erekat or Hanan Ashrawi or any of the other veteran terror apologists who hog the airwaves at CNN and the BBC celebrating the deaths of their loved ones the way Miss Jaradat's brother did. "We are receiving congratulations from people," said Thaher Jaradat. "Why should we cry? It is like her wedding day, the happiest day for her."

The problem is not the security fence, but the psychological fence— a chasm really—that separates a sizable proportion of the Palestinian population from all Jews. For one side, there is no common humanity, even with people they know well, who provide them with jobs, and much else: Wafa Samir Ibrahim al-Biss, a twenty-one-year-old woman who has received kind and exemplary treatment at an Israeli hospital in Beer-sheba, packs herself with explosives and sets off to blow apart that hospital and the doctors and nurses who've treated her.

Oh, well. If you're pro-Palestinian, you shrug that their depravity is born of "desperation." If you've had it with the Palestinians, you figure that after decades of UN coddling and EU funding and wily Arab manipulation they're the most comprehensively wrecked people on the planet. In either case, it's a very particular circumstance.

But what if that "desperation" goes global? What if it's shared by large numbers of other people around the planet?

Here's another death scene. Photographed from above, the body bags look empty. They seem to lie flat on the ground, and it's only when you peer closer that you realize that that's because the bodies in them are too small to fill the length of the bags. They're children. Row upon row of dead children, over a hundred of them, 150, more, many of them shot in the back as they tried to flee.

It was a picture from the Beslan massacre—the pupils of a Russian schoolhouse, taken hostage and slaughtered in September 2004. And, as Ken Bigley did, the very last thing they heard as they departed this world was the voice of their killer screaming "Allahu Akhbar!"

God is great.

This virus has been a long time incubating. In 1971, in the lobby of the Cairo Sheraton, terrorists shot the prime minister of Jordan at point-blank range. As he fell to the floor dying, one of his killers began drinking the blood gushing from his wounds. Thirty-five years later, the Palestinian Authority elections were a landslide for Hamas and among the incoming legislators was Mariam Farahat, a mother of three, elected in Gaza. She used to be a mother of six but three of her sons self-detonated on suicide missions against Israel. She's a household name to Palestinians, known as Umm Nidal—Mother of the Struggle—and, at the rate she's getting through her kids, the Struggle's all she'll be Mother of. She's famous for a Hamas recruitment video in which she shows her seventeen-year-old son how to kill Israelis and then tells him not to come back. It's the Hamas version of *42nd Street*: you're going out there a youngster but you've got to come back in small pieces.

It may be that she stood for parliament because she's got a yen to be junior transport minister or deputy secretary of fisheries. But it seems more likely that she and her Hamas colleagues were elected because this is who the Palestinian people are, and this is what they believe. After sixty years as UN "refugees," they're now so inured they're electing candidates on the basis of child sacrifice. When you're there, in Gaza or the West Bank, that culture of death is pervasive. You go into a convenience store and they're affable and friendly and you exchange some pleasantries, and over the guy's shoulder you're looking at the Martyrs of the Week he's got proudly displayed on the wall. On my last visit, Palestinian schools were in the midst of a national letter-writing competition. Among the education ministry's first-prize winners was twelve-year-old Mahmoud Naji Chalilah for this epistle to the Zionist Entity: "My heart has turned into a sad block of pain. One day I will buy a weapon and I will blow away the fetters. I will propel my living-dead body into your arms...."

The famously "moderate" mullah Yusuf al-Qaradawi, the favorite imam of London mayor Ken Livingstone, was invited to speak at the 2004 "Our Children Our Future" conference sponsored and funded by the Metropolitan Police and Britain's Department for Work and Pensions. When it comes to children and their future, Imam al-Qaradawi certainly has it all mapped out: "Israelis might have nuclear bombs but we have the children bomb and these human bombs must continue until liberation."

Thank heaven for little girls; they blow up in the most delightful way. We are not dealing with "enemies" like the Soviets, or "terrorists" like the IRA. We are a long way from the common humanity that bound those German and British soldiers at Christmas Eve 1914. Try to imagine what a jihadist feels when he looks at a Russian schoolchild or an Israeli diner or a British contractor or an American pacifist.

Now try to imagine how he'd feel if asked to participate in a nuclear plot, and to kill vastly greater numbers of Russians and Israelis and Britons and Americans.

That moment is now upon us. Or as the *Daily Telegraph* in London reported in 2006: "Iran's hard-line spiritual leaders have issued an unprecedented new fatwa, or holy order, sanctioning the use of atomic weapons against its enemies."

Well, there's a surprise.

●   ●   ●

WHAT PART OF "KNOW" DON'T WE UNDERSTAND?

In 2003, Donald Rumsfeld made a much quoted rumination. "Reports that say that something hasn't happened are always interesting to me," the defense secretary began, "because, as we know, there are known knowns; there are things we know we know. We also know there are known unknowns; that is to say we know there are some things we do not know. But there are also unknown unknowns—the ones we don't know we don't know."

A lot of people jeered at Rummy. The witless twits at Britain's Plain English Campaign gave him that year's award for the worst use of English. But Rumsfeld is perhaps the best speaker of Plain English in English-speaking politics, and it would be a less despised profession if there were more like him. His little riff about known knowns, known unknowns, and unknown unknowns is in fact a brilliant distillation of the dangers we face. Let's take an example close to the heart of arrogant Texas cowboys: John Wayne is holed up in an old prospector's shack. He peeks over the sill and drawls, "It's quiet out there. Too quiet."

What he means is that he knows the things he doesn't know. He doesn't know the precise location of the bad guys, but he knows they're out there somewhere, inching through the dust, perhaps trying to get to the large cactus from behind which they can get a clean shot at him. Thus he knows what to be on the lookout for: he is living in a world of known unknowns. But suppose, while he was scanning the horizon for a black hat or the glint of a revolver, a passenger jet suddenly ploughed into the shack. That would be one of Rumsfeld's unknown unknowns: something poor John Wayne didn't know he didn't know—until it hit him.

That's how most of the world reacted to September 11: we didn't know this was one of the things we didn't know. For most people in the developed world, terrorism meant detonating bombs in shopping streets, railway stations, and park bandstands—killing a couple dozen, maiming another thirty, tops. As Thomas Friedman wrote in the *New York Times*: "The failure to prevent September 11 was not a failure of intelligence or co-ordination. It was a failure of imagination."

In other words, it was an unknown unknown: we didn't know enough to be alert for the things we didn't know.

There's a legitimate disagreement about that. Given al Qaeda's stated ambitions, given its previous targeting of the World Trade Center, given the number of young Arab men taking flight lessons in America, one can make the case that September 11 should have been a known unknown—one of those things we ought to have been scanning the horizon for. Friedman insists that "even if all the raw intelligence signals had been shared among the FBI, the CIA, and the White House, I'm convinced that there was no one there who would have put them all together, who would have imagined evil on the scale Osama bin Laden did." For the sake of argument, concede that. After all, the Cold War was a half century of very well-known unknowns. We didn't know the precise timing or specifics of what would happen, but we knew the rough shape—a mushroom cloud—so well that, from *Dr. Strangelove* on, the known unknowns generated the most numbingly homogeneous body of predictive fiction ever seen.

It's trickier now. This is an age of unknown unknowns. If you've ever been at an airport counter buying a ticket when the computer goes down and the clerk explains that he can't do anything until the system's back up, you'll know that blank look on his face as he sits and waits and sits and waits, an able-bodied man effectively disabled. It wasn't like that if you were at the desk buying your ticket in 1937. He tore the stub off the book in his cash drawer and that was that. Today our system has a million points of vulnerability. Some of those are known unknowns—some type of terrorist-sparked electromagnetic pulse that wipes out every bank account in the United States and Canada and crashes the financial markets. We know some of the other things we don't know—who North Korea's been pitching its wares to, where the missing Soviet nuke materials have gone walkabout, who else has the kind of "explosive socks" found by Scotland Yard in 2003—but we have no real idea in what combination these states and groups and technology and footwear might impress themselves on us, or what other links in the chain there might be. And we might not know until we switch on the TV and the screen's full of smoke again, but this time it's May 7 in Frankfurt, or February 3 in Vancouver, or October 22 in Dallas. Or we might not be able to switch on the TV at all, because the unknown unknown is a variation of technological catastrophe we haven't imagined.

Yet what we're confronted with in Iran are known knowns: a state that's developing nuclear weapons, a state that's made repeated threats to use such weapons against a neighboring state, a state with a long track record of terrorist sponsorship, a state whose actions align with its rhetoric very precisely. What's not to know?

So the question is: will they do it?

And the minute you have to ask the question you know the answer. It's the same answer to the same question: Will they go ahead and slaughter the Beslan schoolchildren? Will they decapitate the bumbling Englishman? Will they kill the Iraqi aid worker and the American "Christian peacemaker"?

In 1993 a Hezbollah suicide bomber killed twenty-nine people and injured hundreds more in an attack on the Israeli embassy in Argentina. The following year, the Argentine Israel Mutual Association was bombed in Buenos Aires. Nearly a hundred people died and 250 were injured— the worst massacre of Jewish civilians since the Holocaust. An Argentine court eventually issued warrants for two Iranian diplomats and two former cabinet ministers. The chief perpetrator had flown from Lebanon a few days earlier and entered Latin America through the porous "tri-border" region of Argentina, Brazil, and Paraguay. Suppose Iran had had a "dirty nuke" shipped to Hezbollah, or even the full-blown thing: Would it have been any less easy to get it into the country? And if a significant chunk of downtown Buenos Aires were rendered uninhabitable, what would the Argentine government do? Iran can project itself to South America effortlessly, but Argentina can't project itself to the Middle East at all. It can't nuke Tehran, and it can't attack Iran in conventional ways.

So any retaliation would be down to others. Would Washington act? It depends how clear the fingerprints were. "Mutually Assured Destruction" only works if you know who lobbed the thing your way in the first place. One reason Iran set up Hezbollah and other terror franchises is to have "plausible deniability." Actually, it's implausible deniability, but that's good enough for the UN. So, if the links back to the mullahs were just the teensy-weensy bit tenuous and murky, how eager would the United States be to reciprocate? Bush and Rumsfeld might, but an administration of a

more Clinto-Powellite bent? How much pressure would there be for investigations under the auspices of the UN? Perhaps Hans Blix could come out
of retirement, and we could have a six-month dance through Security
Council coalition-building with the secretary of state making a last-minute
flight to Khartoum to try to persuade Sudan to switch its vote.

The Iranian version of No Dong will be able to hit not just Tel Aviv
but also Rome, Berlin, Paris, Madrid, and London. How will the European political class react? Will it stand firm against threats from Tehran?
Or will it take the view that there are ways to avoid having to confront
incoming Islamonukes? You might, for example, approve the spectacularly large mosque wealthy Muslims have been wanting to build in your
capital city. Or make certain well-connected heads of Muslim lobby
groups members of a special government commission. You might appoint
a minister for Islamic education to your cabinet. In other words, "the
Muslim bomb" is likely to accelerate the Islamification of Europe, because
Islamification more or less brings you under the Persian nuclear umbrella
and encourages Tehran and its clients to turn their attentions elsewhere.

● ● ●

OUR WORD IS OUR BOMB

"Men of intemperate mind never can be free; their passions forge their
fetters," wrote Edmund Burke. From the ayatollahs to the freelance
jihadists, there are, in the end, no "root causes"—or not ones that can
be negotiated by troop withdrawals from Iraq or the flag-raising ceremony for a Palestinian state. There is only a metastasizing cancer that
preys on whatever local conditions are to hand. Five days before the
slaughter in Bali in 2005, nine Islamists were arrested in Paris for report-
edly plotting to attack the Metro. Must be all those French troops in
Iraq, right? So much for the sterling efforts of President Chirac and his
prime minister, the two chief obstructionists to Bush-Blair-neocon-Zion-
ist warmongering since 2001.

In the months after the Afghan campaign, France's foreign minister, Hubert Védrine, was deploring American "*simplisme*" on a daily basis, and Saddam understood from the get-go that the French veto was his best shot at torpedoing any meaningful UN action on Iraq. Yet the jihadists still blew up a French oil tanker. If you were to pick only one Western nation not to blow up the oil tankers of, the French would surely be it.

But they got blown up anyway. And afterwards a spokesman for the Islamic Army of Aden said, "We would have preferred to hit a U.S. frigate, but no problem because they are all infidels."

No problem. They are all infidels.

When people make certain statements and their acts conform to those statements I tend to take them at their word. As Hussein Massawi, former leader of Hezbollah, neatly put it, "We are not fighting so that you will offer us something. We are fighting to eliminate you." The first choice of Islamists is to kill Americans and Jews, or best of all an American Jew like Daniel Pearl, the late *Wall Street Journal* reporter. Failing that, they're happy to kill Australians, Britons, Canadians, Swedes, Germans, as they did in Bali. No problem. We are all infidels. You can be a hippy-dippy hey-man-I-love-everybody Dutch stoner hanging out in a bar in Bali, and they'll blow you up with as much enthusiasm as if you were Dick Cheney.

Back in February 2002, Robert Fisk, the veteran Middle East correspondent (i.e., he's reliably wrong about practically everything), wrote a column headlined "Please Release My Friend Daniel Pearl." It followed a familiar line: please release Daniel, then you'll be able to tell your story, get your message out. Taking him hostage is "an own goal of the worst kind," as it ensures he won't be able to get your message out, the message being—Fisky presumed—"the suffering of tens of thousands of Afghan refugees," "the plight of Pakistan's millions of poor," etc.

Somehow the apologists keep missing the point: the story did get out. Pearl's severed head *is* the message. That's why they filmed the decapitation, released it on video, circulated it through the bazaars and madrassas and distributed it worldwide via the Internet. It was a huge hit. The message got out very effectively.

In our time, even the most fascistic ideologies have been canny enough to cover their darker impulses in bathetic labels. The Soviet bloc was comprised of wall-to-wall "People's Republics," which is the precise opposite of what they were—a stylistic audacity Orwell caught perfectly in *1984*, with its "Ministry of Truth" (i.e., official lies). But the Islamists don't even bother going through the traditional rhetorical feints. They say what they mean and they mean what they say—and we choose to stay in ignorance. Blow up the London Underground during a G-8 summit and the world's leaders twitter about how "tragic" and "ironic" it is that this should have happened just as they're taking steps to deal with the issues—as though the terrorists are upset about poverty in Africa and global warming. Even in a great blinding flash of clarity, we can't wait to switch the lights off and go back to fumbling around on the darkling plain.

A world without order eventually liberates all restraints. Even in low-level conflicts there's no monopoly of depravity: Americans think of "Northern Ireland" as being the IRA versus the Brits. But it doesn't stop there: there were plenty of "loyalist" paramilitaries too, groups that took the view that if the other side was blowing up their civilians maybe a little reciprocity was in order. Islamists are foolish to assume that freelance nukes go one way. If a dirty bomb with unclear fingerprints goes off in London or Delhi, it's not necessary to wait for the government to respond. As in Ulster, there'll always be groups who think the state power is too pussy to hit back. So unlisted numbers will be dialed hither and yon, arrangements will be made, and bombs will go off in Islamabad and Riyadh and Cairo. There will be plenty of non-state actors on the non-Islamic side. In the end the victims of the Islamist contagion will include many, many Muslims.

But we surely don't need to wait for Iranian nukes, do we? The Bali bombs and Madrid bombs and London bombs have already lit up the sky: they make unavoidable the truth that Islamism is a classic "armed doctrine"; it exists to destroy. One day it will, on an epic scale.

Chapter Eight

The Unipole Apart

AMERICA VS. EVERYONE ELSE

In the end it will be America vs. the Rest of the World. Whose side will you be on?

MATTHEW PARRIS, *SPECTATOR* (UNITED KINGDOM), FEBRUARY 2, 2002

Can America win its "long war"? If you think the question's ridiculous, well, other countries are certainly asking it. Because, if America can't, nobody else in the developed world can, and they'd be well advised to begin reaching their accommodations with the new realities, an Islamic Europe and a nuclear Iran being merely the warm-up acts. A good place to start any consideration is the Sunni Triangle. A few weeks after the fall of Saddam Hussein, I drove into Fallujah. What a dump—no disrespect to any Fallujans reading this. I had a late lunch in a seedy cafe full of Sunni men. Not a gal in the joint. And no

Westerners except me. As in the movies, everyone stopped talking when I walked through the door, and every pair of eyes followed me as I made my way to a table.

I strongly dislike that veteran-foreign-correspondent look, where you wander around like you've been sleeping in the back of the souk for a week. So I was wearing the same suit I'd wear in Washington or New York, from the Western Imperialist Aggressor line at Brooks Brothers. I had a sharp necktie I'd bought in London the week before. My cuff links were the most stylish in the room, and also the only ones in the room. I'm not a Sunni Triangulator, so there's no point pretending to be one. If you're an infidel and agent of colonialist decadence, you might as well dress the part.

So I ordered the mixed grill, which turned out to be not that mixed. Just a tough old stringy chicken. My tie would have been easier to chew. The locals watched me—a few obviously surly and resentful, the rest somewhere between wary and amused. Or so it appeared. But in cultures that are as foreign to one as a just-liberated Arab dictatorship it's hard to say for sure. Even facial expressions don't always mean what they seem: at times my fellow diners appeared to be grinning in another language. Still, I've had worse welcomes in Berkeley, so I chewed on, and, washed down with a pitcher of coliform bacteria, the unmixed grill wasn't bad. As a parodic courtesy, mein host switched the flickering black-and-white TV from an Arabic station to the BBC, which as usual was full of doom and gloom about the quagmire.

And I gave no further thought to Fallujah until a year later, when four American contractors working in Iraq—Scott Helvenston, Wesley Batalona, Jerry Zovko, and Michael Teague—were ambushed while driving through town. They were dragged from their vehicles, shot, burned, mutilated, and what was left was dangled from a bridge over the Euphrates while the natives danced in the streets. The "insurgents" were pleased as punch, made a video of the attack, and distributed it around the world.

There's not a lot to be said for the oh-my-God-that-could-have-been-me routine. But, watching the scenes on TV, I did think back to my lunch eleven months earlier, and wondered about some of those inscrutable toothy grins at the adjoining tables. Would those fellows have liked to kill me? Well, I'll bet one or two would have enjoyed giving it a go. And if they had, I'll bet three or four more would have enthusiastically beaten my corpse with their shoes. And five or six would have had no particular feelings about me one way or the other but would have been generally supportive of the decision to kill me after the fact. And the rest might have had a few qualms but they would have kept quiet.

So why didn't they kill me? I'm not brave, and certainly not suicidally brave. And, if I'd known the Sunni Triangle was the most dangerous place on Earth, I wouldn't have been there driving around on my own in some beat-up rented Nissan.

But, of course, Fallujah wasn't dangerous in those days. Why? Because, as Osama gloated after September 11, when people see a strong horse and a weak horse, they go with the strong horse. And in May 2003, four weeks after the fall of Baghdad, the coalition forces were indisputably the strong horse. They'd removed Saddam Hussein—the self-declared new Saladin—in nothing flat. And so, even when a dainty little trotting gelding of a touring writer comes through the door, they figure he's with the strong-horse crowd and act accordingly.

What happened within the next year was that America ceased to be perceived as a strong horse. It was a range of factors, from the West's defeatist media to the Bush administration's wish to be seen as, so to speak, a compassionate crusader. Nice idea. But to the Arab mindset there's no such thing. So the compassion got read by the locals not as cultural respect but as weakness. And the quagmiritis diagnosed by the media from Day One suggested that a hyperpower of historically unprecedented dominance didn't have the stomach for a body count that in the course of a year added up to little more than a quiet week's internal policing for Saddam. By comparison, some four million people died in the Congo in the couple of years either side of the turn of the century—and how many books or TV investigations have you seen on that subject?

Before I got to Fallujah, on the deserted highway between the Jordanian border and the town of Rutba, I came across my first burnt-out tank. You'd see them periodically—a charred wreck blocking the lane or shoved over to the shoulder. With that first one I stopped, walked around it, and pondered the fate of the men inside. Sobering. Yet as the great strategist of armored warfare Basil Liddell Hart wrote: "The destruction of the enemy's armed forces is but a means—and not necessarily an inevitable or infallible one—to the attainment of the real objective."

The object of war is not to destroy the enemy's tanks but to destroy his will. As Liddell Hart put it: "Our goal in war can only be attained by the subjugation of the opposing will.... All such acts as defeat in the field, propaganda, blockade, diplomacy, or attack on the centres of government and population are seen to be but means to that end."

America is extremely good at destroying tanks. If you make the mistake of luring the United States into a hot war—i.e., tanks, bombers, ships, etc.—you'll lose very quickly. The Taliban did, and so did Saddam Hussein. That's why my lunch in Fallujah required no personal courage on my part: just about the safest time to visit anywhere in the Muslim world is in the month after the United States has toppled its dictator.

But an enemy folds when he knows he's finished. In Iraq, despite the swift fall of the Saddamites, it's not clear the enemy did know. Even during the combat phase we were playing the compassionate crusader. The Western peaceniks' prewar "human shields" operation proved to be completely superfluous, mainly because the Anglo-American forces decided to treat not just Iraqi civilians and not just Iraqi conscripts but virtually everyone other than Saddam, Uday, and Qusay as a de facto human shield. Washington made a conscious choice to give every Iraqi the benefit of the doubt, including the fake surrenderers who ambushed the U.S. Marines at Nasiriyah. The main victims of Western squeamishness in those few weeks in the spring of 2003 turned out to be not American or coalition troops but the Iraqi civilians who two years later were providing the principal target for "insurgents." It would have been better for them had more Baathists been killed in the initial invasion. It would have been preferable, too, if the swarm of foreign jihadi from neighboring countries had occasionally been met with the "accidental" bombing of certain targets on the Syrian side of the border. Wars fought under absurd degrees of self-imposed etiquette are the most difficult to win—see Korea and Vietnam—and one lesson of Germany and Japan is that it's easier to rebuild totalitarian states if they've first been completely smashed. Colin Powell famously framed Iraq in Pottery Barn terms: you break it, you own it. But Saddam's Baathist apparatus and other parties concluded the opposite: we didn't have the guts to break it; therefore, we didn't own it.

I'm not worried about Iraq. Its political class has behaved with both amazing restraint and impressive resolve: the country won't be New Hampshire or Singapore, but it will be good enough and (even if it dissolves into three separate states) better governed than any of its neighbors. That's fine if you live in Mosul or Basra, where the Iraq question is a question about Iraq. But, for the rest of the world, what's at issue in the Iraq war is not the future of Iraq but the future of America. Can the world's leading nation still lead, or is John Kerry's Vietnam Syndrome "seared" (as he'd say) into its bones? If so, how likely is it that America can stick out the "long war"? Especially if it's fought not in sudden swift total devastating military campaigns but in arenas where our military and technological advantage is peripheral and other factors come into play. Facing a foe who has nothing but will and manpower, do we have the strength to (in Liddell Hart's phrase) subjugate that will? The enemy was certainly impressed by the speed with which U.S. forces raced to Baghdad. But the invasion becomes a liberation and the liberation becomes a policing operation and the further you get from that first month of hard power the more constrained the hyperpower becomes, the less willing to use any but a tiny proportion of his awesome might until in the end he's Gulliver ensnared by more motivated Lilliputians.

Do you remember when that statue of Saddam came down? It proved to be hollow. The Islamists think Western Civilization's like that: tough exterior, but empty inside; protected by a layer of hard steel—the U.S. military—there's nothing underneath.

Why would they get that idea? Well, from a million and one little things—itsy-bitsy foot-of-page-thirty-seven news items, none too important in itself but cumulatively an avalanche. Take one trivial example: just before Christmas 2003, Muslim community leaders in California

applauded the decision of the Catholic high school in San Juan Capis-
trano to change the name of its football team from the Crusaders to the
less culturally insensitive Lions.

Meanwhile, twenty miles up the road in Irvine, the schedule for the
Muslim Football League's New Year tournament promised to bring
together some of the most exciting Muslim football teams in Orange
County: the Intifada, the Mujahideen, the Saracens, and the Sword of
Allah.

That's the spirit. I can't wait for the California sporting calendar circa
2015: the San Diego Jihadi vs. the Oakland Culturally Sensitives, the
Malibu Hezbollah vs. the Santa Monica Inoffensives, the Pasadena
Sword of the Infidel Slayer vs. the Bakersfield Self-Deprecators, the San
Jose Decapitators vs. the Berkeley Mutually Respectfuls.

I suppose the rationale, conscious or not, behind such trivial concessions as school sports team names is that a big powerful wealthy culture
can afford to be generous to a weaker culture. Unfortunately, magnanim-
ity is often seen as weakness by those on the receiving end. It's easy to be
sensitive, tolerant, and multicultural—it's the default mode of the age—
yet, when you persist in being sensitive to the insensitive, tolerant of the
intolerant, and impeccably multicultural about the avowedly unicultural,
don't be surprised if they take it for weakness.

If this is a "long war," then in the long run, which is the real battlefield? The sands of Araby? Or the football fields of Orange County and a
thousand others? When it chose to expose the U.S. Treasury program for
tracking terrorist finances, the *New York Times* was heavily criticized for
damaging national security and responded that, au contraire, it took its
responsibilities very seriously and would never reveal "troop movements."
But this isn't a "troop movement" war: in asymmetrical warfare, the troop
movements are the wire transfers—getting the money from Saudi Arabia
to America not just to pull off September 11 but to advance its cause in all
manner of slyer ways. We know the jihad hasn't got anything to match the
Third Infantry Division. But what about the other fronts?

If you go to war colleges or strategic studies institutes in almost any
country, they teach the importance of looking at all elements of national

power. For example, from the 2004 U.S. Department of Defense Strategic Deterrence Joint Operating Concept: "Strategic deterrence requires a national deterrence strategy that integrates and brings to bear all elements of national power: diplomatic, informational, military, and economic."

Nothing unusual about that. I'd add a fifth element: judicial power, law enforcement. The difference between military power and the others is obvious: with military power, you give the orders and somewhere at the other end someone carries them out. With the other elements of national power, the chain of command isn't that direct. So let's consider how they're going:

Military Power

The United States has the most powerful armed forces on the planet. The fact that Washington's responsible for 40 percent of the planet's military spending pales in comparison to the really critical statistic: it's responsible for almost 80 percent of military research-and-development spending, which means the capability gap between it and everyone else widens every day. In Afghanistan, a handful of prototype robots assisted in the cave-by-cave search for al Qaeda nutters. If these innovations have certain snot-nosed Brit toffs pining for the dash and élan of old-school imperialism, America's enemies project their own prejudices onto them, too: the Great Satan prefers antiseptic technological warfare because he can't stomach a three-figure death toll. Therefore, the trick is not to provoke him into walloping you with daisy cutters and bunker busters but to gnaw away at him incrementally, with one or two casualties per evening news bulletin.

As for America's "friends," there's another paradox of the non-imperial hyperpower: the United State garrisons not remote ramshackle colonies but its wealthiest allies, thereby freeing them to spend their tax revenues on luxuriant welfare programs rather than on tanks and aircraft carriers and thus further exacerbating the differences between America and the rest of the free world. Like any other form of welfare, defense welfare is a hard habit to break and damaging to the recipient. The

peculiarly obnoxious character of modern Europe is a logical consequence of America's willingness to absolve it of responsibility for its own
security. In 1796 George Washington wrote to Alexander Hamilton:
"The nation which indulges towards another an habitual hatred, or an
habitual fondness, is in some degree a slave. It is a slave to its animosity
or to its affection, either of which is sufficient to lead it astray from its
duty and its interest."

That neatly sums up the Euro-American relationship: the United
States has become a slave to its habitual if largely misplaced fondness for
Europe, while Europe has become a slave to its habitual if entirely irra-
tional hatred for America. There's a line conservatives are fond of when
they're discussing welfare: what's better for a man—to give him a fish or
to teach him to fish for himself? That goes double for defense welfare.

So, just as the only guy in town with a tennis racket isn't going to be
playing a lot of matches, the logic of America's military dominance is that
both its allies and enemies have every interest to find some other form of
battlefield, whether (for France) the international talking shops or (for
Islamist clerics) the suburban mosques of North America, just to name
two venues where the hyperpower is far less confident.

Judicial Power

What about law enforcement as an element of national power? Well, in
the words of the so-called "twentieth hijacker" Zacarias Moussaoui,
upon being sentenced to life imprisonment: "America, you lose."

Hard to disagree. On the day Mr. Moussaoui was led out of court to
begin his sentence, some pompous member of the ghastly 9-11 Commission turned up on one of the cable shows to declare proudly that jihadists
around the world were marveling at the fairness of the U.S. justice system. The leisurely legal process Mr. Moussaoui enjoyed had lasted longer
than America's participation in World War Two. Around the world,
everybody was having a grand old laugh at the U.S. justice system.

Except for Saddam Hussein, who must be regretting he had the misfortune to fall into the hands of the Iraqi justice system. Nine out of
twelve U.S. jurors agreed that the "emotional abuse" Mr. Moussaoui suf-

fered as a child should be a mitigating factor. Saddam could claim the same but his jury wasn't operating on the legal principles of the Oprah-fonic Code. Criminal prosecution gives terrorists all the rights of criminals, including the "Gee, Officer Krupke" defense: I'm depraved on account of I'm deprived.

It's a very worn cliché to say America is over-lawyered but the extent of that truism only becomes clear when you realize how overwhelming is our culture's reflex to cover war as just another potential miscarriage-of-justice story. In the Moussaoui case, the first instinct of the news shows to the verdict was to book some relative of the September 11 families and ask whether they were satisfied with the result, as if the prosecution of the war on terror is some kind of national-security Megan's Law on which they have inviolable proprietary rights. Sorry, but that's not what happened that Tuesday morning. The thousands who died were not targeted as individuals: they were killed because they were American, not because somebody in a cave far away decided to murder Mrs. Smith. Their families have a unique claim to our sympathy and a grief we can never truly share, but they're not plaintiffs and war isn't a suit. It's not about "closure" for the victims; it's about victory for the nation.

Agreeing to fight the jihad with subpoenas is a declaration that you're willing to plea bargain. Instead of a Churchillian "We will never surrender!" it's more of a "Well, the judge has thrown out the mass murder charges, but the D.A. says we can still nail him on mail fraud." And even that may prove increasingly difficult. In 2005, the British authorities finally moved against the most famous of the country's many incendiary imams. Abu Hamza is a household name in the United Kingdom thanks to the tabloids anointing him as "Hooky"—he lost his hands in an, er, "accident" in Afghanistan in 1991. On trial in London for nine counts of soliciting to murder plus various other charges, he retained the services of a prestigious Queen's Counsel, who certainly came up with an ingenious legal strategy: "Edward Fitzgerald, QC, for the defence, said that Abu Hamza's interpretation of the Koran was that it imposed an obligation on Muslims to do jihad and fight in the defence of their religion. He said that the Crown case against the former imam of Finsbury Park

Mosque was 'simplistic in the extreme.' He added: 'It is said he was preaching murder, but he was actually preaching from the Koran itself.'"

If the Koran permit, you must acquit? Brilliant. To convict would be multiculturally disrespectful: if the holy book of the religion of peace recommends killing infidels, who are we to judge? SIAC, the United Kingdom's anti-terrorist court, found in 2003 that a thirty-five-year-old Algerian male had "actively assisted terrorists who have links to al Qaeda." But he was released from Belmarsh Prison the following year because jail causes him to suffer a "depressive illness."

By Western standards, every Islamic terrorist is "depressive"—for a start, as suicide bombers, they're suicidal. What's impressive about these "unassimilated" Islamists is the way they pick up on our weaknesses so quickly—the legalisms, the ethnic squeamishness, the bureaucratic inertia. The courtroom evens the playing field to the enemy's advantage.

Diplomatic Power

What of U.S. diplomacy as an element of national power? At the dawn of the American era, after the Second World War, Washington chose not to be an active promoter of America's values, America's ideas, America's voice, but instead opted to be what Michael Mandelbaum called an *ordnungsmacht*—an "order maker." In the interests of economic order, the United States set up a network of international bodies—the World Bank, the International Monetary Fund, the General Agreement on Tariffs and Trade. In the interests of geopolitical order, it created transnational institutions in which the non-imperial hegemon was so self-deprecating it artificially inflated everybody else's ideas and values and voices. In recent years, for example, I can find only one example of a senior UN figure having the guts to call a member state a "totalitarian regime." It was the former secretary-general Boutros Boutros-Ghali in 2004, and he was talking about America.

The organization's more artful critics agree that yes, the UN's in a terrible state, what with the Oil-for-Fraud and the Congolese child-sex racket and the flop response to genocide in Darfur and the tsunami, but that's all the more reason why America needs to be able to build consensus for much-needed reforms. The problem with that seductive line is that most of the proposed reforms are likely to make things worse. For most of its leading members, the organization is not a reflection of geopolitical reality but a substitute for it. The UN is no longer a latter-day Congress of Vienna, a permanent talking-shop for the world's powers, but instead an alternative power in and of itself—a sort of ersatz superpower intended to counter the real one. Look at the eighty-five yes-or-no votes America made in the General Assembly in 2003:

- The Arab League members voted against the U.S. position 88.7 percent of the time.
- The ASEAN members voted against the U.S. position 84.5 percent of the time.
- The Islamic Conference members voted against the U.S. position 84.1 percent of the time.
- The African members voted against the U.S. position 83.8 percent of the time.
- The Non-Aligned Movement members voted against the U.S. position 82.7 percent of the time.
- And European Union members voted against the U.S. position 54.5 percent of the time.

Yay! Go, Europe, America's steadfast 45 percent friends! You can take the view of the European elites that this is proof of America's isolation and that the United States now needs to issue a "Declaration of Interdependence" with the world. Or you can be like the proud mom in Irving Berlin's Great War marching song: "They Were All Out of Step but Jim." But what the figures really demonstrate is that the logic of the post–Cold War UN is to be institutionally anti-American.

Washington could seize on the embarrassments of the Kofi Annan regime and lean hard on Turtle Bay to reform this and reorganize that and reinvent the other and, if they threw their full diplomatic muscle behind it, they might get those anti-U.S. votes down to—what, a tad over 80 percent? And along the way they'd find that they'd "reformed" a corrupt dysfunctional sclerotic anti-American club into a lean mean effectively functioning anti-American club. Which is, if they're honest, what most reformers mean by "reform."

Economic Power

The Sufi theologian and jurist al-Ghazali, regarded by many as the greatest Muslim after Mohammed, died a millennium ago but his words on the conduct of *dhimmis*—non-Muslims in Muslim society—seem pertinent today: "The dhimmi is obliged not to mention Allah or His Apostle. . . . Jews, Christians, and Majians must pay the jizya."

The *jizya* is the poll tax paid by non-Muslims to their Muslim betters. One cause of the lack of economic innovation in the Islamic world is that they've always placed the main funding burden of society on infidels. This goes back to Mohammed's day. If you take a bunch of warring Arab tribes and unite them as one *umma* under Allah, one drawback is that you close off a prime source of revenue—fighting each other and then stealing each other's stuff. That's why the Prophet, while hardly in a position to deny Islam to those who wished to sign up, was relatively relaxed about the presence of non-Muslim peoples within Muslim lands: they were a revenue stream. If one looks at their comparative dissemination patterns, Christianity spread by acquiring believers and then land; Islam spread by acquiring land and then believers. When Islam conquered infidel territory, it set in motion a massive transfer of wealth, enacting punitive taxation to transfer money from non-believers to Muslims—or from the productive part of the economy to the non-productive. It was, in its way, a prototype welfare society. When admirers talk up Islam and the great innovations and rich culture of its heyday, they forget that even at its height Muslims were never more than a minority in the Muslim world, and they were in large part living off the energy of others. That's still a useful rule of thumb: if you take the least worst Muslim societies, the reason for their dynamism often lies with whichever group they share the turf with—the Chinese in Malaysia, for example.

But eventually almost all Muslim societies tend toward the economically moribund, if only because an ever-shrinking infidel base eventually wises up. You can see it literally in the landscape in rural parts of the Balkans: Christian tradesmen got fed up paying the *jizya* and moved out of the towns up into remote hills. In other parts of the world, non-Muslims found it easier to convert. That's in part what drove Islamic expansion. Once Araby was all-Muslim, it was necessary to move on to the Levant, and to Persia, and to Central Asia and North Africa and India and Europe—in search of new infidels from which to extract the *jizya*. As engines of growth, the Muslim world and the European Union suffer a similar flaw: both encourage defections to the non-productive segment of the economy.

But the Muslim world has effortlessly extended the concept of *jizya* worldwide. If you're on the receiving end, it's possible to see the American, European, and Israeli subsidies of the Palestinian Authority as a form of *jizya*. Or even the billions of dollars Washington has lavished on Egypt, to such little effect (other than Mohammed Atta coming through the window). Not to mention every twenty bucks you put in the gas tank. The telegram has been replaced by the e-mail and the victrola has yielded to the CD player, but, aside from losing the rumble seat and adding a few cupholders, the automobile is essentially unchanged from a century ago. If you can't sell the country on the need for new energy sources when your present ones are funding your enemies, when can you?

Yet, five years on from September 11 and after a torrent of information on Saudi funding of the jihad, America had changed its policy to Riyadh only to this degree: we're lavishing even more dough on them than we did before.

The oil revenue collected by the House of Saud not only buys off their subjects but buys up other countries' subjects around the world. Americans are paying for the rope that will hang them.

Information Power

The fifth element of national power—"information"—speaks for itself, incessantly: the *New York Times*, CNN, Hollywood, the universities, Michael Moore...—i.e., quagmire, Islamophobia, BUSH LIED!!!!!, "exit strategy."

In World War Two, the sands of Iwo Jima were the main event, and rounding up enemy sympathizers in Michigan was the sideshow. One can argue that this time around the priorities are reversed—that bombing Baby Assad out of the presidential palace in Damascus is a more marginal battlefield than turning back the tide of Islamist support in Europe and elsewhere. America and a select few other countries have demonstrated they can just about summon the "war will" on the battlefield. On the cultural front, where this war in the end will be won, there's little evidence of any kind of will. If you look at the United Kingdom and the impunity with which imams like Abu Hamza incite treason, it requires a perverse genius on the part of Tony Blair to have found the political courage to fight an unpopular war on a distant shore but not the political courage to wage it closer to home, where it would have commanded far more support. That's the sad lesson of July 7: Her Majesty's forces can police southern Iraq more effectively than southern England.

If this were World War One, with their fellows in one trench and us in ours facing them over some boggy piece of terrain, it would be over very quickly. Which the smarter Islamists have figured out. They know they can never win on the battlefield, but they figure there's an excellent chance they can drag things out until Western Civilization collapses in on itself and Islam inherits by default. An army is only one weapon a civilization wields, and the weapon of last resort, too. But when you add up those elements of national power—military, judicial, diplomatic, economic, informational—it's hard not to conclude that (as was said of the British after the fall of Singapore) at least four of those five guns are pointing in the wrong direction. The point of the media is to speak truth to (domestic) power, the point of transnationalism is to constrain American power, the point of law is to upgrade the defendant—and the upshot of economic power in a time of plenty is that every time you gas up you're funding an enemy who's flusher than he's been since the fall of Constantinople. Meanwhile, we fight the symptoms—the terror plots—but not the cause: the ideology. The self-imposed constraints of this war—legalistic, multilateral, politically correct—are clearer every day.

"Know your enemy," they say. They know us very well. Do we know them at all?

● ● ●

THE FAINTHEARTED HYPERPOWER

In 2003, Tony Blair spoke to the United States Congress. "As Britain knows," he said, "all predominant power seems for a time invincible but, in fact, it is transient. The question is: what do you leave behind?"

An excellent question. Today, three-sevenths of the G-7 major economies are nations of British descent. Of the twenty economies with the highest GDP per capita, no fewer than eleven are current or former realms of Her Britannic Majesty. And if you protest that most of those are pinprick colonial tax havens—Bermuda, the Caymans—okay, eliminate all territories with populations lower than twenty million and the top four is an Anglosphere sweep: the United States, United Kingdom, Canada, and Australia. The key regional players in almost every corner of the globe are British-derived—South Africa, India—and, even among the lesser players, as a general rule you're better off for having been exposed to British rule than not: try doing business in Indonesia rather than Malaysia, or Haiti rather than St. Lucia.

And of course the pre-eminent power of the age derives its political character from eighteenth-century British subjects who took English ideas a little further than the mother country was willing to go. As for the allegedly inevitable superpower of the coming century, if China ever does achieve that status, it will be because the People's Republic learned more from British Hong Kong than Hong Kong ever did from the Little Red Book. Sir John Cowperthwaite, the colony's transformative financial secretary in the sixties, can stake a better claim as the father of modern China than Chairman Mao, and, if Beijing weren't so twitchy about these things, his would be the face they'd plaster over all the banners in Tiananmen Square.

I point out the obvious because an Englishman never would. "While some nations suffer from folie de grandeur," wrote President Bush's former speechwriter David Frum a year or two back, "the British seem uniquely disposed to bad-mouth themselves." In the late sixties, Sir Richard Turnbull, high commissioner of Aden, remarked bleakly to Defense Secretary Denis Healey that the British Empire would be remembered for only two things—"the popularization of Association Football [soccer] and the term 'fuck off.'" Instead of their bizarre cultural self-flagellation, the British might usefully deploy the latter formulation toward those kinky Eurofetishists who think the future lies in liquidating English law, custom, and parliamentary democracy within the conglomeration of failed nation states that make up the European Union.

Britain was never an unrivaled colossus, even at its zenith. Yet today, in language, law, politics, business, and the wider culture, there is simply nothing comparable in scale or endurance to the Britannic inheritance.

We now live in the American moment. And, even if nobody's planning on leaving, the "what do you leave behind?" question is worth asking. How does America want to use its moment? What does it wish to bequeath the world?

Even to present the question in those terms feels vaguely un-American. The United States has an unmatched dominance that the British never enjoyed and that is historically unprecedented. Yet it remains a paradox: the non-imperial superpower. For good or ill, the American people don't have an imperialist bone in their body—as we saw, in fact, in post-liberation Iraq.

A week before the president's inaugural address in January 2005, I picked up the *Village Voice* for the first time in years. Couldn't resist the cover story: "The Eve of Destruction: George W. Bush's Four-Year Plan to Wreck the World."

If only. It's so easy to raise expectations at the beginning of a new presidential term. In the wake of September 11, the administration pledged itself to a long-overdue reversal of decades of misguided foreign policy that the Second Inaugural made explicit: Bush committed America to spreading freedom through the Muslim world—or, as a skeptical friend of mine phrased it, we're going to shove liberty down their throats whether they want it or not. It was presented as a kind of lo-carb, organic, environmentally friendly version of "the white man's burden."

But no country has ever seemed more burdened by it. It's America's world; she just doesn't want to live in it.

Almost as soon as American troops entered Iraq, Senate Democrats demanded to know what the "exit strategy" was. "Exit strategy" is a phrase that might have been designed as a textbook definition of lack of will. In war, there are usually only two exit strategies: victory or defeat. The latter's easier. Just say, whoa, we're the world's dominant power but we can't handle an unprecedently low level of casualties, so if you don't mind we'd just as soon get off at the next stop. Taking your ball and going home is a seductive argument in a paradoxical superpower whose inclinations on the Right have a strong isolationist streak and on the Left a strong transnational streak—which is isolationism with a sappy face and biennial black-tie banquets in EU capitals. Transnationalism means poseur solutions—the Kyotification of foreign policy.

For a serious power, the correct answer to "What's the exit strategy?" is: there isn't one, and there shouldn't be one, and it's a dumb expression. The more polite response came in the president's second inaugural speech: "The survival of liberty in our land increasingly depends on the success of liberty in other lands."

If you want an example of "exit strategy" thinking, look no further than the southern "border." A century ago, American policy in Mexico was all exit and no strategy. That week's president-for-life gets out of hand? Go in, whack him, exit, and let the locals figure out who gets to be the new bad guy. If the new guy gets out of hand, go back, whack him, and exit again. The result of that stunted policy is that three-quarters of Mexico's population is now living in California and Arizona—and, as fine upstanding members of the Undocumented American community, they've got no exit strategy at all. Judging from the placards brandished at the Million Mexican Marches held across the United States in 2006 ("Honkies, Why Don't You Take Your Asses Back to Europe?") many of them feel it's the Documented Americans who ought to be planning on an exit.

By contrast, the British went in to India without an exit strategy, stayed for generations, and midwifed the world's most populous democracy and a key U.S. ally in the years ahead. Which looks like the smarter approach now? Those American conservatives—the *realpolitik* crowd—who scorn "nation-building" ought to reflect on what the Indian subcontinent would look like if the British had been similarly skeptical: today, it might well be another Araby—a crazy quilt of authoritarian sultanates, Hindu and Muslim, punctuated by thug dictatorships following Baath-type local variations on Fascism and Marxism. It would be a profoundly unstable region with a swollen uneducated citizenry of little use for call centers or tech support. Any American who's found himself at three in the morning talking to Suresh or Rajiv in customer service will appreciate the benefits of an Indian education. He can thank Lord Macaulay and his famous 1835 government memo on the subject for that: London dispatched generations of English, Scots, and Irish schoolma'ams and masters to obscure outposts of empire because they thought that by introducing them to Shakespeare and the Magna Carta and Sir Isaac Newton they were effectively giving their colonial subjects a passport to the modern world.

Failed states destabilize their neighbors, and Americans don't have to pore over maps of West Africa to figure that out. Insofar as four of the September 11 killers obtained the picture ID with which they boarded their flights that morning through the support network for "undocumented" workers, it's not unreasonable to argue that, if you're looking for really deep "root causes" for what happened that day, you could easily start with America's failure to nation-build in Mexico. And the problem with "exit strategy" fetishization is that these days everywhere's Mexico—literally, in the sense that the September 11 killers were part of the Undocumented American community, and more figuratively in the sense that if you've got a few hundred bucks and an ATM card you can come to America and blow it up. Everyone lives next door now.

The United States, almost in inverse proportion to its economic and military might, is culturally isolated. I know, I know—you've read a thousand articles about America's "cultural imperialism." And that's fine if you mean you can fly around the world and eat at McDonald's, dress at the Gap, listen to Hilary Duff, and go see *Charlie's Angels 3* or *Dude, Where's My Car? 7* pretty much anywhere on the planet. But so what? *The Merry Widow* was both a blockbuster sensation on Broadway and Hitler's favorite operetta. If I sent my profile in to the average computer dating agency, they'd fix me up with Saddam Hussein: he and I have the same favorite singer (Frank Sinatra) and favorite candy (Britain's Quality Street toffees). It's not enough. You can easily like American pop culture without liking America: in London, the broadsheet newspapers that devote most space to U.S. cultural trends—the *Guardian*, the *Independent*—are the most vehemently anti-American. Then again, if you despise America's trash pop culture, it'll make you despise America even more. Thus Jean-Pierre Chevènement, former French foreign minister, and his celebrated assertion that the United States is dedicated to "the organized cretinization of our people"—a claim that's a lot more persuasive if you've never had the misfortune to sit through a weekend of French TV. In 2002, there was a shoot-out in a French town hall by some left-wing eco-loon, and one of the country's presidential candidates, Alain Madelin, deplored it as an "American-style by-product." One Frenchman kills eight other Frenchman and somehow it's proof of America's malign cultural influence.

You can sort of see what he's getting at. With very few exceptions, wherever you live in the world the landscape of the imagination is America: in the movie in your mind, the car chase takes place on the Los Angeles freeway, the love scene in Central Park, the massive explosion at the World Trade Center. The world watches Hollywood's America in a kind of post-neutron-bombed way: you get the sex and drugs and rock n' roll, the shoot-outs and fireballs, but the spirit of the country remains as foreign as ever. This is not a healthy phenomenon. On the things that matter—which, no disrespect, Hilary Duff doesn't—the gap between America and the rest of the world is wider than ever. If you define "cultural dominance" as cheeseburgers, America rules. But in the bigger cultural sense, it's a taste most of the world declines to pick up.

"Europe and America," said George W. Bush in Ireland in 2004, "are linked by the ties of family, friendship, and common struggle and common values." If so, the president and many other Americans have an all too common struggle articulating what those common values are. In Prague in 2002, Mr. Bush told fellow NATO members, "We share common values—the common values of freedom, human rights, and democracy."

Big deal. In a post-Communist world, these are vague, unobjectionable generalities to everyone except the head hackers in the Sunni Triangle. The "common values" stuff is the transnational equivalent of "Have a nice day." It's when you try to flesh it out that it all gets more complicated. The United States spends 3.4 percent of GDP on defense, the other NATO members spend on average 1.9 percent. So, if they do share "common values," Europe's prepared to spend a lot less defending them. On a raft of other issues, from guns to religion, America is also the exception. In North American terms, it's Canadian ideas, from socialized health care to confiscatory taxation, that are now the norm in the other Western democracies and, alas, in many of the emerging democracies.

The raucousness of American pop culture—jazz, showgirls, hard-boiled cops—belies the hyperpower's geopolitical circumspection. And, on the receiving end, the Americanization of global pop culture puts a greater premium on being un-American in every other respect. Almost all the supranational bodies—from the EU to the International Criminal Court—are, if not explicitly hostile to American values, at the very least antipathetic to them. In the face of this rejection of the broader American culture, the popularity of Brad Pitt and Angelina Jolie isn't much consolation. Britain exported its language, law, and institutions around the world to the point where today there are dozens of countries whose political and legal cultures derive principally from London. On islands from the Caribbean to the South Pacific, you can find miniature Westminsters proudly displaying their maces and Hansards. But if England is the mother of parliaments, America's a wealthy spinster with no urge to start dating. Of all the new nations that have come to independence since 1945 not one has adopted the American system of republican decentralized federalism—even though it's arguably the most successful ever invented.

The United States has zero interest in empire, for obvious reasons. For one thing, it's already as big as an empire, and most countries that controlled that big a land mass would probably run it in imperial fashion. Instead, America took a federation designed for a baker's dozen of ethnically homogeneous East Coast colonies and successively applied it across the continent and halfway over the Pacific. It's not strictly true that the sun never sets on the American Republic, but it's up an awful lot of the time.

Beyond that, Americans are deeply suspicious of the notion that you can swan around the world "giving" freedom to people. They have to want it, like the first Americans did—as we say in New Hampshire, live free or die. If the Iraqis want a free society badly enough, they'll stick with it; if they don't and they take the easy option of falling for some puffed-up strongman, that's their problem, not America's.

While this might be philosophically admirable, the practical drawback is that power abhors a vacuum. If America won't export its values— self-reliance, decentralization—others will export theirs. In the eighties, Paul Kennedy warned the United States of "imperial overstretch." But the danger right now is of imperial understretch—of a hyperpower reluctant to sell its indisputably successful inheritance to the rest of the world.

After Mao's victory, America's anti-Communists famously demanded to know, "Who lost China?"

Answer: Nobody. China wasn't lost. Chiang Kai-shek had never won it in the first place. He was merely an early beneficiary of American foreign policy's faith in unreal *realpolitik*—the system embodied in the cynical line that so-and-so may be a sonofabitch but he's our sonofabitch. In the case of Mubarak, the House of Saud, and many others, the obverse is more to the point: he may be our sonofabitch but in the end he's a sonofabitch. Even if it wasn't licensing anti-Americanism as a safety valve for what might otherwise be more locally directed grievances, the Cairo government would not be a meaningful friend. There's a huge difference between having a regime as an ally and having a nation as one, the difference being Egypt's Mohammed Atta and fifteen Saudi citizens flying through the windows of the World Trade Center and the Pentagon— which suggests considerable limitations to the theory that, as long as

America gets along fine with President Mubarak and key Saudi princes, it doesn't matter if everyone else in Egypt and Saudi Arabia is shouting "Death to the Great Satan!" That, too, is a lesson in demography.

So instead of waiting ten years and demanding to know "Who lost Japan? Who lost Russia? And Europe? Oh, and who lost Britain?" analysts might be better advised to ponder why a supposed moment of unprecedented unipolar dominance doesn't feel like it.

Most Americans are familiar with their stereotype abroad: the ugly American, loud, brash, ignorant, arrogant. It is, in most respects, the inversion of reality: America may be the most modest and retiring hegemon in history. "You're either with us or you're with the terrorists"? Most of America's European "allies" checked the Neither of the Above box and most Middle Eastern "allies" checked the Both of the Above box. Belgium isn't exactly with the terrorists but it isn't with us in any meaningful sense. Saudi Arabia is with us but also funding the terrorists in every corner of the world. And both countries get away with it.

America has huge advantages. On the Continent, the Euroconsensus is shrinking both its economy and its population; America is managing to grow both. Why then project American power through transnational institutions disproportionately in thrall to European ideas? Especially when the one consistent feature of twenty-first century politics is the comprehensive failure of the over-Europeanized international order: UN staff facilitates Saddam's subversion of the Oil-for-Food program; the EU subsidizes the Palestinian intifada; the International Atomic Energy Agency provides cover for Iran's nuclear ambitions; the UN summit on racism is a grotesque orgy of racism. As we've learned since September 11, if there is a "white man's burden" in the early twenty-first century, it's not the burden of doing one's bit for the natives, but doing so under a hail of continual sniping from Chirac, Schröder, the Belgian guy, Kofi, Oxfam, the BBC, and a gazillion others. There's something a little bizarre about a so-called unipolar world in which it's the unipole that gets shafted every time.

And, as the various local demographic adjustments start to take effect, America is in danger of finding itself in the same lonely camp as

Israel. Nudge things half a decade down the road. There'll be an informal Islamo-veto over many areas of French and European policy. Russia and China have already determined that, whatever their own little local difficulties with Muslims, their long-term strategic interest lies in keeping the jihad as an American problem. The internal logic of the demographic shifts will be to make much of the world figure it makes sense to be on the side America's not.

Al Qaeda thinks it's got America pegged—an effete, fleshy sultan sprawled languorously on overstuffed cushions, lost in sensual distractions. The choice for the United States is between those who believe America can take the lead in shaping the times and those who think the most powerful nation in human history can simply climb in the Suburban and go to the mall for its entire period of dominance. That's what the great Democratic Party all-purpose "multilateral" cure-all for United States foreign policy boils down to: "We need to hand power back to the UN. Or the EU. Or the Arab League. Or the Deputy Fisheries Minister of the Turks and Caicos Islands." Or as Thomas Friedman, the hilariously tortured foreign-policy grandee of the *New York Times*, agonized: "Mr. Bush needs to invite to Camp David the five permanent members of the UN Security Council, the heads of both NATO and the UN, and the leaders of Egypt, Jordan, Saudi Arabia, and Syria. There, he needs to eat crow, apologize for his mistakes," etc, etc.

Why would it be in America's interest to inflate the prestige of Boy Assad and Mubarak? This lame-o multilateral outsourcing is the geopolitical equivalent of subcontracting your lawn care to "undocumented" immigrants: here you are, we don't mind giving you the money, just take care of it, we don't want to know the details, we want to go back to watching *American Idol*. Is foreign policy just another one of those "jobs Americans won't do"?

"Common values" and "universal values" are not all that common and universal, and the willingness to defend those values is even rarer. They've been sustained over the long haul by a very small group of countries. In the years ahead, America has to take the American moment seriously—in part, to ensure that the allies of tomorrow don't make the mistakes Western Europe did. That means at the very minimum something beyond cheeseburger imperialism. In the end, the world can do without American rap and American cheeseburgers. American ideas on individual liberty, federalism, capitalism, and freedom of speech would be far more helpful.

In 2004, Goh Chok Tong, the prime minister of Singapore and a man who talks a lot more sense than most Continental prime ministers, visited Washington at the height of the Democrats' headless-chicken quagmire frenzy. He put it in a nutshell: "The key issue is no longer WMD or even the role of the UN. The central issue is America's credibility and will to prevail."

The prime minister of Singapore apparently understands that more clearly than many Americans.

Chapter Nine

The Importance of Being Exceptional

CITIZENS VS. DEPENDENTS

Were I a Kerry voter, though, I'd feel deep anger, not only at them returning Bush to power, but for allowing the outside world to lump us all into the same category of moronic muppets. The self-righteous, gun-totin', military-lovin', sister-marryin', abortion-hatin', gay-loathin', foreigner-despisin', non–passport ownin' red-necks, who believe God gave America the biggest dick in the world so it could urinate on the rest of us and make their land "free and strong."

BRIAN READE, *DAILY MIRROR* (LONDON), NOVEMBER 5, 2004

In the film *Superman Returns*, Superman returns—to fight not for "truth, justice, and the American way" but instead for "truth, justice, and all that stuff." In the not so subtle elision from "the American way" to "all that stuff" much peril lies. "The American way" is human and thus imperfect, but the European way leaves you well and truly stuffed, like a dead parrot after a trip to the taxidermist. In the end, hard wars are won on the hardest ground—at home. Whatever changes America makes in its foreign policy and transnational relationships, the home front is critical. You can't win a war of civilizational confidence with a population of nanny-state junkies. Take Brian Reade's list of American deformities—gun-totin', sister-marryin', foreigner-despisin', etc. It goes without saying that that's why I supported Bush in 2004, but I'm not sure it entirely accounts for the other 62,039,073 urinating rednecks. Mr. Reade, though, does usefully enumerate the distinctions that separate the American republic from the rest of the West, differences that will become even more important in the years ahead.

1. Self-righteous

Who exactly is being self-righteous here? If you want a public culture that reeks of indestructible faith in its own righteousness, try Europe—especially when they're talking about America: if you disagree with Euro-conventional wisdom, you must be an idiot. Or a Nazi. As Oliver James told the *Guardian* the day after the 2004 U.S. elections, "I was too depressed to even speak this morning. I thought of my late mother, who read *Mein Kampf* when it came out in the 1930s [sic] and thought, 'Why doesn't anyone see where this is leading?'"

Mr. James is a clinical psychologist and appears to have a bad case of projection. With respect to *Mein Kampf*, it's Europe that has resurgent anti-Semitism (the French intifada), explicitly racist parties (the British National Party), and neo-Fascists who, if not yet their countries' leaders, have gotten near enough to be in the presidential run-off (Jean-Marie Le Pen) or form part of the governing coalition (Austria).

2. Gun-totin'

Americans tote guns because they're assertive, self-reliant citizens, not docile subjects of a permanent governing class. At dinner in Paris a couple of years ago, I was asked about "this American sickness with guns."

"Americans have guns," I said, "because a lot of Americans like having guns."

My host scoffed. "A lot of people here would like to have guns too. But they don't."

"Exactly," I said.

3. Military-lovin'

What's not to love? Americans take pride in their military on absolute grounds, but, if they were to go all comparative about it, they'd point out there's something contemptible about Europeans preening and posing as a great power when they can't even stop some nickel n' dime Balkan genital-severers piling up hundreds of thousands of corpses on their borders.

4. Sister-marryin'

Back to demography: you can't be a redneck in Germany, Spain, or Italy. When the birth rates are 1.1 children per couple, there are no sisters to bunk up with.

5. Abortion-hatin'

Is Brian Reade saying he loves it? Abortion is one manifestation of what John Paul II called the reduction of sexuality into an "instrument for self-assertion." Mr. Reade might respond, "Yeah, that's what's so great about it!" But whatever one's tastes in this area, as the pope understood, sex as mere self-assertion is a dead end. If the progressives either abort or decline to conceive their progeny, the progeny of the redneck knuckle-draggers will be the only fellows around.

6. Gay-loathin'

More projection. It's Amsterdam where the poor gay guys now have to watch what street they turn down. It's Paris where the gay mayor was stabbed by a gay-loathin' Muslim. Homophobia-wise, America's funda-mentalist Christians have nothing on Europe's fundamentalist Muslims.

7. Foreigner-despisin' non–passport ownin'

The only despisin' of foreigners that's going on here seems to be by Europeans toward Americans. Recall Margaret Drabble's diatribe from the beginning of this book. We only skimmed the surface:

> My anti-Americanism has become almost uncontrollable. It has possessed me, like a disease. It rises up in my throat like acid reflux, that fashionable American sickness. I now loathe the United States and what it has done to Iraq and the rest of the helpless world. I can hardly bear to see the faces of Bush and Rumsfeld, or to watch their posturing body language, or to hear their self-satisfied and incoherent platitudes.

Etc. When one examines Brian Reade's anatomy of redneck disfigurements most of them are about the will to survive, as individuals and as a society. If one were to formulate it less disapprovingly, "self-righteous, gun-totin', military-lovin', sister-marryin', abortion-hatin', gay-loathin', foreigner-despisin', non–passport ownin' red-necks" equals "culturally confident, self-reliant, patriotic, procreative, religious, democratic, constitutional rednecks who believe in national sovereignty rather than ineffectual poseur multilateralism."

As for Mr. Reade's bit about "the biggest dick in the world so it could urinate on the rest of us"—if it bothers you that much, why not try urinating back? Ah, but in Europe it seems even that simple act is in the process of being feminized. *Stehpinkeln*—standing while urinating—is disapproved of in Germany, to the point where toilets can now be fitted with voice alarms triggered when the seat is raised. "Hey, stand-peeing is not allowed here and will be punished with fines, so if you don't want any trouble, you'd best sit down," orders the "toilet ghost" in a voice that imitates former chancellor Gerhard Schröder.

The notion of German government leaders commanding you in the privacy of your own home to urinate like a woman seems almost too poignant an image of the peculiarly European blend of state-enforced docility. In contrast to the swaggering Texan cowboy, it's the Last Stand of the EU-Corraled. Yet millions of these devices have been sold and

Klaus Schwerma has written a book on the phenomenon called *Steh-pinkeln: Die Letzte Bastion der Männlichkeit?*—or "Standing Urinators: The Last Bastion of Masculinity?"

This hardly seems the time to open up yet more unbridgeable cultural divides between the Old World and the New. The British TV historian Simon Schama defined the Bush/Kerry divide as "Godly America" and "Worldly America," hailing the latter as "pragmatic, practical, rational, and skeptical"—which is, naturally, exactly the wrong way around: it's the Christian fundamentalists, Holy Rollers, born-again Bible Belters, and Jesus freaks of Godly America who are rational and skeptical, especially of Euro-delusions. It's secular Europe that's living on faith. Uncowed by Islamists, undeferential to government, unshriveled in its birth rates, redneck America is a more reliable long-term bet.

● ● ●

THE PASTEURIZATION IS PROLOGUE

Lest you think this is veering close to the jingoistic xenophobia deplored by America's East Coast media, let me do a bit of America-bashing. The softening and feminization of the Western world isn't merely a matter of gun confiscation. I've never been one of those Americans who's just plain old anti-foreigner—mainly because I'm not an American, I'm a foreigner. And so I'm quite partial to foreigners, apart from myself. I blush to say it but I like French food, I like French coffee, I like French women. To be honest, I'd rather see some interminable French movie where Isabelle Adjani or Isabelle Huppert or pretty much any other Isabelle sits naked on the end of the bed smoking a cigarette and discussing with her husband how each of their affairs are going than watch Arnold Schwarzenegger in *Terminator XII*. Please don't throw the book away in disgust until after you've paid for it. I've never subscribed to that whole "cheese-eating surrender-monkey" sneer promoted by my *National Review* colleague Jonah Goldberg. As a neocon warmonger, I yield to no one in my contempt for the French, but that said, cheese-wise I feel they have the edge.

When I'm at the lunch counter in America and I order a cheese-burger and the waitress says, "American, Swiss, or cheddar?" I can't tell the difference. They all taste of nothing. The only difference is that the slice of alleged Swiss is full of holes, so you're getting less nothing for your buck. Then again, the holes also taste of nothing, and they're less fattening. But either way, cheese is not the battleground on which to demonstrate the superiority of the American way. In America, unpas-teurized un-aged raw cheese that would be standard in any Continental *fromagerie* is banned. Americans, so zealous in defense of their liberties when it comes to guns, are happy to roll over for the nanny state when it comes to the cheese board.

Personally, I want it all: assault weapons and Camembert, guns and butter and all the other dairy products that U.S. big-government federal regulation has destroyed the taste of. The French may be surrender mon-keys on the battlefield, but they don't throw their hands up and flee in ter-ror just because the Brie's a bit ripe. It's the Americans who are the cheese-surrendering eating-monkeys, who insist that the only way to deal with this sliver of Roquefort is to set up a rigorous ongoing Hans Blix–type inspections regime. France, for all its faults, has genuinely federalized food: a distinctive cheese every twenty miles down the road. In America, mean-while, the food nannies are lobbying to pass something called the National Uniformity for Food Act. There's way too much of that already.

The federalization of food may seem peripheral to national security issues, and the taste of American milk—compared with its French or English or even Quebecois equivalents—may seem a small loss. But take almost any area of American life: what's the more common approach nowadays? The excessive government regulation exemplified by American cheese or the spirit of self-reliance embodied in the Sec-ond Amendment? On a whole raft of issues from health care to educa-tion the United States is trending in an alarmingly *fromage*-like direction. As they almost say in New Hampshire, live Brie or die. Amer-icans should understand that the softening of a state happens incremen-tally. You can reach the same point as the Europeans by routes other than gun confiscation.

Could America wind up as just another enervated present-tense Western nation? Well, it's halfway there. I've no wish to be "partisan." Not because attacking the Democrats is, as the media say, "mean-spirited," but because the Democrats have chosen to make themselves all but irrelevant to the great questions of the age. You can understand why the Dems miss the nineties. There was nary a word about war. Okay, you'd get the odd million-man genocide in Rwanda, but you tended to hear about it afterward, usually as a late-breaking item in the Clinton teary-apology act. Instead, it was an era of micro-politics, a regulation here, an entitlement there, a bike path and a recycling program everywhere you looked. Venusian Americans assumed they'd entered an age of permanent post-Martian politics, and they resented September 11 as an intrusion on their minimalism. When you're at an event for the "antiwar" movement, you realize it's no such thing: it's an I-don't-want-to-have-to-hear-about-this-war movement. So they mock Bush, Cheney, Rummy, and Co. as the real terrorists—the ones determined to maintain America in a state of "terror." Oddly enough, this was how the Left chose to live during the Cold War, when the no-nukes crowd expected Armageddon any minute. If you believe in a two-party system, in the end even the integrity of the dominant party isn't served by the self-marginalization of the only alternative: the Democratic Party needs to get back in the game. But to do that they've got to get over the bike-path micro-politics and back on the unlovely central thruway of geopolitical reality.

● ● ●

MY WAY OR THE HIGHWAY

Conservatives, on the other hand, embrace big government at their peril. The silliest thing Dick Cheney ever said was a couple of weeks after September 11: "One of the things that's changed so much since September 11 is the extent to which people do trust the government—big shift—and value it, and have high expectations for what we can do." Really? I'd say September 11 vindicated perfectly a decentralized, federalist, conservative view of the state: what worked that day was municipal government, small government, core government—the firemen, the NYPD cops, rescue workers. What flopped—big-time, as the vice president would say—was federal government, the FBI, CIA, INS, FAA, and all the other hotshot, money-no-object, fancypants acronyms. Under the system operating on that day, if one of the many Algerian terrorists living on welfare in Montreal attempted to cross the U.S. border at Derby Line, Vermont, and got refused entry by an alert official, he would be able to drive a few miles east, attempt to cross at Beecher Falls, Vermont, and they had no way of knowing that he'd been refused entry just half an hour earlier. No compatible computers. Yet, if that same Algerian terrorist went to order a book online, Amazon.com would know that he'd bought *The A-Z of Infidel Slaying* two years earlier and their "We have some suggestions for you!" box would be proffering a 30 percent discount on *Suicide Bombing for Dummies*. Amazon is a more efficient data miner than U.S. Immigration. Is it to do with their respective budgets? No. Amazon's system is very cheap, but it's in the nature of government to do things worse, and slower.

Here's another example of Dick Cheney's government—the one we "trust and value and have high expectations for"—from the morning of September 11:

> FAA Command Center: Do we want to think about scrambling
>   aircraft?
> FAA Headquarters: God, I don't know.
> FAA Command Center: That's a decision somebody's going to
>   have to make, probably in the next ten minutes.
> FAA Headquarters: You know, everybody just left the room.

Most of what went wrong on September 11 we knew about in the first days after. Generally, it falls into two categories:

1. Government agencies didn't enforce their own rules (as in the terrorists' laughably inadequate visa applications).

or

> 2. The agencies' rules were out of date—three out of those four planes reached their targets because their crews, passengers, and ground staff all blindly followed the FAA's 1970s hijack procedures until it was too late, as the terrorists knew they would.

The next time a terrorist gets through and pulls off an attack, it will be for the same reasons: there'll be a bunch of new post–September 11 regulations, and some bureaucrat somewhere will have neglected to follow them, or some wily Islamist will have rendered them as obsolete as his predecessors made all those thirty-year-old hijack rules. That's an abiding feature of government: 90 percent of its ever-proliferating agencies just aren't very good, and if you put your life in their hands, more fool you.

But, on the fourth plane, they didn't follow the seventies hijack rituals. On Flight 93, they used their cell phones, discovered that FAA regulations weren't going to save them, and then acted as free men, rising up against the terrorists and, at the cost of their own lives, preventing that flight carrying on to its target in Washington. On a morning when big government failed, the only good news came from private individuals. The first three planes were effectively an airborne European Union, where the rights of the citizens had been appropriated by the FAA's flying nanny state. Up there where the air is rarified, all your liberties have been regulated away: there's no smoking, there's 100 percent gun control, you're obliged by law to do everything the cabin crew tell you; if the stewardess—whoops, sorry—if the flight attendant's rude to you, tough; if you're rude back, you'll be arrested on landing. For thirty years, passengers surrendered more and more rights for the illusion of security, and, as a result, thousands died. On the fourth plane, Todd Beamer and others reclaimed those rights and demonstrated that they could exercise them more efficiently than government. The Cult of Regulation failed, but the great American virtues of self-reliance and innovation saved the lives of thousands: "Let's roll!" as Mr. Beamer told his fellow passengers.

By contrast, on March 11, 2002, six months to the day after Mohammed Atta and Marwan al-Shehhi died flying their respective planes into World Trade Center Tower One and Tower Two, their flight school in Florida received a letter from the Immigration and Naturalization Service informing it that Mr. Atta and Mr. al-Shehhi's student visas had been approved. Even killing thousands of people wasn't enough to impede Mr. Atta's smooth progress through a lethargic bureaucracy. And the bureaucrats' defense—which boiled down to: don't worry, we're only issuing visas to famous dead terrorists, not obscure living ones—is one that Americans largely have to take on trust. A furious President Bush insisted that the INS take decisive action against those responsible, which it did, moving Janis Sposato "sideways" to the post of "Assistant Deputy Executive Associate Commissioner for Immigration Services." I don't know what post she was moved sideways from—possibly Associate Executive Deputy Assistant Commissioner. Happily, since then, the INS has changed its name to some other acronym and ordered up a whole new set of business cards, extra-large if Ms. Sposato's title is anything to go by.

Given the difficulty of reforming the torpid bureaucratic culture, the best we can hope for is to constrain its size—and leave enough space so that a nimble and innovative citizenry don't degenerate into mere subjects of an overbearing state. In 2004, *Wired* magazine ran an interesting featurette about a fellow called Hans Monderman, a highway engineer in northern Holland for the previous three decades. A year or two back, he'd had an epiphany. As *Wired*'s Tom McNichol puts it: "Build roads that seem dangerous, and they'll be safer."

In other words, all the stuff on the streets—signs for everything every five yards, yellow lines, pedestrian crossings, stoplights, crash barriers, bike lanes—all that junk clogging up the highway, by giving you the illusion of security, in fact makes driving more dangerous. The town of Christianfield in Denmark embraced the Monderman philosophy, removed all the traffic signs and signals from its most dangerous intersection, and thereby cut the number of serious accidents down to zero. These days, when you tootle toward the junction, there's no instructions from the Department of Transportation to tell you what to do. You have to figure it out for yourself, so you approach it cautiously and with an eye on what the other chaps in the vicinity are up to.

Mr. Monderman's thesis feels right to me—that by creating the illusion of security you relieve the citizen of the need to make his own judgments. Howard Zinn, in his introduction to Cindy Sheehan's book *Dear President Bush*, pens this paean to the plucky underdog: "A box-cutter can bring down a tower. A poem can build up a movement. A pamphlet can spark a revolution."

But the only reason "a box-cutter can bring down a tower" is because on September 11 our defenses against such a threat were exclusively the province of the state. If nineteen punks with box-cutters had tried to pull some stunt in the parking lot of a sports bar, they'd have been beaten to a pulp. The airline cabin, however, is the most advanced model of the modern social-democratic state, the sky-high version of the wildest dreams of big government; it's Massachusetts in cloud-cuckoo land. So on September 11 on those first three flights the cabin crews followed all those Federal Aviation Administration guidelines from the seventies. By the time the fourth plane got into trouble, the passengers knew the government wasn't up there with them. And, within ninety minutes of the first flight hitting the tower, the heroes of Flight 93 had figured out what was going on and came up with a way to stop it.

That's been my basic rule of thumb since September 11: anything that shifts power from the individual judgment of free citizens to government is a bad thing, not just for the war on terror but for the national character in a more general sense. Charles Clarke, formerly Britain's home secretary, gave a revealing glimpse into the big-government mentality in a column for the *Times* defending the latest allegedly necessary security measure: "ID cards will potentially make a difference to any area of everyday life where you already have to prove your identity—such as opening a bank account, going abroad on holiday, claiming a benefit, buying goods on credit and renting a video."

"Renting a video"? That sounds about right. When you go to Blockbuster, you'll need your national ID card. But if you're an Algerian terrorist cell coming in on the Eurostar from Paris to blow up Big Ben, you

won't. And its requirement for the routine transactions of daily life—
"opening a bank account...buying goods on credit"—will have the
same impact as all those street signs and traffic lights at that Danish
intersection: it will relieve bank managers and store clerks of the need to
use their own judgment in assessing the situation. You'd have to have an
awful lot of faith in government to think that's a good thing.

Britain's religious "hate crimes" law is another example of excessive
street signage applied to the byways of society. It attempts to supplant
human judgment with government management: the multicultural state
is working out so well that we can no longer be trusted to regulate our
own interactions with our neighbors. Islam, unlike Anglicanism, is an
explicitly political project: sharia is a legal system, but, unlike English
Common Law or the Napoleonic Code, for the purposes of public debate
it will henceforth enjoy the special protection of Her Majesty's Government. Given that the emerging Muslim lobby groups are already the
McDonald's coffee plaintiff of ethno-cultural grievance-mongers, you can
be certain they'll make full use of any new law. Political debate in Europe
is already hedged in by excessive squeamishness: Holland's "immigration
problem" is a Muslim problem, France's "youth problem" is a Muslim
problem, the "terrorism threat" that necessitates those British ID cards
is in reality an Islamic threat. How is preventing honest discussion of the
issue going to make citizens any safer? The term "nanny state" hardly
covers a society where you need retinal-scan ID in order to rent *Mary
Poppins* but you're liable for prosecution if you express your feelings too
strongly after the next bombing.

●   ●   ●

CRADLE TO GRAVE

Restoring the balance between the state and the citizen is most urgent
when it comes to reversing the biggest structural defect of the developed
world. You'll recall that during the Iraq war, we heard a lot of talk
about ancient Mesopotamia—the land of the Sumerians, Akkadians, and

Hittites—being "the cradle of civilization." That's a very pertinent for-mulation: without a cradle, it's hard to sustain a civilization. Demography is not necessarily destiny: today's high Muslim birth rates will fall, and probably fall dramatically, as the Catholic birth rates in Italy and Quebec have. But it's no consolation that Muslim birth rates will be as bad as yours in 2050 if yours are off the cliff right now. The last people around in any numbers will determine the kind of society we live in, and right now the last people around Europe will be Muslim.

For many nations, it's already too late. As Romania and other Com-munist countries belatedly discovered, even a repressive dictatorship has a hard job coercing the populace into breeding once they've lost the habit. When I've mentioned the birth dearth in newspaper columns on abortion, pro-"choice" readers have insisted it's due to other factors—the generally declining fertility rates that affect all materially prosperous societies, or the high taxes that make large families prohibitively expen-sive in materially prosperous societies. But this is a bit like arguing over which came first, the chicken or the egg—or, in this case, which came first, the lack of eggs or the scraggy old chicken-necked women desper-ate for one designer baby at the age of forty-eight. Whether or not Rus-sia, Japan, and Europe's fertility woes derive from abortion, what should be obvious is that the way the abortion issue is posited—as an issue of personal choice—is in and of itself symptomatic of the existential crisis of the dying West. In a traditional society—a seventeenth-century farm-ing village, say—children are an advantage, not just economically but in more general social ways. We're not doing a lot of seventeenth-century farming these days, so we need to find a way to restore advantage to par-enthood in the context of a modern society.

All we know is that the modern social-democratic state is not the answer. The EU figures it needs another fifty million immigrants in the next few years just to maintain a big enough working population to fund the lavish social programs its vast retired army of baby boomers expects to enjoy. And the only available sources of immigrants are North Africa and the Middle East. Whether these are the chaps to keep Pierre and Gerhard in the style to which they've become accustomed is highly doubtful: according to some Scandinavian statistics, 40 percent of those on welfare are immigrants. Elsewhere, the picture is similar: welfare regimes work a lot better for their Islamist beneficiaries than for native Continental ones.

When one contemplates the demographic catastrophe, it's easy to say, well, maybe we should reduce the tax burden on young fertile adults, make it easier for them to afford to buy a home and start a family. But the economic argument is, in the larger scheme, marginal. In traditional rural societies, children were a necessary insurance for one's old age: by the time you were too stooped and worn to plough the field and hunt for dinner, Junior would do it for you. Today, when you're stooped and worn (and, in fact, long before that point), the state steps in to take care of you. Reconnecting nanny-state populations with cross-generational solidarity requires much more than the marginal tax breaks the Portuguese government announced or the nine thousand bucks the Russian state is now offering for second children. The most important action in reacquainting individuals with a larger sense of life is the one that governments recoil from: shrink the state.

They could at least reorient as many benefits as possible toward children: In America, a lot of welfare is inadvertently natalist (albeit in not always helpful ways, like single motherhood) in the sense that for most of the big-time benefit gravy you need babies. But those nations farther down the death spiral will need to embrace serious uber-natalism: for example, if you've got four dependents, your taxable income ought to be divided by five; an employed man with a stay-at-home wife and three children pays a fifth of what an employed single man does. If they both earn $50,000, the swingin' bachelor pays tax on $50,000, which still leaves enough for him to hit the singles bars; the married stiff pays tax on $10,000, which makes a family affordable.

Another constraint on family size is available housing. Acre for acre, America is the cheapest developed country in which to buy a big home with plenty of space for plenty of kids. That helps explain why Canada's fertility rate is so European: partly for reasons of climate but partly because of more recent Trudeaupian social developments and immigration trends, the Northern Dominion's population is more concentrated than America's—i.e., more urban. If you were designing a "master plan" for Canada, you'd want to provide some way of encouraging still fecund young couples to move from their poky Toronto and Vancouver apartments to the great outdoors. In Western Europe, the cost of housing is extraordinarily high. Whenever I read about the ever-larger number of Italians in early middle age still living with mom and dad, I'm reminded of an old Benny Hill sketch in which he and his dolly bird are bikers who can't get public housing. The BBC interviewer says, "Why don't you move back in with your parents?" Benny grunts, "We would do, but they've moved back in with theirs."

That gets closer to the nub of the matter. It's not just a question of tax breaks and affordable housing. The chief characteristic of our age is "deferred adulthood." All over North America and Europe there are millions of people going to college for no good reason. Certainly, there's no reason why the sum of knowledge the average American has accumulated by the time he's completed a bachelor's degree should take twenty years to inculcate. We need to redirect the system to telescope education into a much shorter period. Instead, we've implicitly accepted that our bodies mature much earlier than our great-grandparents' but that our minds don't. We enter adolescence much sooner and leave it much later—in some cases, not until middle age. We've created a world where a thirty-one-year-old European male can stroll into a nightclub, tell the babes he lives at his mom and dad's place in the same bedroom he's slept in since he was in diapers—and he can still walk out with a hot-looking date. This guy would have been a laughingstock at any other point in human history.

The state and its citizens would be better off if we gave students a terrific high school education and then let 'em get on with earning money so they can afford to have two or three kids in their twenties instead of one fertility-treatment special delivery in late middle age. It won't be easy to do that, particularly in America, where schools are a bastion of over-unionization dedicated to expanding their privileges and protections at the expense of their pupils. But our refusal to rein in deferred adulthood is one reason why developed societies are ever more dependent on unsustainable levels of immigration. That includes the United States, where the Hispanicization of large parts of the country is setting up America for the most destabilizing aspects of bicultural and bilingual societies.

By 2015, almost every viable political party in the West will be natalist, and the cannier ones will be supporting policies—like a flat tax—that help restore the societal architecture vandalized by careless governmental social engineering. As much as Europe and Islamism, social and fiscal policy are now a matter of national survival. In the end, it's not about cash: after all, materialism and self-gratification are why Eutopians gave up on the future in the first place. The best reason to diminish social programs is not to put more money in people's pockets but to put more responsibility in people's pockets.

Because, if we don't, the unthinkable solutions are the only ones left.

In his final book, the distinguished British commentator Anthony Sampson claimed that after September 11 "the fear of terrorism strengthened the hands of all governments." It certainly shouldn't have. In Hans Monderman's Netherlands, they show some signs of acknowledging that the multiculti pieties of the last thirty years were a dangerous fantasy; in the rest of the developed world, they're still larding it on. If America is to avoid the Continent's fate, she needs to talk up self-reliance and individual innovation instead of being sheepish (as Democrats often sound) that their Neanderthal citizenry aren't more enlightened and European. Free citizens have a shot at winning this existential struggle; nanny-state charges don't. The road ahead will be difficult enough; cluttering it up with "no parking" signs isn't going to make it any safer.

Chapter Ten

The Falling Camel

LAST LEGS

Nature has made up her mind that what cannot defend itself shall not be defended.

RALPH WALDO EMERSON, *SOCIETY AND SOLITUDE* (1870)

This book isn't an argument for more war, more bombing, or more killing, but for more will. In a culturally confident age, the British in India were faced with the practice of "suttee"—the tradition of burning widows on the funeral pyres of their husbands. General Sir Charles Napier was impeccably multicultural: "You say that it is your custom to burn widows. Very well. We also have a custom: when men burn a woman alive, we tie a rope around their necks and we hang them. Build your funeral pyre; beside it, my carpenters will build a gallows. You may follow your custom. And then we will follow ours."

India today is better off without suttee. If you don't agree with that, if you think that's just dead-white-male Eurocentrism, fine. But I don't think you really do believe that. Non-judgmental multiculturalism is an obvious fraud, and was subliminally accepted on that basis. After all, most adherents to the idea that all cultures are equal don't want to live in anything but an advanced Western society. Multiculturalism means your kid has to learn some wretched tribal dirge for the school holiday concert instead of getting to sing "Rudolph the Red-Nosed Reindeer" or that your holistic masseuse uses techniques developed from Native American spirituality, but not that you or anyone you care about should have to live in an African or Native American society. It's a quintessential piece of progressive humbug. But if you think you genuinely believe that suttee is just an example of the rich, vibrant tapestry of indigenous cultures, you ought to consider what your pleasant suburb would be like if 25, 30, 48 percent of the people around you really believed in it too. Multiculturalism was conceived by the Western elites not to celebrate all cultures but to deny their own: it is, thus, the real suicide bomb.

The rest of us—the ones who think you can make judgments about competing cultures on liberty, religious freedom, the rule of law—need to recover the cultural cool that General Napier demonstrated.

Instead, as his first reaction to the controversy over those Danish cartoons, the EU's justice and security commissioner, Franco Frattini, said that Europe would set up a "media code" to encourage "prudence" in the way they cover, um, certain sensitive subjects. As Signor Frattini explained it to the *Daily Telegraph*, "The press will give the Muslim world the message: we are aware of the consequences of exercising the right of free expression.... We can and we are ready to self-regulate that right."

"Prudence"? "Self-regulate our free expression"? No, I'm afraid that's just giving the Muslim world the message: you've won, I surrender, please stop kicking me.

But they never do. Because, to use the Arabic proverb with which Robert Ferrigno opens his novel *Prayers for the Assassin*, "A falling camel attracts many knives." In Denmark and France, the Netherlands and Britain, Islam senses the camel is falling and this is no time to stop knifing him.

Or as Simeon Howard said in a sermon preached to the Ancient and Honorable Artillery Company in Boston in 1773:

> An incautious people may submit to these demands, one after another, till its liberty is irrecoverably gone, before they saw the danger. Injuries small in themselves, may in their consequences be fatal to those who submit to them; especially if they are persisted in. And, with respect to such injuries, we should ever act upon that ancient maxim of prudence; obsta principiis. The first unjust demands of an encroaching power should be firmly withstood, when there appears a disposition to repeat and encrease such demands. And oftentimes it may be both the right and duty of a people to engage in war, rather than give up to the demands of such a power, what they could, without any incoveniency, spare in the way of charity. War, though a great evil, is ever preferable to such concessions, as are likely to be fatal to public liberty.

After the Madrid bombing, the *Spectator*, the oldest continuously published magazine in the English language, ran an editorial headlined "We Are Not at War." They wished to assure Britons that the jihad would not be taking possession of Buckingham Palace: "Osama bin Laden is no more likely to march triumphantly down the Mall than is a little green man from Mars. Al Qaeda has means but no end."

Well, no, Osama won't be going down the Mall and through the Palace gates, unless it's his surviving granules of DNA on a gun carriage. But it doesn't have to be that dramatic: the al Qaeda air force won't be having dogfights with the RAF over the White Cliffs of Dover before the Queen signs the instrument of abdication in the presence of the Acting First Ayatollah of the Islamic Republic of Britain. Yet you can reach the same point of surrender very gradually, almost imperceptibly. In that respect, the editors of the *Spectator* have it exactly backward: al Qaeda haven't the means, but their end—the Islamification of the West—is shared by millions of law-abiding Muslims. Recall one of the most famous images of terror, from Joseph Conrad's great novel *The Secret Agent* (1907) and its signature scene of the lone terrorist padding the streets of London with a bomb strapped to his chest:

> He had no future. He disdained it. He was a force. His thoughts caressed the images of ruin and destruction. He walked frail, insignificant, shabby, miserable—and terrible in the simplicity of his idea calling madness and despair to the regeneration of the world. Nobody looked at him. He passed on unsuspected and deadly, like a pest in the street full of men.

The power of the image lies in the bomber's isolation from the tide of Londoners all around him, all blissfully unaware. But, as became clear very quickly after the 2005 Tube bombings, that's not quite the world we live in. It's not black (the bomber) and white (the rest of us); there's a lot of murky shades of gray in between: the terrorist bent on devastation and destruction prowls the streets, while around him are a significant number of people urging him on, and around them a larger group of cocksure young male co-religionists gleefully celebrating mass murder, and around them a much larger group of "moderates" who stand silent at the acts committed in their name, and around them a mesh of religious and community leaders openly inciting treason against the state, and around them another mesh of religious and community leaders who serve as apologists for the inciters, and around them a network of professional identity-group grievance-mongers adamant that they're the real victims, and around them a vast mass of elite opinion in the media and elsewhere too squeamish about ethno-cultural matters to confront reality, and around them a political establishment desperate to pretend this is just a managerial problem that can be finessed away with a few new laws and a bit of community outreach.

It's these insulating circles of gray—the imams, lobby groups, media, bishops, politicians—that bulk up the loser death-cult and make it a potent force. And way out at the end of this chain of shades of gray is the general population. And sometimes enough of them bleed into the gray blur of passivity and defeatism, as in Spain. Sometimes they don't, yet, as in America. And sometimes, as in the United Kingdom, they talk about defiance and the old Blitz spirit, but they make a thousand trivial concessions day by day. That's how great nations die—not by war or conquest, but bit by bit, until one day you wake up and you don't need to sign a formal instrument of surrender because you did it piecemeal over the last ten years.

So, unlike Conrad's lone bomber, this enemy is able to hide in plain sight—a pest in a street full of pests, in an America where half the political establishment wants to upgrade enemies into defendants with their day in court and full legal rights, in a Europe paralyzed by fear of its own immigrant populations, in a Western world whose media dignify our killers as "militants," "activists," and "insurgents." "Why do they hate us?" was never the right question. "Why do they despise us?" is a better one.

After the carnage in Spain, Sheikh Omar Bakri Mohammed told Lisbon's *Publica* magazine that a group of London Islamists were "ready to launch a big operation" on British soil. "We don't make a distinction between civilians and non-civilians, innocents and non-innocents," he said, clarifying the ground rules. "Only between Muslims and unbelievers. And the life of an unbeliever has no value." The cleric added he expected to see the banner of Islam flying in Downing Street. "I believe one day that is going to happen. Because this is my country, I like living here," he said. "If they believe in democracy, who are they afraid of? Let Omar Bakri benefit from democracy!"

You think that sounds ridiculous? The Islamic crescent flying over 10 Downing Street? You'd be surprised how quickly the question of what flag should fly over government buildings can become an issue. In 2005, Anne Owers, Her Majesty's chief inspector of prisons, banned the flying of the English national flag in English prisons on the grounds that it shows the cross of St. George, which was used by the Crusaders and so is offensive to Muslims. The Drivers and Vehicles Licensing Agency has also banned the English flag from its offices. So has Heathrow Airport.

So Britain's already crept a little way toward the *Spectator*'s allegedly as-kooky-as-men-from-Mars scenario: the old flag's unflyable, de facto if not quite de jure, and it's just a matter of what new and appropriate multicultural swatch is selected to fly in its place.

If it were just terrorists bombing buildings and public transit, it would be easier: even the feeblest Eurowimp jurisdiction is obliged to act when the street is piled with corpses. But there's an old technique well understood by the smarter bullies. If you want to break a man, don't attack him head on, don't brutalize him: pain and torture can awaken a stubborn resistance in all but the weakest. But just make him slightly uncomfortable, disrupt his life at the margin, and he'll look for the easiest path to re-normalization. There are fellows rampaging through the streets because of some cartoons? Why, surely the most painless solution would be if we all agreed not to publish such cartoons.

Fast-moving demographic changes provide immense challenges for any society. In the wake of the No Mexican Left Behind illegal-immigration come-on-down bonanza passed by the Senate and cheered by the president in 2006, *National Review*'s John Derbyshire noted the enrolment statistics for his school district on suburban Long Island, 1,400 miles from the southern border:

> High school: 17 percent Hispanic
> Intermediate: 28 percent Hispanic
> Elementary: 31 percent Hispanic

There's no jihad, no honor killings, no polygamy issues with Latinos. But transformative demographic trends at the very minimum impose huge costs even for quiet communities far from the political front lines. Derbyshire's numbers suggest that at some point every school board in America will have to factor in ever-swelling bilingual and other related education programs. That's aside from the bigger cultural shifts less easy to quantify in budgetary line items.

You might say, as "open borders" advocates do, oh well, the American idea is so strong that all those 31 percent grade school Hispanics will be perfectly assimilated by the time they're in high school. Maybe. To put it at its mildest, that requires taking a very optimistic view of the assimilationist power of contemporary multiculturalism. Now put yourself in Europe's shoes, up against a surging demographic more self-segregating and more explicitly opposed to the Continent's cultural and political inheritance. Will plus demography is a potent combination: it's why you can't dismiss Sheikh Omar Bakri Mohammed as a fringe nutcake—because he can command just enough support from just enough people to put just enough of what he wants just within the realm of political possibility.

After September 11, the first reaction of just about every prominent Western leader was to visit a mosque: President Bush did, so did the Prince of Wales, the prime minister of the United Kingdom, the prime minister of Canada and many more. And, when the get-me-to-the-mosque-on-time fever died away, you couldn't help feeling that this would strike almost any previous society as, well, bizarre. Pearl Harbor's been attacked? Quick, order some sushi and get me into a matinee of *Madam Butterfly*! Seeking to reassure the co-religionists of those who attack you that you do not regard them all as the enemy is a worthy aim but a curious first priority. And, given that more than a few of the imams in those mosque photo-ops turned out to be at best equivocal on the matter of Islamic terrorism and at worst somewhat enthusiastic supporters of it, it involved way too much self-deception on our part. But it set the tone for all that followed, to the point where with each bomb or plot—from September 11 to London to Toronto—the protestations of Islam's good faith grew ever more fulsome. "Minority rights doctrine," wrote British author Melanie Phillips, "has produced a moral inversion, in which those doing wrong are excused if they belong to a 'victim' group, while those at the receiving end of their behavior are blamed simply because they belong to the 'oppressive' majority.... It is impossible to overstate the importance—not just to Britain but to the global struggle against Islamist extremism—of properly understanding and publicly challenging this moral, intellectual, and philosophical inversion, which translates aggressor into victim and vice versa."

Consider the name given to the current conflict: "war on terror."
Wait a minute. Aren't wars usually waged against named enemies? Yes,
but, to the progressive mind, the very concept of "the enemy" is obsolescent: there are no enemies, just friends whose grievances we haven't yet
accommodated. In part, it's societal forgetfulness. In an electronic age, a
present-tense culture, we assume that social progress is like technological progress: it can't be reversed. Just as you can't disinvent the internal
combustion engine, so you can't disinvent women's rights. Just as the
horse and buggy yielded to the steam train and the Ford Model T and
the passenger jet, so the advanced social-democratic society will march
onward to state day care and thirty-hour work weeks and gay marriage
and ever greater ethnic diversity—and nothing can turn it back, certainly
not a lot of seventh-century weirdbeards. Many of us figure the Islamist
plan to re-establish the caliphate is the equivalent of that moment in *The
SpongeBob SquarePants Movie* when Plankton roars, "I'm going to rule
the world!" Towering over him, SpongeBob says, "Good luck with that."

But you never know: it might be that we're the plankton. "Our enemies are small worms," Adolf Hitler told his generals in August 1939. "I
saw them at Munich." In Europe today, as in the thirties, the political class
prostrates itself before an insatiable force that barely acknowledges the latest surrender before moving on to the next invented grievance. Indeed, a
formal enemy is all but superfluous to requirements. Bomb us, and we ago-
nize over the "root causes." Decapitate us, and our politicians rush to the
nearest mosque to declare that "Islam is a religion of peace." Issue blood-
curdling calls at Friday prayers to kill all the Jews and infidels, and we fret
that it may cause a backlash against Muslims. Behead sodomites and muti-
late female genitalia, and gay groups and feminist groups can't wait to
march alongside you denouncing Bush and Blair. Murder a schoolful of
children, and our scholars explain that to the "vast majority" of Muslims
"jihad" is a harmless concept meaning "healthy-lifestyle lo-fat granola
bar." Thus the lopsided *valse macabre* of our times: the more the Islamists
step on our toes, the more we waltz them gaily round the room.

As French philosopher Jean-François Revel wrote, "Clearly, a civilization that feels guilty for everything it is and does will lack the energy

and conviction to defend itself." During the cartoon jihad, the *New York Times* gave a routinely pompous explanation of why it would not be showing us the representations of the Prophet: sensitive news organizations, the editors explained, had the duty to "refrain from gratuitous assaults on religious symbols." The very next day the *Times* illustrated a story on the Danish controversy with a piece of New York "art" from a couple of seasons earlier showing the Virgin Mary covered in elephant dung. Multiculturalism seems to operate on the same even-handedness as the old Cold War joke in which the American tells the Soviet guy that "in my country everyone is free to criticize the president," and the Soviet guy replies, "Same here. In my country everyone is free to criticize your president." Under the rules as understood by the *New York Times*, the West is free to mock and belittle its Judeo-Christian inheritance, and, likewise, the Muslim world is free to mock and belittle the West's Judeo-Christian inheritance. If one has to choose, on balance Islam's loathing of other cultures seems psychologically less damaging than the Western elites' loathing of their own.

Insurgencies, whether explicitly terrorist or more subtle, persist because of a lack of confidence on the part of their targets. The IRA, for example, calculated correctly that the British had the capability to smash them totally but not the will. So they knew that while they could never win militarily, they also could never be defeated. The Islamists have figured similarly. The only difference is that most terrorist wars are highly localized. We now have the first truly global terrorist insurgency because the Islamists view the whole world the way the IRA view the bogs of Fermanagh: they want it, and they've calculated that our entire civilization lacks the will to see them off.

Granted, at a certain level that's preposterous. There's a contradiction at the heart of Islamist confidence, nicely caught in a story from New Zealand about female Muslims driving around in burqas. According to some police representatives, this mode of dress somewhat restricts the field of vision, and also offers opportunities for fleeing bank robbers to disguise themselves as Muslim women. However, nobody wants to be insensitive, do they? And, on the whole, the police were happy to take the Islamic lobby groups at their word that the burqa was a requirement of these women's faith. But as Greg O'Connor, president of the New Zealand Police Association, couldn't resist adding, "If one's belief system was so strong that you didn't want to show one's face then perhaps that belief system should extend to not driving."

Indeed. If your clothing can't evolve out of the camel-train era, maybe your mode of transportation shouldn't either. But that's Islam in the third millennium: they want the certainties of seventh-century society with the conveniences of the twenty-first century. It doesn't work like that, of course. An Islamic States of America, an Islamic Republic of France, an Islamic Kingdom of Belgium, an Islamic Dominion of Canada would all very quickly be societies in decline, living on the accumulated capital of their pre-Muslim past—as, indeed, much of Islam did at its zenith. But do we really want to test that proposition?

Simply as a matter of fact, every year more and more of the world lives under Islamic law: Pakistan adopted Islamic law in 1977, Iran in 1979, Sudan in 1984. In the sixties, Nigeria lived under English Common Law; now, half of it's in the grip of sharia, and the other half's feeling the squeeze. Today, there are more Muslim nations, more radicalized Muslims within those nations, more and more Muslims within non-Muslim nations, and more and more Muslims represented in more and more influential transnational institutions. Will these Muslims live by the laws of Singapore or Denmark or New Zealand or by the laws of Islam? Or is their primary identity a new worldwide Islamic identity?

To ask the question is, in large part, to answer it. Even if a Muslim wanted to, how would he assimilate with, say, Canadian national identity? You can't assimilate with a nullity, which is what the modern multicultural state boils down to. It's much easier to dismantle a society than to put anything new and lasting in its place. And across much of the developed world that's what's going on right now. Multiculturalism makes a nation no more than a holding pen. In the absence of cultural confidence, demography will decide the future. Or in the unimprovable summation of James C. Bennett: "Democracy, immigration, multiculturalism. Pick any two."

At the heart of multiculturalism is a lie: that all cultures are equally "valid." To accept that proposition means denying reality—the reality of any objective measure of human freedom, societal health, and global population movement. Multiculturalism is not the first ideology founded on the denial of truth. You'll recall Hermann Goering's memorable assertion that "two plus two makes five if the Führer wills it." Likewise, we're asked to accept that the United States Constitution was modeled on the principles of the Iroquois Confederation—if a generation of multiculti theorists, the ethnic grievance lobby, and even a ludicrous resolution of the United States Congress so wills it.

Still, it's harmless, isn't it? What's wrong with playing make-believe if it helps us all feel warm and fuzzy about each other?

Well, because it's never helpful to put reality up for grabs. There may come a day when you need it.

Look at the photograph that appeared on the front of a Fleet Street tabloid shortly after the London Tube bombings: a quartet of young men enjoying a weekend's whitewater rafting in Wales—a mini-vacation the killers took to prepare themselves for blowing the Underground to bits. Outwardly, these blokes were no different from any other Yorkshire lads of their age—weaned on chips, fond of cricket, garbed in revolting Brit leisurewear. The London bombers were, to the naked eye, almost perfectly assimilated—at least in respect to sports, fashion, and pop music. The only difference was inside: a willingness to slaughter dozens of their fellow Britons in the interests of the jihad. They'd adopted so many trees that nobody could see they lacked the big overarching forest—the essence of identity, of allegiance.

If Islamist extremism is the genie you're trying to put back in the bottle, it doesn't help to have smashed the bottle. At the core of multiculturalism is an assumption that a non-Western culture is somehow primal and immutable but that an advanced nation is no more than the sum of its constituent parts. It's a kind of societal Stockholm Syndrome—a desperation to identify with anything that comes along other than your own. The great thing about multiculturalism is that it doesn't involve knowing anything about other cultures—the capital of Bhutan, the principal exports of Malaysia, who cares? That's the stuff the old imperialist wallahs used to be well up on. But multiculturalism just involves feeling warm and fluffy about everyone, making bliss out of ignorance. If the guy's rich vibrant cultural tradition involves standing over you with a scimitar shouting "Allahu Akhbar!" well, you can't complain you're not getting your share of cultural diversity. Given the growing Muslim populations in Europe and the remarkable success hitherto obscure Muslim lobby groups have had in constraining certain aspects of the war on terror, it seems almost certain that Islamist political parties will arise on the Continent within the next decade. And, given the very few degrees of separation between very prominent Western Muslims—ambassadors, princes, professors—and the terrorists, it seems likely that many prominent figures in these parties will be supportive of the terrorists' ends. And given the governing principle of multicultural society—that Western man demonstrates his cultural sensitivity by pre-emptively surrendering—any smart Islamist, surveying the Madrid bombing and the aftermath, must be contemplating the benefits of a twin-track strategy.

There are three possible resolutions to the present struggle:

1. Submit to Islam
2. Destroy Islam
3. Reform Islam

Because most of us don't take number one as a serious possibility, we're equally unserious about being forced to choose between two and three. But submission to Islam is very possible, and to many it will still seem ridiculous even as it happens; like John Kerry during the 2004 campaign, we'll be spluttering that we can't believe we're losing to these idiots. But we *can* lose (as I've always believed) and (as I've come to believe) we might lose more easily than even the gloomiest of us thought.

By "we might lose," I mean "the good guys"—and I define that term expansively. There are plenty of good guys in Australia and Poland and Iraq and even Pakistan. And I'm a little unnerved at the number of readers who seem to think the rest of the world can go hang but America will endure as a lonely candle of liberty in the new Dark Ages. Think that one through: a totalitarian China, a crumbling Russia, an insane Middle East, a disease-ridden Africa, a civil war-torn Eurabia—and a country that can't even enforce its borders against two relatively benign states will somehow be able to hold the entire planet at bay? Dream on, "realists."

As for option two, it doesn't bear thinking about. Even if you regard Islam as essentially incompatible with free societies, the slaughter required to end it as a force in the world would change America beyond recognition. That doesn't mean that, a few years down the line, if some kooks with nukes obliterate, say, Marseilles or Lyons that the French wouldn't give it a go in some fairly spectacular way. But they're unlikely to accomplish much by it, any more than the Russians have by their scorched-earth strategy in Chechnya.

That leaves option three: Reform Islam—which is not ours to do. Ultimately, only Muslims can reform Islam. All the free world can do is create conditions that increase the likelihood of Muslim reform, or at any rate do not actively impede it. We can:

1. Support women's rights—real rights, not feminist pieties—in the Muslim world. This is the biggest vulnerability in Islam. Not every Muslim female wants to be Gloria Steinem or Paris Hilton. But nor do they want a life that starts with genital mutilation and ends with an honor killing at the hands of your brothers. The overwhelming majority of females in Continental battered women's shelters are Muslim—which gives you some sense of what women in the Middle East might do if they had any women's shelters to go to. When half the population of these societies is a potential source of dissent, we need to use it.

2. Roll back Wahhabi, Iranian, and other ideological exports that have radicalized Muslims on every continent. We have an ideological enemy and we need to wage ideological war.

3. Support economic and political liberty in the Muslim world, even if it means unsavory governments: an elected unsavory government is still better than a dictatorial unsavory government. It's not

necessary for Syria and Egypt to become Minnesota and New Zealand. All that's necessary is for them to become something other than what they are now. And on the bumpy road to liberty, every Muslim regime that has to preoccupy itself with internal dissent has less time to foment trouble beyond its borders.

4. Ensure that Islamic states that persecute non-Muslims are denied international legitimacy and excluded and marginalized in international bodies.

5. Throttle the funding of mosques, madrassas, think tanks, and other activities in America and elsewhere by Saudi Arabia, Iran, and others.

6. Develop a strategy for countering Islamism on the ideological front. Create a civil corps to match America's warrior corps and use it to promote alternative institutions, structures, and values through a post-imperial equivalent to Britain's Colonial Office, albeit under whatever wussy name is deemed acceptable: Department of Global Community Outreach or whatever (this, by the way, is what Washington should have created instead of the bloated bureaucracy of the Department of Homeland Security).

7. Marginalize and euthanize the UN, NATO, the International Atomic Energy Agency, and other September 10 transnational organizations and devote the energy wasted on them to results-oriented multilateralism. We need real allies now.

8. Cease bankrolling unreformable oil dictatorships by a long-overdue transformation of the energy industry.

9. End the Iranian regime.

10. Strike militarily when the opportunity presents itself.

Aside from numbers nine and ten, these are important but undramatic objectives—i.e., the kind of stuff our side does very badly. The problem with redesignating the "war on terror" as "the long war" is that it's easy for it to degenerate a step further and lapse into non-war mode entirely. But what are the alternatives? Retreat behind Fortress America? What fortress? The one Congress built on the Rio Grande as a Latino Welcome

Center? The hyperpower has to be engaged with the world, if only because splendid isolation is rarely seen as such by others. What was the biggest single factor in the radicalization of young British Muslims? The then Conservative government's conclusion in the 1990s that it had no dog in the Balkans junkyard. As Osama bin Laden put it: "The British are responsible for destroying the Caliphate system. They are the ones who created the Palestinian problem. They are the ones who created the Kashmiri problem. They are the ones who put the arms embargo on the Muslims of Bosnia so that two million Muslims were killed."

How'd a list of imperial interventions wind up with that bit of non-imperial non-intervention? Because, for great powers, detachment from the affairs of the world is not an option: even-handedness by Washington will be received as a form of one-handedness by the time its effects are felt in Wackistan or Basketkhazia. Isolation doesn't travel.

Americans and other Westerners who want their families to enjoy the blessings of life in a free society should understand that the life we've led since 1945 in the Western world is very rare in human history. Our children are unlikely to enjoy anything so placid, and may well spend their adult years in an ugly and savage world unless we decide that who and what we are is worth defending. To a five-year-old boy watching Queen Victoria's Diamond Jubilee procession on the Mall in 1897, it would have been inconceivable that by the time of his eightieth birthday the greatest empire the world had ever known would have sunk to an economically moribund strike-bound slough of despond whose tax rates drove its best talents abroad, and whose most glittering colonial possessions now valued ties to Communist Russia over those to the mother country. It's difficult to focus on long-term trends because human life is itself short-term. So think short-term: huge changes are under way right now.

The threat to U.S. power comes not principally from Chinese innovation or Indian engineering graduates but from America's own cultural indolence, just as the sack of Rome was a symptom of the fall of the empire rather than the cause. The governing class found themselves, to quote Cole Porter, "fighting vainly the old ennui"—and that's harder to do than fighting off an invading army. Bernard Lewis, the West's preeminent scholar of

Islam, worked for British intelligence through the grimmest hours of World War Two. "In 1940, we knew who we were, we knew who the enemy was, we knew the dangers and the issues," he told the *Wall Street Journal*. "In our island, we knew we would prevail, that the Americans would be drawn into the fight. It is different today. We don't know who we are, we don't know the issues, and we still do not understand the nature of the enemy."

The advantage for the United States and, to a lesser extent, other parts of the English-speaking world is that Europe is ahead in the line, and its fate may wake up even the most blinkered on this side of the Atlantic. Islamism is militarily weak but ideologically confident. The West is militarily strong but ideologically insecure. The suicide bomber is a symbol of weakness, of a culture so comprehensively failed that what ought to be its greatest resource—its people—is instead as disposable as a firecracker. But in our self-doubt the enemy's weakness becomes his strength. We simply can't comprehend someone like Raed Abdel Mask, pictured in the papers in 2004 with a big smile, a checkered shirt and two cute little cherubs, a boy and a girl, in his arms. His wife was five months pregnant with their third child. So he kissed her goodbye and then big, smiling Raed strapped an eleven-pound bomb packed with nails and shrapnel to his chest and boarded the number 2 bus in Jerusalem.

We heard a lot about "root causes" in the weeks after September 11—mostly the usual ones: "poverty breeds despair," etc. But the September 11 murderers were middle class and educated, which is one reason why they were so skilled at their job that day. It was carefully plotted. They hijacked long-haul flights with the most fuel at the time of day when airport security would be even more careless than usual. It was brilliantly planned, superbly executed. The perpetrators trained to become jet pilots—a profession that would guarantee a good life anywhere around the world. They could be pulling down six-figure salaries instead of Manhattan skyscrapers. But they went to pilot school and trained in a highly disciplined fashion so they could make one flight, one time, one way: into a tall building.

We cannot fathom men such as Mohammed Atta and Raed Abdel Mask. But, if you were the late Messrs. Mask and Atta following events in North America and Europe, wouldn't we strike them as a little odd too?

When we hear about some guy in a cave dreaming of the new caliphate, we think he's nuts. But if you were in the cave watching a CNN bulletin in which legal analysts explain why the U.S. Supreme Court decided to confer Geneva Convention rights on unlawful combatants under an unprecedented reading of Common Article 3 or watching *New York Times* executives explain proudly how important it was for them to reveal fatally damaging details of a national security terror-tracking program for no good reason whatsoever, wouldn't you conclude that we're the ones who are nuts? If you'd been in the cave and had your radio tuned to National Public Radio for the following exchange, wouldn't you have been splitting your sides (and not because your suicide-bomber belt went off early)? This was an interview on NPR's *Morning Edition* with the mayor of Toronto, after the arrest of seventeen alleged terrorist plotters. I was laughing so much I drove off the road. There ought to be a health warning before these cockamamie public broadcasting gagfests. Hizzoner David Miller warmed up with a bit of boilerplate Islamoschmoozing: "You know, in Islam, if you kill one person, you kill everybody. It's a very peaceful religion. And they're as shocked as Torontonians are. And—"

Renee Montagne, the NPR anchorette, instantly spotted the ghastly breach of PC etiquette and leapt in: "Well, they sort of are Torontonians," she pointed out.

"Sorry," gulped the mayor, hastily re-smothering Muslims within the great diversity quilt. "They're shocked as every Torontonian is."

Ms. Montagne then expressed bafflement that these allegedly alleged fellows would have wanted to commit a terrorist atrocity in what was, compared to the Great Satan next door, "a very open society, very liberal immigration policy, very good social services."

Mayor Miller agreed. "More than half of the people who live in Toronto, including myself, were not born in Canada. And I think that's why Canada works."

"Although it didn't work in this case," Ms. Montagne noted, somewhat maliciously.

"Well, we don't expect these kinds of occurrences, exactly because of our public services, because of diversity," blah, blah, blah. Insofar as there's any relation between jihadists and "good social services," the latter seem to attract the former—at least in the sense that the millennium bomber, the shoe-bomber, the Tube bombers, etc., were all products of the Euro-Canadian welfare system. But go ahead, pretend that these guys were upset about insufficient "social services," that they wanted to behead the prime minister to highlight the fact that wait times for the beheaded at the Toronto General are now up to eighteen months, and they don't always reattach the right head. It's easy to scoff that a chap who can be bothered to blow up the Canadian Parliament must be insane, but if you were a jihadist sitting in the cave back in the Hindu Kush listening to Renee Montagne and David Miller compete to abase themselves before the most irrelevant PC platitudes, wouldn't you conclude that they're way more suicidal than you and Ahmed?

A suicide bomber may be a weak weapon, but not against a suicide culture.

● ● ●

THE SICK BED

Shortly after September 11, I reread an old potboiler I vaguely remembered from my childhood: Sir Arthur Conan Doyle, the creator of Sherlock Holmes, had a sick wife and in 1895 they went to Egypt, hoping the climate would alleviate her tuberculosis. No writer likes to waste local color, so in 1898 Conan Doyle published *The Tragedy of the Korosko*, the story of a party of Anglo-American-French tourists on a trip up the Nile who wind up getting kidnapped by the al Qaeda of the day—the followers of the Mahdi. What's striking is how familiar it all is. The sudden intrusion of an unbending savagery upon modern man:

> When, but a year before, he had wandered under the elms of Cambridge, surely the last fate upon this earth which he could have predicted for himself would be that he should be slain by the bullet of a fanatical Mohammedan in the wilds of the Libyan Desert.

Even the techniques are much the same:

> "What do you suppose that they will do with us, Cochrane?" he
> asked, after a pause.
>   "They may cut our throats, or they may take us as slaves to
> Khartoum. I don't know that there is much to choose."

Then as now, the Islamists believe the infidels are looking at things back
to front, that the advanced scientific mind is, in fact, an effete arrogant
weakness in the face of unquestioning faith:

> "As to the learning of which you speak, my lamb," said the mul-
> lah, in answer to some argument of Fardet's, "I have myself stud-
> ied at the University of Alazhar at Cairo, and I know that to
> which you allude. But the learning of the faithful is not as the
> learning of the unbeliever, and it is not fitting that we pry too
> deeply into the ways of Allah. Some stars have tails, oh my sweet
> lamb, and some have not; but what does it profit us to know
> which are which? For God made them all, and they are very safe
> in His hands. Therefore, my friend, be not puffed up by the fool-
> ish learning of the West, and understand that there is only one
> wisdom, which consists in following the will of Allah as His cho-
> sen Prophet has laid it down for us in this book. And now, my
> lambs, I see that you are ready to come into Islam."

And in the face of such clarity there are among the tourists those who
take refuge in conspiracy theories. Just as many Westerners believe Bush
cooked up the whole war-on-terror scam as a pretext to invade
Afghanistan and Iraq, so at the beginning of Conan Doyle's adventure a
character believes the Mahdists have been concocted by the British government to provide a pretext for intervention:

> "I repeat that there are no dervishes. They were an invention of
> Lord Cromer in the year 1885."

"You don't say!" cried Headingly.

"It is well known in Paris, and has been exposed in *La Patrie* and other of our so well-informed papers."

And when the conspiracy theorist is kidnapped and learns that there are, indeed, dervishes, his initial reaction—like those of the misnamed "Christian Peacemaker Teams" seized in Iraq—is to emphasize how much he agrees with their point of view:

> The Frenchman waved his unwounded hand as he walked. "Vive le Khalifa! Vive le Mahdi!" he shouted, until a blow from behind with the butt-end of a Remington beat him into silence.

For, as did the kidnappers of those Iraqi "Peacemakers," the dervishes see even a supportive infidel only as an infidel.

So what is different between a late Victorian "shocker" and our time? Conan Doyle's Britons and Americans and Europeans were men and women of the modern world even then:

> None of them, except perhaps Miss Adams and Mrs. Belmont, had any deep religious convictions. All of them were children of this world, and some of them disagreed with everything which that symbol upon the earth represented.

Yet in the end the English, Irish, and Americans among the party have an instinctive civilizational confidence. They respect their foe, in part because they understand that's what he is. It was an odd sensation rereading *The Tragedy of the Korosko* after September 11. As innumerable Western academics lined up across the TV studios and public prints to insist that "poverty breeds desperation," I came across this passage:

> "It isn't safe to reckon upon a dervish's fears," remarked Brown. "We must always bear in mind that they are not amenable to the same motives as other people. Many of them are anxious to meet

death, and all of them are absolute, uncompromising believers in destiny. They exist as a reductio ad absurdum of all bigotry—a proof of how surely it leads towards blank barbarism."

It *is* absurd: how can the most advanced society in human history fall to a bunch of ignorant death cultists? Well, who do you think advanced societies do fall to? Something worse, something barbarous, something that's prepared to fight when you're not. One hundred and eight years later, there was a latterday Cook's Tour atrocity in Egypt—a terrorist bombing at the popular Western holiday destination of Dahab. Egyptians were polled as to whom was responsible: 4 percent thought it was al Qaeda; 21 percent thought it was internal terrorist groups; 49 percent thought it was the Mossad. Denial really is a river in Egypt.

How many Egyptians or Arabs or Muslims living in, say, Brussels or London or Dearborn, Michigan, feel the same?

The key difference between the Anglo-American hostages in *The Tragedy of the Korosko* and their successors today is that they accepted their obligations. It's never easy, and certainly not for Conan Doyle's dramatis personae in 1898, when the "white man's burden" seemed especially burdensome:

> "It's my opinion that we have been the policemen of the world long enough. We policed the seas for pirates and slavers. Now we police the land for dervishes and brigands and every sort of danger to civilization. There is never a mad priest or a witch doctor, or a firebrand of any sort on this planet, who does not report his appearance by sniping the nearest British officer. One tires of it at last. If a Kurd breaks loose in Asia Minor, the world wants to know why Great Britain does not keep him in order. If there is a military mutiny in Egypt, or a jihad in the Sudan, it is still Great Britain who has to set it right. And all to an accompaniment of curses such as the policeman gets when he seizes a ruffian among his pals. We get hard knocks and no thanks, and why should we do it? Let Europe do its own dirty work."

"Well," said Colonel Cochrane, crossing his legs and leaning forward with the decision of a man who has definite opinions, "I don't at all agree with you, Brown, and I think that to advocate such a course is to take a very limited view of our national duties. I think that behind national interests and diplomacy and all that there lies a great guiding force—a Providence, in fact—which is forever getting the best out of each nation and using it for the good of the whole. When a nation ceases to respond, it is time that she went into hospital for a few centuries, like Spain or Greece—the virtue has gone out of her. A man or a nation is not placed upon this earth to do merely what is pleasant and what is profitable. It is often called upon to carry out what is both unpleasant and unprofitable, but if it is obviously right it is mere shirking not to undertake it."

We have been shirking too long, and that's unworthy of a great civilization. To see off the new Dark Ages will be tough and demanding. The alternative will be worse.

Acknowledgments

would like to thank Harry Crocker and his colleagues at Regnery for their support and wise counsel. I am indebted as always to my assistants Tiffany Cole and Chantal Benoît for their excellent research and brilliantly compressed summations of reams of statistics and numbers. Above all, I am grateful to readers in America, Canada, Britain, Europe, the Middle East, Africa, Asia, Australia, New Zealand, and elsewhere for many useful insights and anecdotes into our fast-changing world.

Index